I0815297

DISCOVERING UZBEKISTAN

DISCOVERING UZBEKISTAN

Dariya Sirotina

Cover
Khiva Old City, a view from Islam Khoja Minaret

Back Cover
A view of the Zaamin National Park

Head of Business Development
Edoardo Ghizzoni

Design
Luigi Fiore

Editorial Coordination
Vincenza Russo

Copy Editing
Laura Colosi
Sara Tedesco

Layout
Faycal Zaouali

Translations
Konstantin Kalinin

Photos by
Dariya Sirotina

First published in August 2025 by
Skira editore srl
via Agnello, 18
20121 Milan, Italy
skira-arte.com

ISBN: 978-88-572-5409-8

This book was printed by RGM Printing on FSC®-certified paper

Distributed in USA, Canada, Central & South America by ARTBOOK | D.A.P., 75 Broad Street, Suite 630, New York, NY 10004, USA.
Distributed elsewhere in the world by Thames and Hudson Ltd., 181A High Holborn, London WC1V 7QX, United Kingdom.

Uzum, Uzbekistan's first IT unicorn. The company has built the country's leading digital ecosystem, integrating a national e-commerce marketplace, fintech solutions, and banking services tailored for both individuals and businesses. Today, over 17 million people across Uzbekistan rely on Uzum's ecosystem every month —a testament to the company's central role in transforming everyday digital services and enabling economic opportunity at scale.

CONTENTS

FOREWORD

The brightest recollection of my first trip to Uzbekistan was the true, authentic life it embodies; the way Uzbekistan is so unlike anything I was accustomed to and, at the same time, how surprisingly relatable it was; and the love of everyone I met to the country. The love that quickly grew on me.

I was captivated by the blue domes of Samarkand, the ancient streets of Bukhara, the abyss of the starry sky above the desert of Kyzyl Kum, and the carving on the pillars of the Juma Mosque in Khiva, but all that was secondary. It was the people, not the monuments, that really got under my skin. People are the greatest treasure of Uzbekistan.

For many people, Uzbekistan still is an unknown and rather underestimated country. When you travel here, you feel like a trailblazer, you enjoy discovering the country that remains, for many, "terra incognita."

Guide books will provide countless stories of how some city or another was founded, or recount stories of time immemorial, but there are no up-to-date reliable publications that can help tourists see and fall in love with Uzbekistan. My desire to write this book stems not just from my vivid recollections of the Uzbek civilization, but also from the urge to fill in the numerous gaps of other stories.

Uzbekistan is still a country of personal contact and communication. This means that the Internet can hardly be of any help there. One needs to ask and ask again. This is a unique book of reference of restaurants, wineries, artisan workshops across the entire country, from Karakalpakstan to Namangan. I have traveled over Uzbekistan and chosen the best of the best. This volume is your guide in order to plan your journey and to get the most out of your time in Uzbekistan.

This book concentrates on the unique nature of decorative and applied arts and crafts of the country. I chose only the most authentic workshops that preserve centuries-old traditions to share my admiration of the vibrancy and polyphony of Uzbek culture with you.

It is also an attempt to conceptualize and systematize the regional diversity of Uzbek cuisine that is by no means limited to plov. Besides, it is the only book focusing on the culture of winemaking in Uzbekistan. You will learn not only that Uzbekistan does, in fact, produce wines, but also which Uzbek wines are really worth drinking.

One of my goals was to give artisan, craftsmen, cooks and winemakers of Uzbekistan some new ideas, bring them new customers, new stimuli, to give them the opportunity to stay in their home country with their family, to keep the ancestral traditions, and to develop their business. I also wanted to draw attention to the local schools and recipes and, in this way, contribute to their preservation.

Yet my main goal was to show Uzbekistan as a rich, diverse, vibrant country full of life—to show it the way I see it.

A HISTORY OF UZBEKISTAN

People, Events, and Empires

With no pretense of making an extensive historical sketch, I would like to talk about the history of Uzbekistan through the optics of religion, best-known names and phenomena, and influence of different empires. I choose this approach because throughout all history there simultaneously existed different historical and geographical regions and states, and different dynasties ruled and fought one another. I believe that it will be more illustrative to speak of the history of Uzbekistan in the chapters dedicated to different regions, and, at the same time, to draw parallels with the monuments that one can see. I think it will be clearer.

Uzbekistan and Religion

Uzbekistan is a secular state, the majority of whose citizens practices **Islam**. The process of Islamization of Central Asia began with the Arabic conquest in the late 8th century. In this way, the Arabic culture formed a synthesis with indigenous cultures, Turkic or Persian, on the territories of present-day Uzbekistan, Kyrgyzstan, Tajikistan and Kazakhstan, and Islam became the prevalent religion. In the 9th century, representatives of the Persian dynasty of Samanids, based in their capital city of Bukhara, were engaged in intense missionary activities solidifying the new belief. It was at that time that Imam al-Bukhari was born in Bukhara, the author of one of canonical collections of hadith, or accounts about the Prophet. Adherents of the Islamic faith believe in Allah, the one Almighty Creator, and consider the Muhammad the last Prophet of the True Faith.

Prior to establishment of Islam in the territories of the present-day Uzbekistan, there were practiced other religions, such as Zoroastrianism and Buddhism. We know **Zoroastrians** as fire-worshippers, for them is the light, including that of the fire burning in the hearth, that is the visible image of the God; the fire itself is the symbol of purity and moral. The monuments of those times are the Magoki-Attari Mosque in Bukhara built on the site of the Temple of Fire, the ancient settlement of Mingorik in Tashkent, where items used in cult ceremonies were found, or the ancient settlement of Gyaur-Kala, an oasis of Zoroastrianism in the land that had already been influenced by Islam. The archeologist and ethnographer Sergey Tolstov believed that the birthplace of Zoroastrianism was the land of the ancient Khorezm, or the regions around today's Khiva and Nukus.

The legacy of Zoroastrianism in today's Uzbekistan is the **holiday of Navruz**, celebrated annually on March 21, symbolizing the advent of the New Year.

Buddhism spread in some areas of the present-day Uzbekistan in the beginning of the Common Era and is related to the reign of the Kushan Dynasty. The prominent King of Kushan and the best known Buddhist of Uzbekistan in the Emperor Kanishka, who ruled in the early 2nd century. The Buddhists believe in spiritual awakening, whose the principles of achievement were found by Buddha in the course of meditative contemplation of his own spirit and of all things.

In the territory of Uzbekistan, in the Surxondaryo Region, almost on the border with Afghanistan, there are the most important Buddhist monuments. Those are the remains of the Kara Tepe Monastery, the temple complex of Fayaz Tepe, the Zurmala Stupa. The archeological museum in Termez keeps a world-class collection of artifacts of the Buddhist era found in the excavations in the region.

Uzbekistan and Great Warlords

The territories of modern Uzbekistan regularly found themselves at the center of global processes and events, giving birth to their own great commanders and falling under the influence of invaders from outside.

Alexander the Great, the King of Macedonia, a Greek state in the Balkan Peninsula, set out to Samarkand in 4th century BC. During the campaign, he defeated the Persian Empire of the Achaemenides and subdued immense territories. He was moving to Samarkand through the areas of the present-day town of Boysun in the Surxondaryo Region. Around Derbent, one can still see the remains of the fortresses besieged by Alexander, and the city itself was likely the place of wedding of Alexander to Roxana, daughter of the Bactrian nobleman Oxyartes. In 329 BC, Alexander the Great conquered the regions usually referred to as Bactria and Sogdiana, controlling the territories from Afghanistan to Fergana Valley, and vast Sogdian territories with the center in Samarkand. However, the prideful Samarkandians, headed by Spitamenes, rose in a revolt and defeated an army of Macedonians, this being the only defeat of Alexander in his Eastern campaign.

Genghis Khan is another name linked with Uzbekistan. In 1219, the war with Khorezm broke out, and in 1220, it was the turn of Bukhara: the besieged city fell in March. One of the few pre-Mongolian monuments that survived to this day is the Kalyan Minaret built in the 12th century. After Bukhara, Samarkand surrendered on the third day of the siege. According to contemporaries, the Mongols wrecked utter devastation. The Mongolian conquest of the Central Asia threw back the once prosperous regions; and it was almost a deathly blow.

Tamerlane, or **Amir Timur**, was the person who was able to raise the country

The construction of Registan Square began with the Ulugh Beg Madrasah in the early 15th century. Ulugh Beg, the grandson of Timur (Tamerlane), was renowned as an eminent mathematician, astronomer, scholar, and poet of his era.

Inner courtyard of the Ulugh Beg Madrasah in Samarkand

SILK WEAVING
WORKSHOP

from its knees, as some would have put it now. Born in the suburbs of the present-day Shahrisabz, he became the ruler of the empire in 1370 making Samarkand the capital. Timur was not a direct descendant of Genghis Khan and did not bear the title of the *Khan*; his title was *Amir*, i.e. ruler or commander. Timur's Empire occupied the lands of the modern Iran, Caucasus, Afghanistan, Syria, India and Pakistan, to say nothing of Central Asia. Timur has some love in Uzbekistan, because he restored the country lying in ruins after the Mongol conquest. His reign was the time when architecture, crafts and sciences flourished. The well-distinctive profiles of Uzbek mosques and madrasahs are due to Timur; the multitude of decorative techniques used to adorn them are due to Timur; the bloom of poetry, theology, and the renaissance of the school of miniature also pay credit to Timur. He would send to his homeland the artisans, scholars and artists that he met during his campaigns and, according to testimonies of contemporaries, paid them well for their labors for the sake of his land. Timur turned Samarkand and Shahrisabz into prospering spectacular cities surrounded by belts of gardens in bloom. The way those cities were made had an extraordinary effect on European travelers contemporary to Timur: at home, they simply did not have anything like it.

Uzbekistan and Great Scientists

Al-Khwarizmi, the great Persian mathematician and geographer, was born in Khorezm, near Khiva, in late 8th century. He is the founder of algebra as a separate science who presented to the world the trigonometric tables with functions of the sine, cosine, tangent and cotangent. The very name "algebra" comes from the title of Al-Khwarizmi's mathematical treatise.

Al-Farghani, one of the most important scientists of the Middle Ages, was born in Fergana Valley. The team of astronomers in Baghdad that he headed made several significant scientific contributions, from the calculation of the meridian arc length to the creation of the celestial chart: all that as early as in the first half of the 9th century! He also made a scientific substantiation of the spherical shape of the Earth.

Avicenna (Ibn Sina) was born near Bukhara in late 10th century, he was the doctor of the Emir of Bukhara and the court doctor of the shah in Khorezm. He is the author of some of the most important medieval treatises on medicine and one of the most influential scholars of the Islamic world.

Omar Khayyam studied at a Samarkand madrasah, and lived and worked in Bukhara for ten years in the early 11th century. He was a recognized scholar, mathematician and astronomer, and his *Rubaiyat* became known as late as in Victorian era. His project of the Iranian calendar is still used as the official calendar in Iran.

Ulugbek, the grandson of Amir Timur, a wise ruler, an eminent intellectual and scholar, poet and astronomer, founded in Samarkand one of the most important observatories of the Middle Ages. The calculations of Ulugbek on the length of the year that date back to the first half of the 15th century are only slightly different from the contemporary data.

He also created the catalog of the stellar sky and calculated the inclination of the Earth's axis.

Babur, a Timurid and a Chingisid, was born in the late 15th century in Andijan, Fergana Valley, he was the founder of the Mughal Empire. His descendants, who ruled the territories of Northern India, built the Taj Mahal. The Baburids remained in power until the British came to the region in the second half of the 19th century.

Uzbekistan and the Silk Road

The Silk Road is a caravan route connecting the East and the West stretching from the Mediterranean to the Eastern Asia. The term "Silk Road" was introduced by the German scholar Ferdinand von Richthofen in 1877. A considerable section of the Silk Road crossed the territory of the present-day Uzbekistan: Fergana Valley, Tashkent, Bukhara, and Khiva. To satisfy the needs of caravans using this route, a whole infrastructure of caravanserais, bazaars, bathhouses, teahouses, and exchange shops was created. Peaches and paper from Samarkand could be bought in various places of Europe and Asia, and coins from Samarkand were in circulation in the German Mainz in the 10th century. In the times of Timur, the caravans with cargo of silk, musk, rubies and diamonds were making their way from China to Samarkand. The number of camels in the caravans dispatched at Timur's orders could reach eight hundred! The horses from the Central Asia were a highly valuable commodity sold at good prices in China. The Silk Road facilitated the invaluable, immense cultural exchange, and in many ways contributed to the formation of the Uzbek culture, as we know it.

Uzbekistan and Russia

Throughout the 19th century, the entire region was the platform where the interests of two empires, the Russian and the British, clashed. These geopolitical processes are known as the Great Game. One may describe it as a curious spy novel, a thriller, and a fine political confrontation. In 1867, the Governorate General of Turkestan was organized which gradually assimilated the Khanate of Khiva, Khanate of Kokand, and the Emirate of Bukhara that existed in the territory of Uzbekistan at the time. The three regions within its structure were headed by military governors. That was a relationship of a liege and the sovereign: the Khanates and the Emirate kept their rulers for a long time, the latter enjoyed quite some respect in the Russian Imperial Court, yet all the external affairs, and the majority of internal ones were taken care of by the central administration.

The attempts to obtain independence after 1917 were not successful. In 1924, the Uzbek Soviet Socialist Republic was formed with the capital in Samarkand, later, in 1930, it was moved to Tashkent. In 1929, the Uzbek writing system was changed from the Arabic alphabet to Latin, and in 1940, to Cyrillic.

Uzbekistan gained its independence after the fall of the Soviet Union. The Republic of Uzbekistan was established on August 31, 1991.

DISTINCTIVE FEATURES OF GASTRONOMY AND WINEMAKING OF UZBEKISTAN

Serving plov in Tashkent—a local variety, with qazi and quail egg

Probably one of the most important features of Uzbekistan gastronomy is that food here is a serious matter, treated almost with a religious ardor. People in Uzbekistan love a good meal, love to get together at the table in large, even great companies, to a foreign eye; people love it when there is not an inch free on the dastarkhan. Dwellers of every region, city, and kishlak will stand passionately for the superiority of their habitual manner of cooking some dishes, and will praise the pomegranates, rice, tomatoes, onions, you name it!—that were grown in their native soil.

There are not too many professional chefs and restaurateurs in Uzbekistan, and they mainly work in Tashkent. It is fascinating to watch them develop: it is quite difficult to engage in restaurant business or build a career as a chef in the country where this profession still is not considered prestigious. For many people in Uzbekistan, a restaurant in the European sense of the word is a place of leisure; one does not go there for tasty food. It happens quite often, therefore, that you do not get delicious food in the places that are on everyone's lips or have flashy signage. European cuisine is considered prestigious, but its Tashkent or Samarkand variant could hardly impress a visitor from abroad. This is why restaurants offering European cuisine seldom make their way into my suggestions, but if they do, they are really, really good.

It will be no exaggeration to say that **food in Uzbekistan varies every 50 or 100 kilometers you travel**: despite the list of specialties of Uzbek cuisine not being extremely long, in every single place the same plov, manti, lagman, samsa, and shurpa will be cooked in different ways, and every cook will be sure that their recipe is the best. At the same time, many dishes are known only within limited territories: for instance, people from Samarkand are not likely to know specialties from Surxondaryo Region or Karakalpakstan. Sometimes it happens that one can buy some product only at a specific market in a specific city or region: Boysun butter in the town of Boysun in Surxondaryo, and Bukhara kaymak at the Green Bazaar in Bukhara.

Seasonality is one of the most important features of Uzbek cuisine. Autumn is the time of fermented and salted vegetables, and quite often, many restaurants and cafés would have those pickles made in-house, in advance, according to a special recipe. Come in spring, and you will try samsa and manti with the first fresh greens. In May, green apricots and alycha, or cherry plum, come to the table. Autumn is pumpkin time, and it goes into manti, samsa and even plov. In winter, apples, pomegranates, persimmons and winter varieties of melon are still available: they are wrapped in tissue paper and stored in cellars and closets, or hung to make sure they are aired.

Food reflects the culture and history of people, or rather peoples living in Uzbekistan: it highlights the cultural, social and historical differences. The country became one quite late: prior to the coming of the Russians to the region in the second half of the 19th century, Uzbekistan consisted of three Khanates uniting people from very different tribes. Iran, Afghanistan, Kazakhstan, Turkmenistan and Kyrgyzstan—all of these countries were parts of Uzbekistan in its present-day boundaries, and all of them left a trace in Uzbek gastronomy. The Soviet reality was no exception! For example, tomatoes and lemons, which we consider as much as signature products of Uzbekistan, appeared here only in the 20th century.

Types of Restaurants

There are three types of restaurants in Uzbekistan (for the sake of simplicity, we will use the term for all places where food is served): some, to satisfy one's hunger (cafés), some, for celebrating special days, and other are venues for tourists and certain locals that adopt European manners. In your journey across the country, you will see many fancy restaurants with glorified interiors and exteriors alike: here, big weddings, anniversaries, and other family events take place. Very often, such restaurants only function as banquet venues, and the rich decorations are their main feature. In simpler cafés, oshxonas, tandoor, and kebab houses, you eat quickly (and enjoy it). Neither the interior, nor the menu call for a lengthy stay. Very often, just one dish is served in such places: just the plov, the samsa, or shashliks (skewered meat). European-style restaurants are located in Tashkent, Bukhara, and Samarkand. The further you go away from the tourist routes, the greater the opportunity to find cafés with national cuisine.

The teahouse, or choyxona, stands out as a cultural institution that flourished particularly in Uzbekistan. It is a fundamental phenomenon, crucial not only for the Uzbek gastronomy, but illustrative organization forms of social life. The term consists of the words choy meaning "tea," and xona meaning "room," "place," or "premise." The rule of not drinking alcohol for the followers of Islam made tea the beverage that structured the Uzbek meals, hospitality, and forms of leisure. Think of the hot climate, and your imagination will picture topchans or pavilions made on the side of a water reservoir or an aryk (canal), under the lace-like shade of a sycamore tree or a mulberry grove, under the ceilings of an aiwan or a terrace. The choyxona is not only for drinking tea, it is also a place to eat. In this sense, it is somewhat closer to a tavern more familiar to us. As a rule, choyxonas appeared near caravanserais or places where merchants following the Silk Road, would stop for rest. Thus, the choyxona became the place to meet people, where city dwellers hurried to talk to visitors from faraway places, and a place of business, where deals were made.

In the present-day Uzbekistan, a classic choyxona is a café with indispensable tapchan platforms, a picturesque courtyard or a shady terrace, a fountain or some other source of water; it is open for everyone, it offers national, or rather regional cuisine. The menu does not focus on one specific dish. Plov is a staple meal, of course. Quite often, you book a

Lunch at a teahouse in Samarkand's Siyob Market: tandoor-baked flatbread, mastava soup, and hot tea

separate room or a tapchan for a specific time and order some plov of your choice. You can also try some signature dishes of the specific region you are visiting. Of course, there will be *babai*, or elderly men, playing checkers or backgammon and drinking tea. Choyxonas attract companies of men to enjoy some pilaf: this is a form of leisure for men; one could say almost a "stag party."

You can see many classic, exemplary choyxonas if you travel the Fergana Valley.

The Uzbek Table

Originally, Uzbek cuisine does not use such terms as "sauce," "entree," or "dessert," neither does it distinguish between the first and main courses, or side dishes. Many national dishes in their consistency are between a soup and a stew, customary to us, whereas the tea and sweet courses such as dried fruit, jams, fresh fruit, and nuts can be eaten several times during a meal, in the beginning, in the middle and in the end. Signature dishes of Uzbek cuisine involve braising or boiling the main and additional ingredients together in a large pot, and the perfect example of it is the plov.

Traditionally, food in Uzbekistan is not served individually: most often, the dishes come to the table on a common plate, and it will be perfectly normal if you eat the same plov with your spoon from a large lagan without putting some on your own plate. Only soups and stocks are served in small individual bowls.

As for spoons and forks, the latter are never used to eat plov: a good cook will make it so fluffy that the rice will simply fall between the prongs of the fork. Therefore, don't be surprised when they offer you a spoon to eat the plov; and don't be surprised when they invite you to eat the plov with your hand, pressing a handful of rice on the rim of the lagan. Mind you, it needs some practice!

The Uzbek table always has some flatbreads. Only seldom does the bread come in the shapes we are accustomed to, such as loaves or baguettes. Flatbreads are almost always served (and sold!) in doubles: when the housekeeper or, more broadly, the host breaks the bread, it is the signal to start the meal.

As the table is laid for the guests, it usually has the flatbreads and pastries (sweet and savory), vegetables (herbs, fresh vegetables, homemade pickles), fresh fruit, sweet dishes (halva, sweets), dried fruit, nuts, and refreshing drinks (lemonades, water, homemade compotes). As soon as the guests sit at the table, teapots with tea arrive, more often it will be green tea rather than black, sometimes with lemon. For Uzbeks, tea is the aperitif, the digestive and the accompaniment to any dishes. Tea is poured in small quantities, showing respect to the guest, as is customary in the Eastern countries. Before serving the tea, the man or the lady of the house pours it from the pot into the bowl and back three times to make sure it is steeped properly.

There is always a lot of food on any table in Uzbekistan: when you visit friends or go to a restaurant. "A lot" is an understatement: food will be abundant, it is the distinctive trait of the nation and the cornerstone of Eastern hospitality. If you are a guest in Uzbekistan, it will be a challenge to have "a bite."

Preparation of typical Bukharan plov. Meat and vegetables are cooked separately

WINEMAKING

November in Parkent's vineyards, Tashkent Region

Winemaking in Uzbekistan is developing, literally, despite everything. The Islam's prohibition of drinking alcohol, the very hot and dry climate, Gorbachev's battle against alcoholism: the winemakers hardly have that in mind when they say that the vine must suffer! Nevertheless, the country is making a slow but steady transition from a supplier of inexpensive base wine to a destination of not only gastronomy but of enogastronomy tourism. There are noteworthy Uzbek wines—a lot more than one can imagine.

A circumstance that impeded a rapid development of winemaking in Uzbekistan is the fact that drinking wine has never been part of the culture, for centuries ruled by the dominant Islamic dogmata. Decades within the USSR taught the locals to drink alcohol, but there is not much talk about the culture of drinking wine in the Western sense. The greater part of alcohol consumed is vodka. In the days of celebrations, in a nod to traditions, sales of sparkling wines would spike (people usually use the word "champagne"). Many people make wines at home as low-alcoholic alternative to traditional hard liquor. Uzbekistan appreciates sweet and fortified wines; the wines from Europe and the New World are scarce, expensive, and drunk by few people.

At the same time, there is another thing to consider, which is the large flow of European tourists, members of the wine culture interested in tasting the local wines. They are the focus of modern small and large winemakers and of the country leadership when it develops winemaking and wine tourism. The boom of the Uzbek tourist spells prosperity for winemaking. Often, wineries grow as tourist attractions focusing on working with group and individual travelers. In those places that still have no tasting rooms, they are sure to open soon.

The climate of Uzbekistan is severely continental, with very hot summers and cold winters. The grapes yield high crops and accumulate a high content of sugar; it is best suited for semi-sweet, sweet and liqueur wine. Speaking of climatic features of grapes growing, the country may be divided into two large areas. The Southern includes the Samarkand, Bukhara and Surxondaryo Regions, and the Northern, the areas near Tashkent, and Fergana Valley. In the Soviet times, the vineyards of the Northern area were considered more suitable for making dry wines; my tasting experience leads me to think that this was a very narrow approach.

The history of modern Uzbekistan winemaking starts with the arrival of the Russians to the region and with gradual Europeanization of the country. In 1867, the Russian merchant **Ivan Pervushin** founded the first distillery to produce wines and alcoholic beverages in Tashkent. He was a successful entrepreneur and traded wine, tobacco and silk in Turkestan. Almost at the same time, in 1868, **Dmitry Filatov** opens the first wine distillery in Samarkand, whose wine would be supplied to the Russian Imperial Court several years later. Another Russian merchant from Orenburg, **Nikolay Ivanov**, founded wine and vodka distilleries in Tashkent, as well as production of ice and fruit drinks. In the Soviet period, the production sites founded by the Russian merchants, the accumulated knowledge, buildings and equipment became the basis of the Uzbek winemaking, a part of the large industrial complex of the great country.

Development of winemaking in Uzbekistan is closely related to the work of **Mikhail Khovrenko**, who became the Head Winemaker of "Uzbekvino" Complex in 1927. He started his operation at the Filatov winery in Samarkand: today, it is the country's only **Museum of Winemaking**. When the Soviets came into power, Filatov had to abandon his business, and his collection was only found decades later, during the reconstruction.

Mikhail Khovrenko systematized everything that Uzbek winemaking had achieved; he planted new grape varieties, created new blends, and brought his wines to international competitions. One can say that what we see in Uzbek winemaking from the perspective of cultivated varieties and that of the technological process are merits of Mikhail Khovrenko.

In 1942, a **sparkling wine factory** was founded in Uzbekistan. In part, it was based on the premises of merchant Ivanov's distillery that had made wine as early as in the second half of the 19th century. The equipment for making the sparkling wine was evacuated to Tashkent from Kharkov, Tsimlyansk, Rostov-on-Don, and Inkerman.

The absolute majority of the wineries now functioning in Uzbekistan were founded on the base of Soviet-era plants and small farms scattered around the country that perform primary vinification and preparation of base wines. Full-cycle companies were a rare phenomenon in the Soviet times, and today the Uzbek winemakers have to face a variety of challenges: some need to find and procure equipment for secondary vinification, some need to gain knowledge of processing the grapes. It is still common for wineries to buy not just the grapes but the base wine without being fully confident of its quality. Greenfield full-cycle wineries began to emerge only in the recent years. The state sees a lot of potential in the development of winemaking, following the example of Western wineries with opportunities of hospitality, and provides benefits for winemakers.

Chaotic branding and immensely broad product ranges of almost every producer are the peculiar features of the Uzbek wine market. Nearly every winery produces dozens of wines trying to fill several price niches at once. Dozens of names are complicated by as many label designs so exotic, that one can hardly guess that the wines on the shelf were made by the same producer. Broadly speaking, this indicates that wineries are still on the quest of the self, of their proper style and expression.

Main Varieties of Grapes

The varieties of grapes popular in Uzbekistan may be divided into three large groups: European, Georgian and Central Asian (Eastern) varieties. A characteristic feature of Uzbek winemaking is the frequent use of all-purpose varieties combining the features of table and technical varieties.

The large group of European varieties includes the traditional Cabernet Sauvignon, Pinot Noir, Chardonnay, Riesling, Aleatico, and Muscat. Some of these, for example, Cabernet Sauvignon, born in the Uzbek terroirs, yield a clear predictable profile; others, such as Pinot Noir and Riesling, usually associated with cooler climates, turn out to be less recognizable. The stellar variety of Uzbek winemaking is the Muscat, foundation of bright, explosive, highly aromatic wines, from semidry to sweet.

Rkatsiteli and Saperavi are two Georgian varieties of grapes widely available in Uzbekistan; largely, it is the result of a cultural exchange of the Soviet period. These are mainly used for mass production of inexpensive wines.

Central Asian or Eastern varieties are the results of selection of regional winemakers and the legacy of the Soviet system that focused on creating high-yield, low-maintenance varieties best adapted to the local climate. These include Soyaki, Bayan Shira, Kuldzhinskii, Taifi, and Rizamat. Bayan Shira and Kuldzhinskii, traditional for Central Asia, are used most frequently; Taifi and Rizamat are table varieties sometimes used in blended wines.

Rizamat Musamuhamedov is a legend of Uzbek viticulture, Hero of Socialist Labor, Merited Vine Grower of Uzbekistan, Merited Agriculturist of the Uzbek Soviet Republic. He started his career in the Ivanov wine factory during the era of the empire; his work in the Soviet period was so successful that his experiments and their results were most highly appreciated by Nikolai Vavilov. Rizamat Musamuhamedov pioneered the projects of growing citrus fruit in Uzbekistan, was the first to implement the use of vine props thus improving the crops. Without knowing how to read or write, he delivered training courses for vine growers. There is a true story that became the basis of the film The Apples of 1941*: Rizamat Musamuhamedov went to the front to see his son bringing with him a railway wagonload of dried fruit. He devoted his entire life to Uzbekistan and Uzbek grapes. One of the dozen varieties bred by him now bears his name.*

Wines to Try

WHITE

- PetNat MSA Family Winery (Parkent, Tashkent District)
- L'Amore Soyaki Château Hamkor (Parkent, Tashkent District)
- Riesling MSA Family Winery (Parkent, Tashkent District)
- Baka Bang White Dry Blend (Surxondaryo District)
- Uzum Fermer Dali Paja (Tashkent District)
- Sultan Porto 2016 (Surxondaryo District)

RED

- Château Hamkor Pinot Noir (Parkent, Tashkent District)
- Chateau Hamkor Cabernet Sauvignon (Parkent, Tashkent District)
- Sultan Cabernet Sauvignon (Surxondaryo District)
- Baka Bang Red Dry Blend (Surxondaryo District)
- Merry Tash Uzumfermer (Tashkent District)

DECORATIVE AND APPLIED ARTS OF UZBEKISTAN

A refined example of Bukhara metal chasing, crafted by the Kasymov workshop

Throughout the centuries, one of the main roles of decorative and applied arts was to decorate interiors, clothing and utensils to animate everyday life, to make it more colorful. Every domain of decorative and applied arts developed in line with the established practices, traditions, and real world of nations. Every single item we buy today is a thread, a bridge connecting us with the past, the legacy of many generations. It is a reflection of everyday life, habits, and fate of people.

In Uzbekistan, the **connection of contemporary decorative and applied arts with tourism is strong and inseparable**. The ancient crafts keep on living only because the intricately painted plates, hammered jars and sharp knives are in demand by visitors from abroad. When traveling across the country in search of artisans who preserve the local style, I had many opportunities to make sure that arts and crafts in Uzbekistan exist only where there are guests.

The Uzbek artisans are facing a multi-faceted complicated task: on the one hand, to preserve the traditions, centuries-old uniqueness that exists in a strong bond with the history and culture of the country, its nation, regions, and families. On the other hand, there is the wish to move forward and the demand of foreign customers to have some shapes and forms, colors and formats that do not always follow the traditions, and the wish to be a commercial success. Embroidery, painting, pottery, hammering and punchwork, as well as any other arts and crafts of Uzbekistan are always a balance between the art and the necessity of earning one's bread.

Hospitality and treatment of guests as treasured ones, and the sheer amount of money that tourism brings to the country became the stimulus for development not of merely small shops, where one can look at the goods and buy them, but rather **workshops combined with showrooms**. You are no longer a buyer there but a dear guest; you will learn the technicalities of the process and enjoy some pilaf, hot flatbreads and fragrant tea. When you visit such workshops, you actually become a guest of a real Uzbek family experience the legendary Eastern hospitality. Of course, if you want to sit to a potter's lathe yourself or take a paintbrush in your hands, Uzbekistan will open immense opportunities. Wherever tourists are, there will be master classes in calligraphy, pottery, and embroidery.

After traveling across the entire country and meeting dozens of people, I asked each of my interlocutors the same question: how they decided on the choice of their career. In the vast majority of cases, it turned out that the choice involved continuing the family business.

Continuity of dynasty. This is the vital feature of Uzbek decorative and applied art. One does not simply abandon the fathers' profession, its continuation is the moral and, in many aspects, religious obligation of the sons, a commitment before one's forebearers. Respect to the elders and the patriarchal structure of life are vital in all spheres of life in Uzbekistan, and arts and crafts are no exception. It was no easy matter to become a master of one's craft in the old times. It was a rite of passage for the apprentice led by the teacher in the present of other artisans. There was even a tradition of marrying the master's daughter to the best apprentice to ensure the continuity of tradition and to keep trade secrets within one family.

In Uzbekistan, the artisans work in the same way their fathers and ancestors did. Great attention is paid to **preservation of old techniques and means**, considerable handiwork, natural, local materials, be it clay or colorants. Almost everything is done the old way, by hand, in the same meticulous and comprehensive manner, as it was a couple of hundred years ago. In most cases, mass production is off the table: the items are unique and represent collector value.

One of the prevalent trends is the **recovery of old crafts**, be it manufacturing of paper out of mulberry trees, decoration of cloth with printed patterns or the time-consuming Tashkent-style embroidery, the important thing is that the initiative comes from the craftsmen themselves. The book has several stories like this. Each of them is a striking example of personal involvement, hard work, and attention to the heritage of the country. Many artisans not only carry on the tradition after the senior generation of the family, but also **recreate the centuries-old traditions** within their craft by learning the archives. They draw inspiration in their native land, archeological discoveries, and museum collections.

Every part of Uzbekistan possesses its own **regional traditions** of crafts. Similar to gastronomy, it will be no exaggeration to say that the forms of decorative and applied arts would change every two or three hundred kilometers of your journey. As you travel Uzbekistan, you discover the country not only by architectural monuments and food, but also by ornaments, patterns, colors of embroidery, drawings, hammered and woven items.

Stark segregation between men's and women's occupations is common in the craft activity of the country. Most professions have been and still are available only to men. Embroidery and home-based carpet weaving have been and still remain the foundation of female independence, especially in rural areas and families with a patriarchal structure. I take special pride in telling stories of female entrepreneurs in my book.

Regardless of gender, all artisans of Uzbekistan that I had the chance to meet **taught children and youth** for free in most cases, not only ensuring the continuity of the tradition, but also handing over the craft, the means to earn a living, to feed their family, to remain with them without going away to earn money. This makes each thing that you buy in your travels across the country just another drop of that special glue that keeps families together.

Things to Bring from Uzbekistan

Textiles and Embroidery

Domestic weaving is one of the vital production areas in the country. Silken, semi-silken and cotton fabrics are woven in Uzbekistan, preserving the traditional ornaments, the uncouth 40 cm width of the cloth due to the dimensions of the loom. These are the bright fabrics with exquisite abstract patterns or stripes, hot and lifeful, carrying the recognizable aesthetics of handiwork. The center of silk weaving is Margilan in the Fergana Valley. The cotton fabrics are masterfully crafted in the Surxondaryo Region.

Without doubt, the **suzani embroidery** is a national vocation, the art in which women of Uzbekistan have attained unparalleled skill. The regional traditions are different, with intricacy of the Nurata style, the suprematism of the Urgut emroidery, the expressive colors and the distinctive themes of Surxondaryo, the *palaks* of Tashkent, where the entire surface of the fabric is covered with millions of minuscule stitches. The suzani and the large canvases lit up with embroidery were used to embellish interiors, and so they serve, being an excellent souvenir to carry from Uzbekistan. Moreover, the embroidery moved from the decorative paintings to the outfits: various types of stitches now adorn the hand and beauty bags, jackets, dresses, and coats.

When packing for Uzbekistan, be sure to bring a foldable shopping bag or leave extra space in your suitcase! For large or fragile items like ceramics, most artisans can easily arrange international shipping to your home.

Gold embroidery is a craft unique to Bukhara. While suzani embroidery was done mostly by women, the gold-stitch embroidery, or goldwork, is the prerogative of men. Embroidery seldom

Traditional Khorezm pottery, made and painted by hand, by Odilbek Matchanov

was used to decorate clothing, because the fabrics were highly ornamental as such, unless it was goldwork for the robes of the Emir and his attendants, and for the palace interiors. To this day, clothing with hand-stitched gold embroidery is manufactured.

Tubeteika embroidery, first of all, from Shahrisabz and Boysun, is widely known in Uzbekistan. These elegant skullcaps are fully decorated, fully embroidered with meticulous stitching.

Cloth printing is a craft that miraculously survived: fabrics are decorated with ornaments printed with hand-carved wooden stamps dipped in dye. Probably due to the intensity of labor and less striking ornamentality than the suzani embroidery, cloth printing, in time past widely spread across the country, has become rare. That's exotics of Uzbekistan! I found an artisan in Samarkand, who revived the old craft; there are also master printers in Margilan.

Metalwork

Jeweller's art. Uzbek women are not wearing so much jewelry as it was customary, say, in the late 19th century. Consequently, few jewelers create true works of art, not mere imitations. The jewelry brands that give a new meaning to the national traditions (specifically, one brand, see chapter on Tashkent) deserve your interest.

Trunk art. No traditional Uzbek house can be imagined without a trunk. However, when traditions changes and the modern furniture appeared, the interest in manufacturing trunks ceased. The craft got its second breath in the manufacturing of trunks, boxes and jewel-cases fully ornated with metal. They are exquisitely decorated.

Copper hammering ornates the kitchenware that has been, and remains, the decorative touch that lights up the interior and shows the owner's good taste and wealth. The renowned centers of copper hammering in Uzbekistan are Bukhara and Kokand.

Knives. Sharp polished knives with bone handles that are so grippy, coming in embossed leather sheaths, are Uzbekistan's long-standing pride. There are household knives (great for meat carving!), and there are collector's knives, with rich encrusted and painted handles. Be sure to look for them in Bukhara, Tashkent, Kokand, and Chust.

Pottery

Glazed ceramics is Uzbekistan's pride and honor with tremendous regional differences. Colored in hues of the sun and the earth, the blue of the lakes and the cerulean color of the skies, masterfully decorated with pointilist ornament or abstract runs of paint, it is manufactured the same way it was hundreds of years ago. Choose to travel the pottery schools of Uzbekistan, and you will see the entire country, literally, because there is not a single region where one cannot find renowned potters. The major centers of pottery are as follows: Tashkent (Rakhimov dynasty), Samarkand (Bobomuradov dynasty and Sharif Azimov), Gidjuvan (Narzullaev masters), Shahrisabz (Muzafarov dynasty), and Rishtan (Alisher and Bakhtiyar Nazirov, Rustam Usmanov). Aside from the master Matchanov, hardly any true masters remain in Khiva. **Unglazed ceramics and small clay plastic** are a fading tradition, primarily associated with Samarkand. Toys for children and every day, rather than festive, household items, such as pitchers, were made from raw clay without any additional treatment. Thanks to a whole constellation of Samarkand masters, this type of pottery not only discovered new forms but thrives today.

Carpet Weaving

Wool carpets are a traditional form of women's domestic artisanship, primarily associated with livestock farming and the necessity of utilizing wool obtained from sheep, and the decoration of living spaces. Uzbekistan boasts a rich legacy in the field of carpet weaving, the diversity of which is closely linked to the country's ethnic variety and the influences of Arabs, Turkmen, Kyrgyz, and Karakalpaks. The art of wool carpet weaving also includes the creation of interior elements for yurts, such as carpets, rugs, bags, and small pouches for storing essentials, as well as the process of felting wool into a material known as *koshma*.

Silk carpets have never been traditional for Uzbekistan; however, today, when one speaks about Uzbek carpets, it is the silk ones that come to mind first of all. The advent of the bew craft, the synergy of ornamental traditions of decoration specific to Uzbekistan and the Turkmenian legacy are the merit of one family, whose story you will find in this book. The craft of weaving silk carpets first appeared in Samarkand, and then in Bukhara and Khiva.

Eastern Miniature

Miniature books, the Persian inheritance, made Bukhara known far and wide. Every painting made with a fine brush is not a mere decoration: it has a deep philosophical significance. What once was illustrations in the books became later interior painting.

Miniature lacquer painting was revived in Tashkent in the 1980s. It adorns items made of papier mâché: small jewelry boxes, small panels, and interior items.

Calligraphy in the East in general, and in Uzbekistan in particular, raised to high degrees of decoration: what seems to us just an ornament of architectural elements of mosques and madrasahs is, in fact, writing. Present-day calligraphers transfer the sophisticated script to handmade paper and create works of art where the picture and the writing merge.

Mulberry paper is indispensable for miniature books and calligraphy. The secret of its production was restored in Samarkand and they continue to make sheets of amazing smoothness without the use of electricity, the old-fashioned way, entirely by hand.

Other Types of Crafts

Woodcarving. In Central Asia, wood was a highly valuable material that required special handling, and it was decorated painstakingly with sophistication. Across the entire country, you will see carved pillars, doors, window-blinds and pieces of furniture. For the visitors who cannot pack a carved door in their luggage, the local artisans offer beautifully worked jewelry boxes.

Ganch carving. The thing guests cannot take away as souvenirs is carved ganch, a mix of clay and gypsum. Nevertheless, one cannot overlook this unique method of interior decoration: the walls, niches, ceilings, either snow-white or covered in brightly-colored ornaments against the white background will forever be etched in the memory. The art of ganch carving is a national honor.

Dressing of furs. It is hard to leave Uzbekistan without buying a caracul, or astrakhan, hat or coat. The art of fur dressers, perfected for centuries, mostly in Bukhara in Khorezm, now produces lightweight versatile items.

Making of dolls is truly an art of synergy, be it interior dolls of theatrical puppets. They combine drawing on papier mâché or ceramics, ornamental textile, adornments, often antique, and unparalleled attention to details of traditional attire that varies from one region to another.

TOURISM IN UZBEKISTAN

The heart of Bukhara: a view of its storied Old Town

Uzbekistan is a country of incredible hospitality, and traveling there is interesting and comfortable. It has no stringent religious restrictions on people's appearance or behavior that travelers need to comply with. People working with tourists speak several foreign languages and are fluent in Russian. There is next to no language barrier, and the price level is quite reasonable. At the same time, Uzbekistan as a tourist destination has its own specifics.

The **tourist season** in Uzbekistan is short due to weather conditions. It is advisable to come in spring (from the middle of March to late May) and in autumn (from early September to early November) to get the best of the mild weather, open restaurants, manufactories, and shops. The summers are very hot, winters are very cold, and all places worthy of tourists' interest are closed, as a rule. The admissible exception is the modern Tashkent, an all-season destination, but even there it is much more pleasant to enjoy the mild weather of spring or autumn, without heat or rain.

Mass tourism is most common in Uzbekistan: the majority of visitors from European and Asian countries travel in groups following the routes made by local agencies with accompanying guides. This scenario, organized group tourism, was the main pattern of tourism development since the Soviet era. Consequently, the infrastructure is tailored to tourists accompanied by a guide at all times, tourists, who do not deal with matters themselves. In the real world, it means that museums have no information books or annotations, tables in restaurants need to be booked in advance during the season, train tickets and hotel reservations also need to be taken care of beforehand. It also means that everything in towns, workshops, restaurants and museums can be perplexing when you try to find your way around. No clear addresses, poorly organized presentations, scarce informational materials are a reality. Knowing this, I decided to write this book. It will not replace a guide, but it will illustrate many small details. I recommend traveling with a local companion, because it is more comfortable. For a social person, not afraid of improvising, there will be no obstacles in getting to know the country on their own. Speakers of Russian have a great advantage: in Uzbekistan, almost all the people working with tourists speak Russian.

The cities of Uzbekistan that are developed best from the standpoint of tourist infrastructure are **Samarkand**, **Bukhara**, and **Khiva**; they are the backbone of conventional routes across the country. Many tourists come to Tashkent, too, but for many of them it is just a place of transfer. Fewer people make their way to Karakalpakstan, although it has an independent tourist system of its own. In other words, if you go to Karakalpakstan, it is advisable to contact local agents, not the large companies based in the center of the country. Even fewer people visit Fergana Valley, and fewer still, the remote areas of the Qashqadaryo and Surxondaryo regions. It is safe to say that these are the areas whose tourist potential is yet to be unlocked. For tourists, it spells fewer hotels and restaurants of a lower level, less guides... with greater authenticity of locations, rituals, arts and crafts, cuisine, and, of course, lower prices.

Uzbekistan is a **large country**. The distance from Tashkent to Samarkand is 300 kilometers, from Samarkand to Bukhara 270, and between Bukhara and Khiva 450. This means that traveling between the cities by car takes almost half a day. Tashkent is the hub for all flight connections within Uzbekistan: if one flies from Termez to Urgench, for example, they will need to transfer in Tashkent. The high-speed train "Afrosiyob" connects Tashkent, Samarkand and Bukhara, but during the high season, it is difficult to procure the tickets due to high demand and blocks of seats being bought out by travel agencies. A high-speed rail will connect Bukhara and Khiva, in the future, but for now, there is only a standard train of sub-standard comfort. There is no regular, easy, comfortable ankhord predictable bus service between the cities: the buses are quite infrequent, the shuttle buses are not safe and very crammed. When traveling the regions of the country, it is worthwhile to rent a car. In most cases, a car is hired privately, or a car is hired with a driver through an agency, and the driver will also be your guide. Rent-a-car services in the European sense of the word are a novelty for Uzbekistan: the agencies are scarce, and tariffs are not very flexible. The traffic and the manner of driving in here are chaotic and unpredictable. The closer you are to tourist locations (Tashkent, Samarkand, Bukhara), the higher the chances to hire a decent car with a driver, but to find an off-road somewhere in Termez might as well be impossible. On the other hand, in Karakalpakstan such vehicles are plentiful, because tours to the Lake Aral are highly popular, and the routes are off-road. Another option of traveling between cities is sharing a taxi with someone; usually the drivers look for their customers in bazaars or markets, and near shopping malls; the locals will give you a hint.

The star rating in Uzbekistan's **hotel business** is rather provisional: save for the hotels of large international chains, there is no sense in looking at the number of stars. Families, not professional hoteliers, privately run the great majority of hotels in the regions. While hospitality may be (often is) above expectations, the housekeeping, quality of communication, and the level of available services may be a problem, as well as the design. Such hotels do not have on-duty restaurants, but in almost every single one of them, you can order dinner or supper in advance.

Limited prevalence of Internet and online booking is something that complicates a traveler's experience. Uzbekistan is not the country where upcoming issues can be dealt with online. The easy way to get an answer to whatever question, to find or to book something is to make a phone call. Uzbekistan is still a country of personal contacts, and it is exactly for this reason that the book gives the current phone numbers of hotels, restaurants, and artisans.

When traveling in Uzbekistan, one should not rely on the availability of cashless payments: **be sure to have cash with you**, because banking cards may not function, even if available. It is better to keep it in mind: cash may be needed.

Making a Route to Visit Uzbekistan for the First Time

Long weekend with no time to prepare?
If you have just three days, your two best options are traveling to Tashkent or Bukhara. Both will not require preparing in advance, looking for a guide, renting a car, or buying hard-to-obtain train tickets. Tashkent is modern and easy to find your way around, the restaurants and shops have proper addresses.
Bukhara is compact, and you can easily get a taxi to go on several drives outside the center of the city.
Samarkand is more difficult to organize a short trip to due to its structure, and Khiva is too small to stay for a few days without leaving it.

Four days and some time to prepare?
Four full days will get you Samarkand and its suburbs covered. The special feature of Samarkand is that it is a big city that has suffered from an ill-thought-out urban layout. It is not easy to walk around it, and you might feel uncomfortable without a local guide with a car.

Four days may get you to Samarkand and Bukhara, leaving the last day for the latter. This is a reliable option that will, most likely, leave you with a feeling that you did not see it all, that you were just short of time.

A whole week and enough time to plan it all?
In a week, you will cover three cities: Tashkent, Samarkand, and Bukhara. Tashkent and Samarkand will require more time than Bukhara. You will fly into the capital and leave from Bukhara, and you will travel between the cities on the high-speed train "Afrosiyob"; be sure to book your tickets early.

A vacation of 8–9 days with some time to get ready?
With so much time you can see the golden triangle of Uzbekistan: Samarkand, Bukhara, and Khiva, but adding Tashkent to that would be quite a challenge. Fly into Samarkand, take the "Afrosiyob" to Bukhara, and hire a car with a driver from Bukhara to Khiva. It is a very frequent request, so ask you hotel's staff to help you.

Tashkent, Tashkent Region, and Regional Areas. The Sunny Side of the Street

Chapter I

Tashkent has several faces… One is the modern Tashkent, seeing the future, looking around, just half a step from common mistakes of urban development, mistakes of the new money and trying so hard to keep up with the neighbors. Sometimes, it is the city made just to look good from a car window.

The other is the Soviet-era Tashkent: a city of broad green avenues, architecture of socialist modernism and an unbelievably beautiful metro system; the city born after the earthquake of 1966. It was powerful, but the direction of the commotion was not vertical but horizontal, so the old mudbrick Tashkent suffered total devastation, but the death toll was just over ten people. An urban legend says that people continued to break down their old houses in the hope of relocation to new, comfortable housing. Only a few districts of that old Tashkent remain. Miraculously surviving the turbulent 20th century, they present yet another face of Tashkent: the wizened face of an old man, a chaotic, complicated labyrinth of a city that still keeps its medieval planning but retreats at the push of the modern age.

Yet another face of Tashkent... An Islamic city with blue cupolas, mosaic façades of madrasahs and mosques, revered for keeping the items valuable for any Muslim, such as the Uthmanic Quran, the oldest manuscript of the Holy Scripture. A city where sheiks, saints and Sufis significant for the Islamic world are buried.

For anyone who starts their journey in Uzbekistan with its capital, Tashkent will be a preface to everything to be seen. Anyone visiting Tashkent in the end of their journey will be surprised by the contrasts of the most Europeanized city of the country and will gladly remember the Eastern details of their journey. The nature hikes around Tashkent, including the suburbs, are some of the most beautiful and easily accessible locations in the country. I do insist that one should not leave Tashkent without several outings from the capital!

Minor Mosque in Tashkent—a modern example of Islamic architecture

A BIT OF HISTORY

A Resort for Warlords, a Republic City, a Mix of Moscow and St. Petersburg

Alisher Navoiy Grand Theater in Tashkent

Tashkent was founded and was growing in the location where the harsh dry climate of Central Asia becomes a little softer and allows people to live and to create. Situated in an oasis and at the crossroads of trade routes, Tashkent has been known since around 4th or 5th century as a target for those dreaming about ruling the region.

In the first half of the 4th century BC, Alexander the Great came to Central Asia. When he was brought to the territory of the present-day Tashkent, he was seriously ill. He was poisoned and so weak that it is said he had to command his last battles while lying—before his healing. The legend has it that the king's salvation was the healthful water from a local spring. Today, the Sheikhantaur Mausoleum is situated where that spring once was. Over the tomb of Sheikh Hovendi at-Tahur, a descent of the Prophet who was buried here in the 16th century, there grows a tree planted in 329 BC, where the drops of the Tashkent healing water fell from the hands of Alexander the Great. It is still possible to see that tree.

In the year 711, the Arabs demolished the northernmost Temple of Fire known in the world, situated to the northeast from the center of modern Tashkent, on the hill of Yunusabad. Another hill, standing 16 meters high, can be found in the center of the city: the Mingorik. Remnants of rhytons made of ivory, and vessels used in the cult rituals of the Zoroastrians were found here. The findings of excavations in the Minogrik allowed identification of the age of Tashkent, 2,200 years. The scientists, however, believe that the age might be elevated to 2,500 years, given more thorough and deeper digging.

The citadel that gave birth to the modern Tashkent was founded in the year 819, not far from where the main city's bazaar, Chorsu, is located. Even then, in the 11th century, the market was next to the fortress and the ruler's palace. Around that citadel and that market, there emerged a city that we know today as the capital of Uzbekistan: a rich city, that made its money, among other things, from silver trade: silver had been mined in the suburbs since the 8th century. The name of the city was *Chach* or *Medina Ach Chach*, in Arabic.

In the end of the 9th century, the Samanid dynasty came to power with their capital in Samarkand, later, in Bukhara, and Tashkent became a part of the Samanid state. The rulers changed: in the 11th–13th centuries, under the Karakhanids, Tashkent was part of their empire and was destroyed in the early 13th century, along with the other cities in the region, by Genghis Khan's armies.

Sheikhantaur Mausoleum in Tashkent

In the late 14th century, the city came under the rule of Tamerlane, but for the first time, the future great military leader was brought here in 1361, at the very start of his military career, as a wounded man without any special rank. It is believed that he was cured by the same healing water that had saved Alexander the Great many centuries before.

In the 16th century, the first Uzbek state of the Sheibanids emerged, and Tashkent became part of it. Before its conquest by the Kokand Khanate in the early 19th century, the independent Tashkent state existed for twenty years, a self-governed republic city. In the 1870s, Tashkent came under the protectorate of the Russian Empire. It was in 1930 that Tashkent became the capital for the first time: the capital of a new state, Uzbek Soviet Socialist Republic, and this status was transferred to it from Samarkand.

The **Anchor Canal** is the nature's border between the old Muslim Tashkent and the new Russian Tashkent. Of course, the division is blurred, but it lives in the people's memories. The Russian part is built according to a city master plan: it was conceived as the Oriental St. Petersburg. However, fortress walls with several gates once surrounded the old city, and the monotonous maze of narrow streets with mud-brick houses was interrupted by the domes of madrasahs and mosques. The way we see Tashkent today, the few monuments and historical buildings, the way Tashkent is so unlike what we think of a traditional city in Central Asia has several reasons. There were devastating earthquakes of the 19th and 20th centuries, there was the wish of the new government to build a city worthy of the title of a capital of a Soviet Republic, and, of course, there are the modern authorities that need a modern capital city. Tashkent had never been a capital city until the Soviet period, which explains the fact that it has no monuments comparable in scale with the Registan in Samarkand. Tashkent suffered from earthquakes, and this is the reason why the historic fabric of a medieval city survived so poorly. This city is a mixture, an alloy, a tangle of a thousand knots.

The ancient sites of **Shoshtepa** and **Mingorik** can still be seen in Tashkent. Mingorik is actually located in the inner yard of one of Uzbekistan's first communal houses built under the project of Georgy Svarichevsky, the chief architect of Tashkent both of the Czarist and the Soviet periods. One can imagine the way the city center looked in the 16th century, under the rule of Sheibanids by visiting the district of **Hazrati Imam** (also known as Hastimom), where the Muyi Muborak Madrasah houses the Caliph Usman Quran that dates back to the 8th century, and a single hair of the Prophet. Nearby, along the Canal of Kalkaus (Keikaus, in the local lingo), there is one of the city's oldest mahallas, that the locals affectionately call the *Venice of Tashkent*, that keeps its traditional structure.

Academic life still goes on in the **Kukeldash Madrasah** built in the second half of the 16th century and restored in the Soviet time: come, and you will see rows of boots and shoes left by the students at the entrance. Places around the **Sheikhantaur Mausoleum** are connected not only with the Saint, not only with Alexander the Great and Timur, cured by the local water, as the legend has it. They are also related to the film production studio, where the famous film *Two Soldiers* was shot; and it was here that Mark Bernes sang his immortal song, *Dark Is the Night*.

The Russian part of Tashkent is home to numerous cultural and historical landmarks, including the **Romanov Palace**. During the Soviet era, it served as the House of Pioneers, where notable persons such as Anna Akhmatova, Nadezhda Mandelstam, and Aleksey Tolstoy, who were evacuated to Tashkent, worked with young people. The buildings of the men's and women's gymnasiums, the State Bank building, the Real School building, and the Treasury Chamber, built under the Russian protectorate, have survived almost unchanged and are examples of Turkestan Art Nouveau. Take a look at the brickwork without plaster: the brick was made using techniques taken from the Muslim world, and you will recognize it when you come to Bukhara and look at the Samanid Mausoleum, built in the 9th century.

Alisher Navoiy Metro Station in Tashkent

Romanov Palace in Tashkent—a remnant of imperial Russian presence

Another layer of Tashkent is the austere and ornate buildings constructed during the Soviet era, which are remarkable monuments of Soviet modernism. These include the **Uzbekistan Hotel**, the **State Museum of Cultural History of Uzbekistan**, the **Alisher Navoiy Cinema Palace**, the **Chorsu Bazaar**, Tashkent **metro stations**, and **residential areas** where mosaics and decorations with national motifs brighten up the familiar Soviet-era mass buildings.

Among the many buildings of Tashkent, I love the **Alisher Navoiy Cinema Palace**, designed by the architect Aleksey Shchusev. Its six foyers are a tribute to the arts and crafts of different regions of Uzbekistan, and the Navoiy Theater is a mix of all Uzbekistan. I believe it is the way to understand Tashkent: a mix of everything there has been and still is, in Uzbekistan.

Places to See

Old Tashkent
Hazrati Imam Complex
Kukeldash Madrasah
Sheikhantaur Mausoleum

Modernist Architecture of Tashkent
Uzbekistan Hotel, Chiming clock, Amir Timur Square
State Museum of Cultural History of Uzbekistan
Alisher Navoiy Cinema Palace
Chorsu Bazaar
Tashkent metro stations (my favorites: Kosmonavtov/Kosmonavtlar, Nezavisimosti/Mustaqillik, Alisher Navoiy)
Residential areas (Chilonzor, and blocks around the Chorsu Bazaar)
Alisher Navoiy Opera and Ballet Theater
Residential complex Zhemchug (Pearl)
Golubie Kupola (Blue Domes) Restaurant

Russian Tashkent
Romanov Palace (closed for reconstruction)
The State Bank Building
State Museum of Applied Arts, Polovtsev's house
Real School Building
Mariinsky Women's School
Evangelical Lutheran Church
Cathedral of the Sacred Heart of Jesus

Tashkent: Highlights

–**Mark Weil's Ilkhom Theater**, the most famous independent theater studio in Central Asia. Their piece *Zeal with a Pomegranate*, a fantasy about the life and paintings of the artist Usto Mumin (Alexander Nikolaev) is a performance enveloped in a cult status.
+998 71 241 22 41, Pakhtakor Street, 5

–**Bonum Factum Gallery** is one of the best-known in Tashkent organizing exhibitions not only on its own premises, but in upscale venues, e.g. Ilkhom Theater and modern restaurants and cafés.
+998 71 232 03 60, Sadyk Azimov 3 Drive, 20A

–**State Museum of Applied Arts**, housed in the mansion of the Russian diplomat Alexander Polovtsov, built in the oriental style. A tour of these halls is an opportunity not only to admire the fantasy interiors, but also to have a closer look at almost every kind of art and craft in the country.
+998 71 256 40 42, Rakatboshi Street, 15

Tashkent: A Schedule

Day 1
Sightseeing tour: Amir Timur Square, Romanov Palace, Independence Square. Lunch. Continuation of the city tour: Hazrati Imam Complex. Visit to one or several handicraft show-rooms. Dinner.

Day 2
Chorsu Bazaar. Lunch. Thematic excursion: seismic modernism, colonial or Russian Tashkent, Tashkent metro. Dinner.

Day 3
Flea market in Yangiobod. Lunch in the city. One or more museums: State History Museum of Uzbekistan, State Museum of Applied Arts. Tasting of Uzbek wines. Dinner. You can also spend the day in the suburbs of Tashkent (Parkent District and Château Hamkor winery or a trip to the mountains, Charvak reservoir and Amirsoy resort).

The façade of the State Museum of Applied Arts in Tashkent, showcasing traditional Uzbek decorative motifs

CUISINE AND WINEMAKING OF TASHKENT, TASHKENT REGION AND NEIGHBORING AREAS:

An Oriental Medley

Traditional bread baked in a kozon, accompanied by homemade butter, Zaamin District

One of the most important factors influencing both the traditional gastronomy of Tashkent and its environs and the city's modern restaurant scene is the large number of ethnic groups living in the region and the proximity of the borders. The cuisine of Tashkent is also the cuisine of the Uyghurs, the Turks who historically lived in China and migrated to Turkestan. It includes the cuisine of the Soviet Koreans who were forcibly resettled here in the late 1930s. And it is also the cuisine of the Kazakhs, because the border is very close, hence the popularity of horsemeat dishes.

The foothills and mountains of Tashkent and neighboring Jizzakh regions with their **cool climate** and winds create good conditions for producing dried meats—beef, mutton, horsemeat—that are the basis of many dishes.

The **specifics of life in mountainous regions** had its effect even on the delicious flatbreads. Here, in Zomin, they are cooked in cooking pots, or kozons, and not in tandoors as is customary in many locations in Uzbekistan.

Another important feature of cuisine is the **availability of fish**. People catch fish in the nearby Syr Daria River, fry and serve it with spicy tomato sauce, or smoke it. Passing through the Syr Daria Region *en route* from Tashkent to Jizzakh, you will see a large fish market and many salespeople standing at their stalls by the road selling bronze-colored smoked fish.

The wineries of merchants Pervushin and Ivanov, which appeared in Tashkent with the establishment of the Russian protectorate, have since become large enterprises producing still and sparkling wines, using traditional methods as well. **O'zbekiston Shampani** is the successor of the Ivanov's distillery, which became the Tashkent Factory of Champagne Wines in the Soviet period. The factory received winemaking equipment, including that for the manufacturing of sparkling wines, from other factories evacuated during the Great Patriotic War. **Tashkentvino** took over the winery of the merchant Pervushin; now it is the largest producer in the country. The **main vineyards are located in Parkent,** where long and hot summers, dry and warm autumns and sufficient altitude provide favorable conditions. It was here that the **Château Hamkor winery** was founded in 1992, on the advice of French oenologists. In recent years, several small and ambitious family wineries (e.g. **Uzum Fermer**) and "garage wineries" appeared in the region.

Dishes to Try

Naryn is a dish of boiled thinly sliced horsemeat and homemade noodles boiled in meat broth and thinly sliced with a knife.

Tashkent plov is usually cooked in enormous pots on special occasions, e.g. weddings. Horse meat sausage (qazi), chick peas, and boiled chicken or quail eggs are added to the dish.

Tashkent flatbread is made from unleavened dough in a tandoor. Its edges are puffy, and it is less dense and smaller than the Samarkand flatbread.

Lochira flatbread is a large thin flatbread of unleavened dough that is baked in the shape of a plate in an oven. It is cooked on special occasions and is used as a plate for the plov, but sometimes can be served for desserts.

Moshkichiri is a hearty wintertime dish highly popular in Uzbekistan. Boiled mung dal beans are stewed in a kozon for a long time with added vegetables and meat, including dried meat.

Gumma is the Tashkent term not simply for small pasties or chebureks, as is the case in other regions, but small pasties filled with giblets (lamb lung, spleen, heart, trachea) deep-fried in oil in a kozon. Hence the street-name given to gumma in Tashkent: "ear-nose-throat." An urban legend says that these pasties first appeared on the Beshagach Square (a meatpacking factory was nearby) as early as in the 1960s at 4 copecks apiece.

Archa kabob is baked meat, usually lamb: they cook it following the same process, as in Surxondaryo and Qashqadaryo Regions. Archa, a local variety of juniper, is used to marinate the meat, and the meat is then baked in tandoors buried in the ground. This dish is cooked mainly in the Jizzakh Region.

Jizzakh samosa is the biggest samosa in Uzbekistan. The ingredients are cut into big pieces, there is a lot of juice inside, and before serving, it is brushed with vegetable oil, to make the taste and presentation better. Vegetable oil with tomato sauce and vinegar are served as the sauce.

Zomin kozon-baked flatbreads. In the mountainous areas of the Jizzakh Region, in the suburbs of the town of Zomin, thick flatbreads are baked in kozons, not tandoors. The dough is made with milk and kaymak. Such flatbreads are enjoyed while still hot, adding whipped homemade butter or drawn butter: it will start melting from the heat of the bread.

So'qoq skewers. Dwellers of Tashkent are sure that the best meat skewers around their native city are made in the town of So'qoq in the Parkent District at the foot of the mountains. Driving to So'qoq on a summer weekend to enjoy the coolness, fresh air and grilled meat is an important ritual.

Lagman is a type of handmade noodle dish served with a rich sauce of lamb, tomatoes, onions, carrots, and bell peppers. Authentic lagman is always prepared by twisting the dough into ropes and stretching it until the noodles become as thin as threads.

Traditional preparation of lagman noodles

Cinara's restaurant in the Bostanlyk District, near Lake Charvak

Mador samsa is a samosa filled with fresh mador greens, a plant from the family of Alliaceae, or onions. Mador appears in the mountainous regions in April and May. The word *mador* translates as "strength," "help," or "assistance."

Dried meat (sur go'sht) is sometimes served as a snack, or added to main courses, for example, to moshkichiri.

Where to Eat: National Cuisine

For a citizen of Tashkent (broadly speaking, for any citizen of Uzbekistan, but we stick to the capital for now), food possesses almost a religious meaning. A conversation about food is full of zeal, and considering that many locations, where this or that dish is an absolute "must-try" have no official names, such a conversation becomes somewhat of a mystery. Visitors will hear such directions as "that samosa at Qo'yliq on your way to the Crossroads," or "that lagman on Sebzar," and will have zero chances of finding their way.
For a resident of any city in Uzbekistan, including the capital, there is no better compliment than your interest in where the best samsa, plov, naryn or beshbarmak is cooked in the neighborhood. For outgoing and adventurous people, I suggest talking to the taxi drivers and asking them to take

you to the most delicious samsa, plov, and so on. Of course, it is impossible to list them all in this book without missing something. Nevertheless, I will give some general instructions without complicated names, passwords and geographical coordinates.

Chorsu Bazaar

A true Oriental market, unkempt and uncouth, not even trying to produce a favorable impression, a market for the locals, yet also visited by tourists. Bins of curds, hundreds of meters of meat cuts, long poles with qazi are on the ground floor of the bazaar under the legendary blue dome. The second floor is more suited for tourists with dried fruit, spices, and teas. On the ground floor, flatbreads are baked in huge gas-fired tandoors.

As you exit the bazaar, don't miss the long lines of food, ready or cooked in front of you: chebureks, samsa, plov, naryn, hasyp, and cabbage rolls, or golubtsi.

Across the road from it, you will find a long gallery of dozens of arches decorated with maroon and white tiles. This is the *besik bazaar* ("cradleboards bazaar"), as the locals sometimes call it, the houseware section of the Chorsu Bazaar. Household items such as children's cradles, furniture, and kitchenware are found here, as well as several stalls with food.

Alay Bazaar

Alay Bazaar is the neat and tidy version of the Chorsu, and expatriates living in Tashkent frequent it to buy food. The range of products is more or less the same, but the place is quieter, there is more light and more space between the stalls. If you talk to an owner of a café in Tashkent or to someone in the hospitality business, and they tell you they buy food at the Alay Bazaar, be sure: that person keeps their standards high.

Flatbread Bazaar of Chig'atoy and Ko'kcha Skewers

If you want to learn the multitude of the Tashkent flatbreads and tandoor-baked samsa, take a ride to the Chig'atoy in the old city, one of the most ancient markets of Tashkent specializing in baked goods. Here, bread is brought from all over the city: homemade artisanal bread carefully shaped by hands of a woman and keeping the heat of the tandoor made for her by her husband. Behind the bazaar, there are several rustic cafés. You will find tables covered with oilcloth, rickety chairs and delicious food. The specialties of Chig'atoy are Bedana sho'rva, a quail soup, and liver skewers. As you go in the direction of the Ko'kcha Street, you will find more kebab houses.

Chig'atoy Art
Most cafés on Chig'atoy are very simple in terms of ambience, service and presentation. If you want something a little more laid back but still authentic, go to Chig'atoy Art, a new café with the atmosphere of old Tashkent and a selection of Tashkent's favorite dishes on the menu. Be sure to try the mashkhurda and beshbarmak.
+998 99 770 99 33, Chamanar Street, 175

Shashleek
If you want a kebab, but nightlife and tables with sticky oilcloths scare you, come to Shashleek, a modern café with panoramic windows overlooking the park. Here they specialize exactly in kebabs and skewers of all possible

Pelmeni (dumplings with meat filling) at Pelmeni Café

kinds: beef, lamb, liver, chicken, fish, vegetables… There is a kebab bar, a counter where you can watch the meat being cooked, high tables for a quick snack and sofa areas for those who are in the mood for a long meal. Enjoy the hot bread from tandoor and Uzbek teas in painted ceramic bowls.
+998 98 101 01 11, +998 88 121 01 11, O'zbekiston Ovozi Street, 49

Tarnov Boshi Barbecue
One of the best places in Tashkent where lagman and other Uyghur dishes are prepared is a café on Sebzar Street (known in Tashkent simply as "lagman on Sebzar"), with a spacious terrace and several darkish inner halls. Besides lagman, the kebab here is worth a try. Pay some attention to ayrimsai, a Uighur-style vegetable sauté, and ganpan, a dish similar to lagman but served with rice.
+998 71 203 52 52, Yuqori Sebzar Mahalla

Gijduvon Milliy Café
Olot samsa is a specialty from Bukhara. Yet you are in Tashkent, and it is the capital city for a reason: dishes from all the country can be found here. If Bukhara is not on your list, come to this simple café to try the samsa the way it should be, with thin crust and juicy filling. It is almost better than they cook in Bukhara! Be sure to ask the waiter to bring tomato sauce and kefir for your samsa.
+998 55 518 08 00, Toshpo'lat Rasulov Street, 2

Ugolok Café
This legendary café was opened back in the 1960s. The interior has lost its space-themed flair over the years, but Tashkent residents still come here for fried chicken,

Nigmatulla Abdullaev, owner of Pelmeni Café

Cooking kebabs at Loza Art Café

a loaf (that's right, not a flatbread, but a factory loaf of bread!) and a simple vegetable salad.
+998 71 233 36 80, +998 99 444 55 51, Mustaqillik Avenue, 10

Pelmeni Café (*Chuchvara dumpling house*)
The dumpling house has not always been here, on the ground floor of this prefabricated apartment block in the center of Tashkent, but Nigmatulla Abdullaev has been working here, across the road from the Cosmonauts Metro Station, since the year 1969. It started as a grocery store, then a deli, then a cafeteria. Now, for several decades, the place is famous for its pelmeni, or dumplings, that many consider the most delicious in Tashkent. In winter, they also cook moshkichiri (adding some dried lamb to the beef), silpildoq (Uzbek-style beshbarmak). In spring, until mid-May, they make dumplings with fresh greens. Spices and condiments are always available: hot pepper, garlic, hot red sauce, fresh greens, and onions. The dumplings (*chuchvara*, as they are called in Uzbekistan) are really good: thin, almost transparent dough and juicy filling. At lunch-time, this simple café is fully packed. In the evening Pelmeni is closed.
+998 94 644 70 20, Yakub Kolas Street, 2

Loza Art Café
Cuisine of the Fergana Valley and Tashkent in the cozy green yard in the Navruz Ethnographic Park with excellent skewers and a must-try plov. The café is only open in the warm season.
+998 97 133 85 55, Navruz Ethnographic Park, Fergana Street, 33

Loft Café
I was talking to Pavel Georganov, young and cheerful Tashkent restaurateur, on a Sunday evening over some plov. We were not in a choyxona, but in a café with loft-style interiors and club music. Next to us, several companies of locals were having plov, too. For a hardcore keeper of Tashkent traditions, this situation could have been unimaginable just a few years before. Never do people cook plov in the evening, let alone on Sunday evening, and people definitely do not come to eat it in a modern café. Pavel says he is headstrong: "We bided our time, and we managed to get a community around us that loved what we do."

A son of a military man, Pavel moved to Tashkent together with his family all the way from Sakhalin in Soviet times. He grew up, his parents left; he got married and had children... He opened a typical café, with coffee and desserts, where he was the pastry chef and the barista. It turned out that people wanted food, not coffee, and this is how the "Loft" came to be, or just the "Café," as it is known in the city.

"We gave some zest to the plov," Pavel says, meaning the modern presentation and the Turkish pickled pepper. The plov is served with the traditional "Achik Chuchuk" salad sprinkled with crumbs of sheep's milk kurt. The café started cooking plov at the traditional time, on Thursday noon, but the demand was high, and Sundays also became plov days. Speaking about the local ways, he adds, "On Sundays people come to have a good drink. We do not have Fridays. In Tashkent, your Friday goes from Thursday to Monday."

Pavel himself taught his team to cook and to communicate with guests. When I come to Tashkent, I pay a visit to the "Café," and I remember my surprise from my first time: such friendly discussion on an equal footing in European style is not frequent in Uzbekistan. "Every day, we have the same people here," comments Pavel, "we serve simple homemade food that people want every day."
+998 95 145 45 45, Beshagach Street, 9

The Choyxona
A teahouse with a modern twist for those who are intimidated by stilted tables and babai drinking tea. It offers an extensive national menu and separate rooms for companies of different sizes, including rooms with their own open terrace.
+998 99 844 88 88, Bog'ishamol Avenue, 131

Khiva Restaurant
A national restaurant located in a large five-star hotel working with international guests, Hyatt Regency Tashkent, no less, faces quite a challenge: give a proper representation of the local cuisine (in the case of Uzbek cuisine, the situation is even more difficult, since the visitors already know how delicious it is) and maintain the Western standards of presentation, service, and taste. I find the approach of Khiva very appealing. They are careful not to intimidate the guests with a multitude of dishes or exotic foods. For example, the naryn is made with beef rather than horse meat, and servings of plov are modest and low on oil. One of my favorite dishes on the menu of Khiva is the dumgaza, or stewed oxtails: tender, sweet meat, in the words of Uzbeks, served over couscous or potatoes. Another advantage of the restaurant is the availability of local wines on the menu. They know how to serve

them, which is not always the case in Uzbekistan. Look out for the Muscat and Cabernet Sauvignon from the local producer, Château Hamkor.
+998 71 207 13 11, +998 99 845 40 22, Navoiy Street, 1A

Caravan
Caravan Group holding is the fruit of an art gallery, a dream about opening a restaurant, and a s food. Natalia Konstantinovna, mother of Timur Musin, owner of Caravan, is a connoisseur of art and theater; more than three years ago, she owned a small gallery dedicated to the art of Central Asia. Problems with rent, lack of interest to items of art on the outside, and the family passion towards food and understanding of gastronomy as a part of the cultural legacy of Uzbekistan led the Musin family to open their first restaurant, Caravan. It became the place, where guests of Tashkent are taken to learn the national cuisine and traditions.
+998 78 150 66 06, +998 78 150 75 55, Abdulla Kahar Street, 22

Tandiriy
A new Uzbek restaurant near the Tashkent City Park, where everything revolves around dishes cooked in a tandoor. If you order a samsa, the tandoor will be brought directly to your table and the freshly baked samsa will be taken out of its fiery interior before your eyes.
+998 881 00 22 55, Ukchi Street, 5

Where to Eat: European, Middle Eastern and Asian Cuisine

Faces Gastrobar
A modern gastrobar with a creative menu from the chef Yegor Ermakov. A mix of European, Asian and Uzbek cuisine, and an excellent bar! Try the Margarita with tree types of oil.
+998 77 704 80 08, Bakhodir Street, 1/1

GŌSHT
A modern restaurant, a kind of Uzbek steakhouse, where they cook mainly locally sourced meat in all kinds of ways, national and international. No alcohol is served, but there is Australian, Japanese, and Russian beef and lamb.
+998 99 516 88 00, Shahrisabz Street, 5A
+998 77 703 88 00, Niyozbek Street, 29/5
+998 77 373 88 00, Ukchi Street, 3

Kurutob House
Kurutob is a national Tajik dish of a layered flatbread, suzma, vegetables and meat, seldom to be found in Uzbekistan restaurants. Thanks to Kurutob House, this dish is available in Tashkent. Apart from the main specialty, there are local and international staples on the menu, such as Caesar salad, mastava and eclairs. A true fusion!
+998 90 094 04 00, Shota Rustaveli Street, 50

City 21 Izakaya Pan Asian Restaurant & Lounge
Perched on the 21st floor of the Hilton Tashkent City, this Pan-Asian restaurant dazzles with craft cocktails infused with local flavors and a one-of-a-kind summer terrace: the highest vantage point of its kind in the city.
+998 71 210 89 06, +998 94 940 10 01, Islam Karimov Street, 2, bldg. 5

Traditional Korean table setting at Kim Sat Gat

In Tashkent, the tastiest food hides in humble settings. Locals—wealthy included—zealously share addresses of these unassuming spots. The city's modest Korean cafes thrive too, partly thanks to kimchi stew's legendary hangover-curing powers.

Sette
For those craving a break from plov, shashlik, and lamb, Sette, the Italian gem of Hyatt Regency Tashkent, delivers flawless pizza, exceptional pasta, and a rare highlight: artisanal tartare, a delicacy scarcely found elsewhere in Uzbekistan. In summer, the open-air terrace offers prime views of the city center.
+998 71 207 13 71, Navoiy Street, 1A

Kim Sat Gat
Soviet Koreans were forcibly relocated to Uzbekistan from the Far East in the late 1930s, establishing a significant diaspora in Tashkent. However, Kim Sat Gat breaks this tradition; it serves authentic South Korean cuisine rather than Soviet-Korean dishes. For over tweenty years, Nelly Vasilyevna Pak has been at the helm—quite unexpectedly, as she never planned to become a chef. Her culinary journey began in 1996 when a South Korean entrepreneur asked for her help opening Tashkent's first authentic Korean restaurant… Over the years, Nelly Vasilyevna has served ambassadors, CEOs, and employees of nearly every South Korean company in Tashkent. Her influence even extends beyond Uzbekistan: she launched successful cafés in Kyiv and Samarkand. Soy sauce, marinades and pickles are all made by her, personally. She recalls how the South Korean ambassador, upon asking how often she had visited her ancestral homeland, was stunned by her reply: "Never." Yet he admitted the food at Kim Sat Gat surpassed what he had tasted back in Korea. When I asked if she had finally made it to Seoul and what she thought of the restaurants there, Nelly Vasilyevna didn't miss a beat: "Let those southerners come here—they'll be the ones learning from me."

At Kim Sat Gat, start with sutbulgogi (marinated beef tenderloin) and moksal (marinated pork neck) served with a dazzling array of condiments: seaweed salad, soy sprouts, chili-marinated radish, vinegar cucumbers, rice crepes, tofu, fermented soybean paste, garlic, scallions in chili oil, sesame oil, and fresh lettuce leaves for wrapping. Complete your meal with two fiery soups: kimchi jjigae (pork stew with fermented cabbage) and yukgaejang (spicy beef soup with bean sprouts and fernbrake).
+998 71 254 54 36, Yusuf Xos Hojib Street, 46/1

Bakinka Café
Bakinka is a true family-run café serving Baku's home-style cuisine. I mean family literally, for in the kitchen you'll find Larisa, a gifted cook with golden hands (born to feed people), while her daughter works the dining room. She never lets anyone into her secrets, and shares no recipes. Her jocular answer is, "I graduated from a home kitchen high school." The guests have just a few tables to enjoy their meals. A parrot chirps, and there is TV in the background. You feel the aroma of spices from the kitchen, and you see jugs of homemade wine and glasses of strong Azerbaijan tea.
The family history is a tragic one. The turbulent early of the 1990s, the escape from Azerbaijan, the split Armenian-Azerbaijani family, and a shattered life. But here, in Tashkent, Bakinka is a true oasis of peace, quiet, and warmth. Homemade pickles and watermelon-rind jam with lemon, a genius shakshuka with köfte, paper-thin kutabs, crackling-skinned fried fish, and melt-in-your-mouth meats. Don't forget to call ahead and book a table!
+998 93 184 72 15, +998 97 131 72 15, Shota Rustaveli Street, 104

Cafés and Coffees

Bon!
A major French café chain offering a rich menu. Think quiches, salads, sandwiches, and fluffy omelets. They even elevate their croissants serving them with a scoop of ice cream.
+998 71 252 56 94, Taras Shevchenko Street, 30
+998 71 280 51 16, Shota Rustaveli Street, 63
+998 71 268 93 02, Akkurgan Street, 14A

ChayKof
ChayKof is a pioneer of Tashkent's tea-and-coffee culture with multiple locations across the city. They serve European-style breakfasts and brew exceptionally balanced coffee, poured into hand-painted ceramic cups. Yet survival is tricky for cafés focusing solely on drinks and pastries here, so ChayKof's menu expands to soups, sandwiches, and pasta.
+998951701666, Kari Niyazov Street, 61
+998909691666, Shota Rustaveli Street, 22
+998781501666, Said Barak Street, 16 B
+998991901666, Buyuk Ipak Yo'li Mavzesi, 24, entrance 1

Socials
Step inside and you will question your coordinates: is this Tashkent, New York, or Dubai? Poached eggs, falafel, burgers, and waffles unite in a culinary alliance. Specialty coffee in perfectly curated cups, plus a charming terrace. Another project from the same creative team is the Arrows & Sparrows café in Tashkent City Park.
+998 99 008 88 11, Taras Shevchenko Street, 36a, Amir Timur Avenue, 86a, Kazakhstan Minor Residence

Community Coffee Bar
A fresh coffee concept that goes beyond brews and breakfasts. The team regularly hosts collaborative dinner series featuring guest chefs.
+998 33 370 0333, Taras Shevchenko Street, 24

B&B Coffee House
B&B stands for Beans&Brews, a growing chain of cafés across the city. Baristas will make you any drink, even off-menu creations, while their desserts rank among the city's best (do try the cheesecake). By day, the menu covers everything from gourmet sandwiches to steaks and pasta.
+998712098448, Fidokor Street, 25
+998 71 281 60 60, Shota Rustaveli Street, 30A

Rassvet
Great specialty coffee and seasonal pastries—think autumn favorites like quince or fig pies. The walls are covered in art by local talents Nigina Mirzadzhanova and Laziza Tulaganova.
+998 50 900 50 11, Chimkent Street, 17

Wine Bars and Restaurants

Just Wine
A modern bar on the Tashkent's Broadway does not make Uzbek wines its main focus. There are some, but most of the shelves and fridges are stocked with European and New World bottles. This makes tasting local wines extra interesting: comparing them with less exotic options.
+998 90 043 59 99, Matbuotchilar Street, 17

Silk96
A wine restaurant and lounge by one of the country's top wine importers. The menu mixes everything from sushi rolls to arugula salads, with plenty of wine-friendly snacks (think cheeses, pâtés,

bruschetta), plus pizza and pasta, and, of course, an extensive wine list.
+998 99 835 85 00, Kari Niyazov Street, 68A

Wine Bazaar
A new wine bar in Tashkent City with an extensive wine list, catering to a younger customer. The menu features a special section dedicated to modern takes on traditional Uzbek dishes.
+998 90 066 63 66, Furkat Street, 1A

Place No.1 bar & store
A tiny, three-table venue that you should keep on your list because you can taste almost all of Uzbekistan's quiet wines by the glass: 17 positions. Sparkling wines are sold only by the bottle.
+998 95 709 50 49, Amir Timur Avenue, 88

If you want to explore Uzbekistan's wine diversity, book a private tasting by reaching out to sommeliers Nadezhda Ivanova (*+998 97 710 04 12*) or Svetlana Fedoseeva (*+998 99 797 93 14*).

DECORATIVE AND APPLIED ARTS OF THE REGION:

A New View of the Old Crafts

Dolls in traditional costumes by Nasiba Akhmedova

Tashkent's arts and crafts scene has one defining feature, its capital city status. As the nation's premier metropolis, it attracts master artisans from across Uzbekistan, all drawn by new commissions, connections, fame and opportunities.

Nowhere in Uzbekistan will you find as many artists as in Tashkent: artists with a freer, more modern take on their craft, less constrained by tourist-driven demand. New styles, **synergy of arts and cultures** from the different regions of the country, transformation and deconstruction of popular heritage, all this happens in the capital. This is where one finds artisans reinventing tradition, creating new forms from ancient techniques and objects while establishing **fresh artistic movements**. Whether it is **straw marquetry paintings, knives** with intricately painted handles, or jewelry-grade **chests and boxes**.

One of the most interesting stories of reviving an old craft and creating a new school based on it is the story of Tashkent **lacquer miniatures**. In the 1980s, this art form combined the nearly lost tradition of book miniatures (characteristic of the East) with the papier-mâché painting technique typical of Russia's Palekh.

Like Shahrisabz, Tashkent features complete-coverage embroidery where no fabric remains visible. **Tashkent palaks**, densely embroidered with a satin-like stitch, may appear unusual and austere from a distance, but reveal meticulous execution and numerous fine details when viewed up close. They are recognizable by the rich red or burgundy base color of the embroidery and stylized solar and lunar motifs, which typically present complex compositions of several circular forms with elaborate ornamentation. The revival story of **Tashkent's embroidery school** unfolded in the 2000s and became possible through the efforts of a single craftswoman.

If you look carefully, Tashkent has representatives of every craft, from Nurata embroidery masters to Shahrisabz potters, from coppersmiths and woodcarvers to weavers, blacksmiths, and ganch artisans. You will find Boysun skullcaps, Qashqadaryo suzanis, and Gijduvan ceramics in tourist areas, mixed with Chinese and Indian knockoffs and items mass-produced in Uzbekistan itself. For this reason, I selected both the people and crafts for this chapter with even greater care and focus, aiming to draw your attention to the most **unusual, unfamiliar, and interesting aspects**, things you are not likely to see when traveling through other regions of Uzbekistan. Whether in gastronomy, history, or craft culture, Tashkent is a great melting pot.

Madina Kasimbaeva's Embroidery Studio
Tashkent embroidery requires two or even three times more work than even the most complex Bukhara or Nurata suzani, where not the entire background is covered, but only various patterns are embroidered. The Tashkent palak requires not only more time but also greater quantities of thread and dye. In the time it takes to embroider one Tashkent palak, an experienced craftswoman could complete two or three suzanis, and sell them. That's basic market economy! By the mid-2000s, the tradition of Tashkent embroidery had faded, primarily due to the labor-intensive nature of the work. It was Madina Kasimbaeva who gave it a second life. Years of dedicated effort resulted in solo exhibitions in Uzbekistan and abroad, a school of embroidery, and collaborations with both Uzbek and international fashion designers. The robes embroidered by Madina's atelier have been worn by Emine Erdoğan and Melania Trump.
+998 90 167 67 04, +998 91 191 34 00, +998 93 555 33 17, +998 90 967 04 75, Suzuk Ota Street, 35

Akbar and Alisher Rakhimov's Ceramic Studio
"I was just playing," tells me Alisher Rakhimov, a descendant of a dynasty of potters, as we make our way through the garden planted with fig, pomegranate, and almond trees to the workshop where he works with his father, son, and students. "Usually, our grandfathers spoil us, and teach us with keen interest, because they have lots of patience." With characteristic Oriental

Embroidery artist Madina Kasimbaeva at work

In autumn 2025, Tashkent will welcome a new museum and workshop space dedicated to Madina Kasimbaeva. Visitors will be able to witness the entire suzani creation process firsthand—from initial sketch to finished piece. The gallery will showcase new works including suzanis, chapan coats, and textile art installations.

Embroidery by Madina Kasimbaeva

Potters Alisher and Akbar Rakhimov, continuing their family's ceramic traditions

subtlety, Alisher sidesteps when I ask if he always wanted to take over the family trade. Alisher's grandfather is one of the most famous potters of Uzbekistan: Mukhitdin Rakhimov, a pioneer among researchers of traditional ceramic art, who made an encyclopedic description of its nuances, forms, and ornaments as early as in 1961. His book *Artistic Ceramics of Uzbekistan* is now a bibliographic rarity. In 2006, in a UNESCO project, it was translated into English, and I, for one, learned the history and nuances of Uzbek pottery through it.

The Rakhimovs' school and studio are impeccably organized. I have visited many artisans, but this is the first time I have seen a gallery where you can study Uzbek ceramic styles and visually trace what was fashionable in the 9th versus the 14th century. While many Uzbek masters work within one technique, only refining the color schemes, patterns, and technologies inherited from past generations, the Rakhimovs master them all. "We put our effort into what needs our help," Alisher says, as we explore the exhibition halls, and I find it hard to believe that the numerous shapes, styles and methods were made in the same family. Alisher skillfully avoids giving a direct answer about where his true passion lies, though he does spend slightly more time describing what he calls his "sunny" ceramics, quite different from the traditional green palette his father prefers.

The shelves of Alisher's father, Akbar Rakhimov's workshop, are filled with

Showroom at Alisher and Akbar Rakhimov's Ceramic Studio

archeological curiosities found in Uzbekistan. The shards of oil lamps, jars and lagans of 9th–10th centuries are the sources of inspiration and the reasons to think, the starting points of contemplation. For the Rakhimovs, the legacy of their homeland and their father's and grandfather's diaries forms the very foundation. Mukhitdin kept meticulous records for over fifty years, documenting both daily life and his experimental results. Alisher continues this tradition in another part of the workshop, building a library dedicated to ceramics.

Mukhitdin Rakhimov was the first from the dynasty to have a specialized education. "He lived an interesting life," recalls Alisher. As a young man, he came to Moscow to visit the first agricultural exhibition and worked there on the potter's wheel. He was invited to study in Moscow, and then returned to Samarkand, the capital of Uzbekistan at the time, and set up the first workshops. When the capital was relocated to Tashkent, Mukhitdin returned to his native city and worked a lot with archeologists to form an understanding of the different styles, schools and techniques that were prevalent in Central Asia for centuries. Alisher's father took over Mukhitdin's work, and now we can have a detailed picture of what were the ceramics of the Timurid period—white and blue, with a distinct Chinese influence, or what precious emerald glow emanated from the traditional pottery of Tashkent.
+998 90 987 20 63, +998 712 49 04 35, Ko'kcha Darvoza Avenue, 15

Human House Gallery
Human House is neither a shop, nor a showroom, nor simply a gallery. It is a genuine home that accommodates everything that interests its owner, Lola Sayfi: from Soviet-era armchairs upholstered in embroidered velvet to photography exhibitions of stray animals and donation boxes for Tashkent shelters. The space hosts lectures, film screenings, workshops, and creative gatherings. Two halls display works by over 200 designers and artisans, not only from Uzbekistan but also Kyrgyzstan, Kazakhstan, and Tajikistan—each of whom Lola knows personally. She explains to each artisan what the client is looking for, how seams should be finished, what treatment the fabric requires. She designs new cuts, provides designers with orders—offering new development directions while serving as a bridge between craftspeople (who know the intricacies of traditional production) and shoppers coming to Human House. She still finds the time to create clothing under her own brand and supervise its production.
+998 90 937 83 73, Kichik Mirobod Street, 43

Bibi Hanum
For Mukhayo Alieva, Bibi Hanum is less a fashion project than a social one, an opportunity to provide employment for women while preserving Uzbekistan's craft heritage. The handmade fabrics used in their collections (which include women's, men's and children's clothing, footwear, accessories, and home goods) come from the Fergana Valley. The embroidery paired with adras-woven patterns originates from Samarkand, Nurata, and Bukhara. Yet all these remarkably beautiful items are designed and produced here in Tashkent. What sets Bibi Hanum apart from numerous brands capitalizing on national fabrics is its contemporary design approach and supreme craftsmanship. This clothing is conceived and sewn by women with impeccable taste, style, and golden hands—making it far more than just another ethnic souvenir.
+998 90 947 91 95, Sagbon Street, 30A, 4th blind alley, bibihanum.com

Alia.7s
Aliya Sharshenbieva works in a unique technique combining hand-felted wool with hand-woven silk. The contrast of colors and textures adds elegance even to the simplest dress, suit, and coat designs. When coats won't fit into your luggage, her versatile shawls will make perfect compact souvenirs.
+998 99 880 00 70, Navruz Ethnographic Park, Samarkand Street, 43

Aliya Sharshenbieva's workshop welcomes families with children—kids will love the wet felting art masterclass! While the little ones craft wool paintings, parents can enjoy shopping in Navruz Ethnographic Park.

Unique dresses designed by Aliya Sharshenbieva

Browsing the stalls at Besik Bazaar, part of Chorsu Bazaar

La Maison du Chapan
Designer Nadira Abdurakhmanova's project in the Navruz Ethnographic Park. The exquisite showroom houses a collection of vintage chapan coats and fabrics, contemporary national-style outfits designed by Nadira herself, and a selection of artifacts from Uzbekistan's master artisans.
+998 77 310 03 33, Navruz Ethnographic Park, Khorezm Street, 15

Kanishka
In Tashkent, Kanishka boasts some of the city's most stylish stores, designed with minimalist aesthetics and subtle nods to traditional Eastern architectural elements. Against this neutral backdrop, the brand's vibrant urban streetwear stands out brilliantly. What truly sets Kanishka apart are its unique leather goods (bags, backpacks, wallets) and playful fur coats combining multiple natural furs, perfect for those who always thought fur coats were hopelessly old-fashioned.
+998 71 268 95 19, Akkurgan Street, 21
+998 71 252 57 77, Afrosiyob Street, 39
+998 71 255 03 93, Shota Rustaveli Street, 39

BJeans
A denimwear brand made in Uzbekistan. The jeans, shirts, dresses, and knitwear are produced in Uzbekistan using locally grown cotton. Collaborations with local designers are especially worth your attention.
www.bjeans.uz

The Black Quail
A contemporary leather workshop specializing in bags, cosmetic cases, wallets, and reinterpretations of national heritage. The brand's boutique also operates in the international departures zone of Tashkent airport.
+998 95 146 09 00, Shota Rustaveli Street, 34

Masar Jewellery
Ulugbek Kholmurodov is one of Uzbekistan's most renowned jewelers, owner of an architecture firm, the man who proves that "contemporary style" and "national heritage" can coexist. His jewelry under the Masar brand does not simply recycle overused folk motifs, but deconstructs and reimagines them. Collections have limited releases, with each piece featuring custom packaging, documentation, and certificates.
+998 90 977 88 78, Nukus Street, 31/7
masar.uz

Nasiba Akhmedova
Nasiba Akhmedova always dreamed of being a fashion designer and creating large-scale national-style collections for people. Instead, she dresses dolls in outfits crafted not just with great taste and care, but based on historical costumes from different regions of Uzbekistan. The coquettish yet modest dolls feature porcelain heads, hands and feet, with bodies made from wire frames, calico, and cotton wool. The dolls are full of movement: here, one balances a jug on her shoulder, another holds a doira tambourine, a third smooths her luxurious braids. Each is completely handmade, with costumes sewn and decorated using antique jewelry and vintage fabrics. The workshop is located within the Navruz Ethnographic Park, designed to showcase Uzbekistan's diversity and rich traditions to visitors.
+998 90 324 26 51, Navruz Ethnographic Park, Samarkand Street, 45, Tumor Art Gallery

The historic Hazrati Imam Complex in Tashkent

Rimma Gazalieva
Rimma Gazalieva was the chief artist of the Kuvasay Porcelain Factory, one of the three in Uzbekistan. She started her business in Tashkent after the collapse of the USSR when she moved to the capital to her relatives. Today, Rimma paints modern tableware with patterns reminiscent of fabric designs and conducts painting workshops for everyone, even absolute beginners. You will spend two hours in the workshop, your creation will stay in the oven for seven hours… and you will take home a plate or a cup decorated by your own hands.
+998 90 167 65 39, Chilanzar District, Block 5, 46/56

Anvar Israilov
Anvar's workshop is located in the Suzuk-Ota residential complex. The artisan became famous for lacquer miniature and knives with exquisitely encrusted handles.
+998 97 425 56 95, Suzuk Ota Street, 40

Mohammaddavlat Umaraliev
If you wander through the mahalla around the Hazrati Imam Complex and you want to pay a visit to an authentic old Tashkent house, see the antique loom, and learn about hand-weaving and block-printing techniques, call Davlat. He comes from a family of hereditary weavers who never abandoned their ancestral craft. His home is a veritable textile museum.
+998 91 131 11 77, Uylanish Street, 2nd blind alley

The Barakhan Madrasah in Tashkent

Where to Shop

Chorsu Bazaar
The household section of the Chorsu Bazaar is full of wares that the locals usually need. Many children's cradles (beshiks), heaps of stamps for flatbreads, stalls with musical instruments (the go-to person here is Mahsud, *+998 33 242 77 24*), quilted gowns, or chapans, and one of the best-known antique shops of the city. Its owner, Botyr (*+998 90 961 89 21*), an antique dealer and screenwriter, is equally knowledgeable about vintage robes, Chinese vases, and copper samovars.

Bodom Gallery
A selection of clothes from Uzbek designers, and crafted items from artisans from across the country.
+998 90 320 03 35, Chigil Street, 42, La Villa Residential Complex, call for appointment

Teplo Store
A modern concept store with a selection of clothes and accessories of Uzbek designers in the national and globes styles.
+998 99 991 20 22, Nukus Street, 31/2

TSUM and shopping pavilions nearby
The old-school Tashkent Central Universal Goods Store, or TSUM, has not yet converted into a modern shopping mall: it is the right place if you have a whim to buy a porcelain teaset with the

traditional Pakhta ornament, or factory-printed cotton with nostalgia-evoking patterns. In a small shady square around there are book stalls where you can find old books on Uzbekistan, and there are some antique dealers with their curiosities.

Adbulkasim Madrasah, Barakhan Madrasah are two ancient madrasahs in the different parts of the city, where the former students' cells have been since transformed into artisans' workshops, where you can watch the artisans work and get acquainted with them.

At Abulkasim Madrasah, Ubaydulla Kasymov (*+998 99 888 40 06*) continues his family's legacy, saving the craft from extinction and elevating the art of chest-making (along with far more compact yet equally beautiful boxes) to new heights.

One of the workshops of the Barakhan Madrasah belongs to Jasyr Jumayev (*+998 99 822 02 01*), an artist who creates pictures not with paints but with straw. Each work begins with a handmade sketch following the techniques of Eastern miniatures, but uses straw fragments instead of paints, adding finer details and shadows by burn.

Yangiobod Flea Market
Open on weekends, the Yangiobod Market offers none of the sophistication found at Europe's famous flea markets like Naschmarkt or Portobello. Yet like all authentic markets worldwide, it shows the urban life, the raw, unvarhished character of Tashkent, complete with its sun-beaten skin and knowing grins. This market is huge! Walk some five kilometers in the dust and old rags, and you will see only a half of it. The best is hidden in the abandoned warehouses beyond the railway tracks (look out for the moving trains!) There, under the long-forgotten ceilings, are stalls with Bohemian crystal, Hungarian porcelain, and silver tableware; there are hangars full of antique furniture, or rickety Thonet chairs, caves filled with carpets from Central Asia, Caucasus, or Persia, and corridors walled with old carved doors. Restoration shops are in full operation, and you hear the rustling of files and whirr of grinding machines. On your way to this collector's heaven, you will see fighting cocks, a gypsy market, and lose your way among old automobile spare part.

Soviet-era porcelain service on display at the Yangiobod Flea Market

SUBURBS OF TASHKENT

Pinot Noir aged in oak barrels from Château Hamkor Estate

Kibray

Sergey Danilov and His "Tasty Uzbekistan"
As an owner of a micro-winery, Sergey Danilov found his interest in wine in his fascination with the gastronomy culture of his country. He recalls that after the country gained its independence, it faced the challenge of forming the national tourist ideology, where architectural monuments became the core. Sergey started working at "Intourist," continued at the national corporation "Uzbektourism," and realized that Uzbekistan could offer no comprehensive gastronomic experience to the tourists.

For the last eight years, Sergey has been working on his own project, "Tasty Uzbekistan," and for the last thirty, with home winemaking. These two areas of his life were destined to come together. He participated in several Moscow and local festivals as a chef, and, with the help of some Moscow partners, organized an event in Moscow where Uzbek dishes were accompanied with family-made Uzbek wines. Then came the realization: this was it!

"We do not claim we make the best wines in the world. We make the wines that reflect our terroir. They are not worse or better, they are different," according to Sergey's honest standpoint. To understand it, one needs to taste the food and the wine together. His objective is to make people come to Uzbekistan and taste, taste, and taste some more, learning the country by its taste.

Sergey and his partners welcome guests in the Kibray District, a twenty-minute drive from the center of Tashkent, in a shady garden by a fast-flowing stream. They organize tasting sessions and master classes of cooking Uzbek dishes, harvest festivals, and invent and deliver various scenarios for private events.
Sergey Danilov: +998 90 977 56 19

Uzum Fermer
What began in 2008 with a purchase of land for a summer house is now a family winery. Uzum Fermer spans 21 hectares: 15 hectares of vineyards plus two hectares of meticulously maintained exotic gardens, a winery, and a ten-room guesthouse. The estate regularly welcomes numerous guests, celebrating everything from Navruz to Easter while organizing photo shoots, weddings, banquets, and garden tours.
+998 90 909 05 45, +998 97 412 09 08, Tashkent Region, Kibray District, Mirobod Street, 1/1, uzumfermer.uz

Parkent

"Just your regular Pinot"

Parkent is Uzbekistan's premier winemaking region. Emerald hues shimmer across the low spring hills, while autumn transforms the vineyards into flowing streams of gold and crimson. Roads wind between saffron-colored poplars and vine-covered slopes, with thick November fogs completing the picture, all just an hour's drive from Tashkent.

In Parkent, table grapes take up to 60% of the land, and technical grapes, the remaining 40%. At the same time, it is more than in any other region of the country. This terroir grows all varieties cultivated in Uzbekistan: Soyaki, Bayan Shirey, Cabernet Sauvignon, Pinot Noir, Riesling, Saperavi, Khindogni... There was a time when Crimean Tatars inhabited these lands after having been relocated here by the Soviet government, and they brought many young grapes to Parkent, including the Muscat of Alexandria.

Château Hamkor is the star of Parkent. Like many Uzbek wineries, it evolved from a Soviet wine collecting point into the nation's first private producer in 1992. The Soviet legacy is preserved and respected here, and both the vines and the equipment are heirlooms of the former superpower's wine industry. Today it is a serious business with savvy branding and results worthy or pride. They love recounting the story of Gérard Depardieu's visit, when he filmed a movie about his Uzbek dream some time ago. The French connoisseur, tasting their Pinot Noir, simply remarked, "Just your regular Pinot." No surprise at its distinctiveness, no mention of "new styles" or avant-garde approaches, just, "Your regular wine. Your regular Pinot." What might have offended French winemakers instead inspired the Uzbek ones. It was proof they are on the right path, albeit a rocky one.

A curious thing, it was a French oenologist who suggested this path to Château Hamkor. Even the brand name with the word *château* is a French idea, as well as the focus of the winery on dry wines, not the highly popular sweet ones. The marketologists waged a veritable campaign for this approach, step by step, bottle by bottle, and Château Hamkor conquered Tashkent. Over 50% of wine retail in the Tashkent's HoReCa segment is the share of this winery.

The Cabernet Sauvignon stands among Château Hamkor's successes: a rich, full-bodied wine with a recognizable peppery note. Their Soyaki is exceptionally good, particularly when young: vibrant, fresh, bursting with fruit-drops tones. The Alexandrian Muscat excels offering a dry, crisp, intensely aromatic palate. However, the winery's true achievement lies in guaranteeing both quality and taste in every bottle of Château Hamkor.
+998 71 226 57 70, +998 99 826 66 61, Parkent, Namdanak settlement, hamkorvino.uz

Ugam-Chatkal National Park
Ugam-Chatkal National Park is a UNESCO World Heritage Site as part of the Western Tien-Shan. These mountains, lakes and waterfalls rank among Uzbekistan's most beautiful landscapes, with more developed infrastructure thanks to its proximity to Tashkent. The park's areas nearest to Tashkent, including Charvak Reservoir and Greater Chimgan, are not subject to the special access restrictions applied to Ugam-Chatkal's more remote zones: a narrow strip of Uzbek territory bordered by Kyrgyzstan on one side and Kazakhstan on the other. Foreign visitors may only enter these distant areas for one daylight period, limiting opportunities for extended treks. Nikita Voinov (*+998 90 941 40 63*) organizes trekking tours in the Tashkent mountains for tourists with different levels of training. Another tested contact is Natalia Shaidullina (*+998 90 995 53 10*).

Wine tasting in Parkent

Lake Charvak
Chirchiq River, the water-abundant tributary of the Syr Darya, is closed with locks between the offsets of the Western Tien-Shan forming a beautiful water reservoir with turquoise water between the mountain peaks, capped with snow for a good half of the year. By the tip of Charvak, situated closest to Tashkent, is the countryside restaurant Cinara's (*+998 78 129 90 09, Bostanlyk District, urban settlement Charvak, open in the warm season*).

The reservoir shoreline features multiple accommodations complete with pools, saunas, and standard recreational facilities for tourists, to name a few, *Krokus Park* (*+998 98 127 99 33, +998 90 356 18 07*) or *Archazor Mountain Resort* (*+998 90 322 22 00*).

Greater Chimgan
Greater Chimgan refers to a mountain range with its highest peak at 3,309 meters, a popular area for mountain sports (skiing, snowboarding, trekking, rock climbing). Known since Soviet times for its slopes and lifts in the Beldersay area, Chimgan has gained new life and ambitious future plans with the opening of the *Amirsoy Mountain Resort* (*+998 71 200 22 90, +998 95 177 55 99*). Here they built Uzbekistan's first gondola lift, reaching an altitude of 2,600 meters. It is worth taking the ride even if you come without skis, just for the breathtaking views of snow-capped peaks shining white against the contrast of blue skies above and folded red soil below.

Zaamin National Park
The border between Uzbekistan and Tajikistan lies along the Turkestan Range, a part of the Pamir-Alay mountain system. This is a beautiful mountainous region considered a national park, home for many birds and animals of the national and international Red Books: the bearded vulture, the Turkestan lynx, and the Himalayan brown bear. A little bit of bad news, if you are coming as a tourist: the most that you can see would be the prints left by some animals in the snow or, if you are really lucky, the soaring eagle.

A trip to Zaamin is worth it for the stunning mountain landscapes and chance to experience local life and food. The most beautiful time in Zaamin (apart from winter, when everything is blanketed in snow) is spring, when tulips and poppies bloom in the foothills, and the mountain slopes are steeped in the scent of archa covering them. The archa and the healing mountain air give Zaamin its resort status.

Zaamin's development as a tourist destination catering not just to locals but also international visitors is a recent undertaking. The town of Zaamin itself happens to be the birthplace of Shavkat Mirziyoyev, President of the Republic of Uzbekistan. The national park has seen the opening of guesthouses and hotels meeting international comfort standards, such as *Wyndham Garden Zomin* (*+998 72 221 53 55*) and *Ramada Encore* (*+998 72 221 51 55*).

The most delicious thing you can try in Zaamin is **kozon non**, a dense flatbread cooked in a kozon rather than a tandoor. The dough is made with kaymak or milk, resulting in a rich, buttery aroma (though not the sterile smell of store-bought milk, but rather the faint animal scent of homemade dairy). The women bakers place a hefty lump of homemade

A view of the Zaamin National Park

butter into the freshly baked bread, which melts from the bread's heat and saturates it with an even richer taste of free-spirited village life. Taken with tea, it is a good nutritious breakfast for hunters and shepherds leaving for a whole day in the mountains. Travelers can benefit from it, too! You will not find flatbreads like this in any restaurant, so do ask your guide or some locals for such a treat to be cooked for you in one of the houses—and be sure to thank the hosts, despite their ardent protests.

Jizzakh

Jizzakh is a gastronomic must-stop in Uzbekistan. The city gifted us its amazing samsa: huge, juicy, and glossy. When driving from Tashkent to Samarkand, plan your route to arrive at lunchtime in Jizzakh and try the samsa you simply will not find elsewhere in Uzbekistan.

The locals think that the best samsa is from the kishlak of Kipchak (for example, *Qipchoq somsa: +998 90 297 02 04, Shodlik Mahalla*). I enjoyed it, too: coarsely chopped lamb and onions, a good amount of lamb fat for juiciness, and crispy crust.

HOTELS OF TASHKENT

Uzbekistan Hotel, one of the iconic landmarks of Tashkent's modernist architecture

Hyatt Regency Tashkent
Hyatt Regency Tashkent is one of Uzbekistan's first international hotels, now seven years old. This large, modern property occupies an entire block in its purpose-built structure, primarily catering to international business travelers: at breakfast, you'll marvel at the diversity of languages spoken. The hotel fully delivers on its five-star promise, skillfully blending chain standards with Eastern hospitality. Its seventh-floor indoor pool offers views of the mountains surrounding the city.
+998 71 207 12 34, Navoiy Street, 1A

Lotte City Hotel Tashkent Palace
The Lotte City Hotel Tashkent Palace occupies a beautiful 1958 building that has always housed hotels. The property takes pride in its balcony-equipped rooms (a rarity in Tashkent) and swan-down bedding. Located in the city center opposite the Alisher Navoiy Opera Theater, the hotel boasts an outdoor pool, which is unusual for the city center. From May through October, its sixth-floor terrace hosts a national cuisine restaurant.
+998 78 120 58 00, Buyuk Turon Street, 56

Hilton Tashkent City
The tallest of Tashkent's five-star hotels, the tweenty-first-story Hilton stands where Uzbekistan's future skyscrapers will soon rise, in the Tashkent City district. Panoramic views from upper floors and a seasonal open-air terrace on the 21st floor rank among its key attractions.
+998 71 210 88 88, Ukchi Street, 1

Courtyard by Marriott Tashkent
Courtyard by Marriott Tashkent offers a central location, proximity to both the airport and train station, spacious European-style rooms, and European service standards. On weekends, breakfast comes with saxophone music and a glass of sparkling wine.
+998 71 202 23 33, Kichik Beshyogoch Street, 126

Apart Hotel Istaravshan
A new apartment hotel next to the Tashkent City Park and the eponymous shopping mall is a perfect location if you want to be in the center of the modern city within a walking distance from the old city.
+998 71 205 20 05, Ukchi Street, 3, Lot 7 Business Center

ATECA Hotel Suites Tashkent
A stylish new hotel in central Tashkent, close to Mingorik Metro Station. Features excellent varied breakfasts, a terrace, and hospitable owners and staff.
+998 55 501 11 16, Kohinoor Street, 44A

Mirzo Boutique Hotel
A lavishly decorated hotel straight from an Oriental fairy tale, Mirzo Boutique is not far from the old part of Tashkent. The spacious grounds are surrounded by buildings with carved balconies and terraces housing the guest rooms. There's even a yurt-themed suite.
+998 97 774 11 61, Zarkaynar Street, 4

Corner Hotel
Just 10 minutes from the train station, this newly built hotel features universal design aesthetics and convenient access to both the airport and downtown.
+998 71 283 79 97, Mirabad District, 1st lock, Sarikol Street, 4

Just an hour and a half from Tashkent, Amirsoy is Uzbekistan's premier winter sports destination. The season typically runs from mid-December to mid-March. Amirsoy offers several red and blue runs, facing different directions, providing surprisingly varied skiing within a compact area.

Amirsoy Mountain Resort, Uzbekistan's top ski destination

Samarkand and Samarkand Region. Enchanted by Turquoise

Chapter II

Samarkand was the first city that came to mind when I thought of Uzbekistan. Like many who had seen its images in albums, books, postcards, and paintings, I felt I knew the place.

At the Shah-i-Zinda necropolis in Samarkand

To see these domes, minarets and arches with my own eyes meant pushing open an imaginary door to the mysterious East, stepping onto a road that seemed to lead straight into the tales of Arabian Nights. Seeing, recognizing, matching the outlines I had in my imagination with reality, and, finally, ticking the box saying, "Dream come true"... with a bit of disappointment. I can clearly remember the moment when the magnificent monuments of the ancient Samarkand went from dream to reality for me, two days after my arrival, and I asked myself: where is the city? Can it be that Samarkand is just some blue domes and highways between them?

A courtyard in Samarkand

Samarkand was Soviet Central Asia's crown jewel—the region's proud showcase to the world. Timur's monuments, which had languished before the Soviets arrived, were meticulously restored. Some warren-like neighborhoods, still clinging to medieval ways, made room for "modern" five-story buildings. Never the capital, Samarkand always stole the spotlight when Uzbekistan came up in conversation. Even now, Samarkand remains Uzbekistan's grand gateway, its postcard-perfect outlook. In their zeal to polish the city's tourist image, the authorities (as often happens in the East) sometimes overdo it, separating the glossy "brochure Samarkand" from the real living city. Moreover, they do that literally: with walls. Finding the authentic city beneath? That's a quest for those who see themselves as travelers, not tourists.

So, where does one look for the real Samarkand? For one, on the great Siyob Bazaar, not among the stalls with identical neat piles of dry apricots, but deep down in its belly, where they sell birdseed and iron hardware; in nondescript teahouses and rustic cafés, where the ceilings are smoky from fried meat or fish, and near fiery-hot tandoors with baking samsa; in some great restaurants (not too cozy, to our liking), where big companies of men and women clad in national clothes celebrate special days and dance away. If you are near, they will surely call you to join the dance.

A BIT OF HISTORY

A Crossroads of Cultures, a Scientific Center, a Country's Showcase

Inside the Shah-i-Zinda necropolis in Samarkand

Samarkand is believed to be one of the oldest cities on the planet. Founded in 8th century BCE, as the capital of the region referred to as Sogdiana, for many centuries it remained a milestone on the Great Silk Road. Skillful merchants, Sogdians spanned their business from the Black Sea to Sri Lanka. This was the intersection of cultures, traditions, and peoples from different places. It was for its nature of being the crossroads of cultures that Samarkand was recorded on the UNESCO World Heritage List in 2001.

Samarkand first rose on the Afrasiyab highlands and grew over its long history—always rooted in roughly the same spot. Today, the ancient **Afrasiyab settlement** lies within the borders of the modern Samarkand. Twenty-five centuries ago, it was a walled city of mighty fortifications, sheltering a citadel, grand mosque, homes, and artisan workshops. Be sure to visit the **Afrasiyab Museum of Samarkand** that still keeps fragments of wall paintings adorning the palaces of Afrasiyob and exhibits items found during the excavations.

Time and again throughout its history, Samarkand faced destruction and rebirth, losing and regaining its capital status. In 329 BCE, the city fell to Alexander the Great, earning its first mention in Greek and Roman records as *Marakanda*. While we cannot say exactly what Samarkand looked like back then, one thing is certain: this was a sophisticated, heavily fortified city, a treasure that aroused the zeal of every ambitious conqueror.

We can only guess, based on countless archaeological clues, what the city looked like in 1220, when Genghis Khan's armies marched in. They conquered it, and nearly wiped it off the map. We do know, however, that when Timur became the Supreme Emir in 1370, he inherited the cities that had not thitherto restored after the Genghis Khan's campaigns. The empire that included parts of the modern Iran, Caucasus, Mesopotamia, Afghanistan, almost the entire Central Asia, parts of Pakistan, India, and Syria had to be built afresh. Timur deployed large-scale military campaigns, and sent the best artisans and scientists he met during his quests to Samarkand. The city was built as the capital of the empire, and as such it had to impress the travelers and make them believe in the glory and power of Timur. It had to be—indeed, it was!—the capital of the world with huge exquisitely decorated palaces, mosques and madrasahs, with glorious gardens, with state-of-the-art technology. The travelers visiting Samarkand in the Timur's period reported, among other things, about a contemporary system of water supply, which Europe had known nothing about at the time.

It was under Timur, the patron and foreman of his constructions, that Samarkand became the jewel of the East. Even today, travelers invoke his name countless times daily. Century after century, he remains the city's presiding genius: woven into its history, architecture, and art; hero of urban legends; Samarkand's eternal guardian. Nearly all its landmark structures bear his imprint: from the **Gur-e-Amir Mausoleum** (his final resting place) to the **Shah-i-Zinda necropolis** (for his family and nobility), **Rukhabad Mausoleum**, and **Bibi-Khanym Mosque**.

Of all Timur's heirs, Ulugbek remains the most celebrated. His name will echo as frequently as his grandfather's as you explore the city. Where Timur blended military genius with visionary ambition, Ulugbek's passion was pure science. His **madrasah** (1417), which launched the architectural ensemble of the **Registan Square**, was conceived as nothing less than a grand Islamic university.

The astronomical measurements taken at **Ulugbek's medieval observatory** were more precise than those Copernicus would make a century later. As you stand before that massive sextant, try imagining this: in the 15th century, they calculated the exact length of a year—with a margin of error of just 58 seconds!

In 1501, Samarkand became part of the Khanate of Bukhara; this was the beginning of the Shaybanid era. When the capital moved to Bukhara in 1533, Samarkand remained the realm's second city, a co-capital of sorts. The Registan ensemble reached completion in the early 1600s with the addition of **Tillya-Kori and Sher-Dor Madrasahs**. Today, artisans work in the *khudjras* (cells) of all three Registan monuments, continuing a tradition that began under Timur, when this was a bustling marketplace, and thrives still in the 20th century. The first half of the 18th century brought fresh devastation when Iran's Nadir Shah stormed and sacked Samarkand. The city remained under Bukhara until Russian forces arrived in 1868. During their capture of the city, the Ark citadel suffered damage. Ironically, artist Vasily Vereshchagin (then working as a military draftsman for General Konstantin Kaufman during Russia's Central Asian conquest) earned a medal for defending this very fortress against local rebels.

Vereshchagin's paintings let us see the condition in which late 19th century found monuments of Timur, Ulugbek and their descendants: tilted minarets, grass-grown cupolas, and the general feeling of decay... The process of restoration started as early as in 1920s and finished only after the Great Patriotic War. The best restoring and artistic talent of the Soviet Union was sent to Samarkand to bring it to its former glory. In 1921, Kuzma Petrov-Vodkin visited the city as a member of such an expedition. He describes Samarkand as a living Eastern fairytale, where monuments, their intricate decorations, and vibrant color schemes outshine even the starry night sky. That electrifying turquoise (the same that stuns every modern visitor) left him awestruck. Studying his Samarkand-series paintings and travel notes, you marvel at how precisely he captured Uzbekistan both through his artist's eye and his heart. One might say these scientific expeditions planted the first seeds of what would grow into Uzbekistan's distinct artistic school.

Samarkand's enduring divide, between its ancient quarters and its Russian colonial district, dates back to the arrival of imperial forces. The European construction began in 1871 under the orders of Governor-General Abramov.

Minaret of the Tilla-Kori Madrasah in Samarkand

Dome of the Tilla-Kori Mosque in Samarkand

This new city center rose with precision: wide tree-lined avenues laid out on a strict grid. Yet most visitors barely glance at this section of the city, their gaze drawn to Timur's legacy. One cannot miss the shady University Boulevard, but one can easily overlook the **Merchant Kalantarov's mansion** (closed for renovation), now the Regional Studies Museum (temporarily closed). This building, with its magnificent interiors, still untouched by the renovator's hand, is unreasonably seldom included in the sightseeing tours.

Samarkand: Highlights

–El Merosi Theater of Historical Costume will take you both to the ancient Sogdiana and to a modern Uzbek wedding, all within one hour. There is an excellent coffee shop by the theater.
+998 66 233 81 25 café, +998 97 288 11 88 theater, Alisher Navoiy Street, 27

–Art Station by Silk Road University. This contemporary exhibition space breathes new life into a former Orthodox church shuttered after the 1917 Revolution. Left abandoned in the early 2000s, the building underwent a dramatic revival a few years back emerging as Samarkand's premier venue for cutting-edge art exhibitions.
+998 99 301 62 96, Beruni Street, 1

–Aysel Gallery and SamArtHub. Exhibition venues next to the Registan feature a gallery of modern arts and crafts, artists' studios, and an art salon in the Do'smatboy Madrasah.
+998 91 553 83 97, Registan Street, 3

–State Museum of Cultural History of Uzbekistan occupies a massive building far from the center of Samarkand (plan at least 20 minutes to get here), housing one of Uzbekistan's finest suzani collections. While the ceramics, jewelry, coins, and archaeological finds certainly deserve attention, my heart belongs to the embroidery exhibits packed with unique pieces that vividly showcase the distinct styles of regional schools.
+998 66 234 05 23, Mirzo Ulugbek Street, 148

–Museum in the Russo-Chinese Bank historical building (branch of the State Museum of Cultural History of Uzbekistan) occupies one of the most beautiful and perfectly restored mansions of Samarkand. Constructed in 1895 for one of the region's leading banks, the building later housed various Soviet institutions before spending its final years hidden behind Samarkand State University slowly crumbling out of sight. Step inside not just for the stunning interiors, but for the compact yet brilliantly curated exhibition showcasing the region's decorative arts and their fascinating Chinese cultural connections.
+998 99 776 17 00, Shohruh Mirzo Street, 94

Samarkand: A Schedule

Day 1
Gur-e-Amir Mausoleum. Registan Square. Lunch. Samarkand Bukhara Silk Carpets Factory. Eternal City Complex or Khoja Doniyor Mausoleum. Dinner.

Day 2
Shah-i-Zinda necropolis. Bibi-Khanym Mosque. Siyob Bazaar. Lunch. Happy Bird Gallery. Kalantarov's Mansion or a walk down the University Boulevard. Dinner.

...if you have more time...

Conventional tourist routes allow a maximum of two days for Samarkand. The must-see list usually includes the Registan Square, Shah-i-Zinda necropolis, Gur-e-Amir Mausoleum with Timur's tomb, and Bibi-Khanym Mosque. The guests are always taken to see the Ulugbek's observatory where the giant sextant has miraculously survived since 15th century, and to the Mausoleum of St. Daniel, whom the Muslims respect as Khoja Doniyor. The fact that these locations are on the tourist route does not make take anything away from them: my heart skips a beat every time I see the turquoise street of Shah-i-Zinda. However, if you want to learn more of Samarkand and its dwellers, you need to go deeper.

The legend has it that the prophet and preacher Dovud (known in Judaism as Prophet David) was hiding from his enemies in the suburbs of Samarkand. There are several versions as to who those enemies might have been, but all stories claim that it was there, in the vicinity of Samarkand, that his prayers were heard, and Allah bestowed upon him with a supernatural power which enabled him to move the boulders and find shelter in the cave. Today, one needs to climb more than a thousand steps to a dizzying height of over 1,250 meters. As one approaches the cave and uses their imagination or their belief, one can see the prints of giant knees and palms of gigantic hands on the stones. Khazrati Dovud is one of the most sacred places for people of Samarkand. The small bazaar nearby is worth your attention, too: I usually buy kurt and medicinal herbs there (believe it or not, they have herbs for every illness). Of course, you will enjoy the breathtaking view from the top of the hill.

Few visitors realize that the Sher-Dor Madrasah, that famous "tiger-lion" adorned landmark of the Registan Square, has a mirror twin in Samarkand. Nicknamed "Sher-Dor's Reflection," the Nadir Divan-Begi Madrasah stands near the modest Khoja Akhror Mosque. When in Tashkent, the tourists are usually shown the legendary Uthmanic Quran. Well, this very mosque safeguarded that sacred text for centuries.
This madrasah adorned with tigers was built nearby under the Shaybanids by the very same vizier whose namesake ensemble graces the center of Bukhara by Lyab-i Hauz. Of course, this place is so much more than just a photo opportunity, but it would be remiss of me not to mention that it's a far less crowded alternative to Registan for those perfect shots.
The ruler himself, Shaybanid governor Bahodir Yalangtosh, who commissioned both Sher-Dor and Tillya-Kori Madrasahs to complete the ensemble of the Registan Square, lies buried 12 km from the center of Samarkand, beside Makhdumi Azam, the revered Islamic theologian and mystic. To locals, this complex remains sacred ground steeped in centuries of prayer. When you visit, you will hear legends whispering of faith, hope, and eternal truths.

University Boulevard in Samarkand

CUISINE AND WINEMAKING OF SAMARKAND:
Medieval Globalism

Fresh Samarkand
flatbread at a local bakery

Timur's genius shaped not just the visual and cultural identity of Samarkand, but its culinary soul too. His building of the empire brought together (and relocated to the capital) skilled artisans from across the continent. This medieval globalization under Timur created the vibrant mosaic of crafts and flavors that defines the city to this day. Still today, there is a large Iranian commune (Central Asian Iranians, to be precise) that lives very close. If you are lucky enough to visit a household true to its recipes and traditions, you may try the Iranian pilaf and sweets.

The same concerns the Jewish and Armenian communities: there are next to zero restaurants serving the national dishes, but the diasporas, however small, still preserve their traditions.
The **Samarkand plov**, considered by many as the gold standard, also owes its existence, at least according to legend, to Timur himself. Or, should we say, to competing legends: one claims Allah revealed the recipe as warrior fuel for endurance, another insists that proper plov must be cooked and served in unmixed layers. This, they say, let Timur verify that the dish was freshly made, not reheated. To this day, whether plov can be stirred remains a favorite good-natured feud between Samarkand and Tashkent dwellers.

No matter what era they belong to, past or present, for every citizen of Samarkand the image of their native city resembles paradise, at least as far as air and water are concerned, the crucial ingredients of the local cuisine. The **most flavorful tea** in Uzbekistan is, of course, in Samarkand, thanks to numerous springs. The glossy, heavy, dense **Samarkand flatbreads** are so delicious, as the legend has it, because of the sweet air of the city. To tell the truth, nowhere in Uzbekistan do they bake them like here.

Samarkand cuisine uses a lot more chickpea and wheat. **Chickpea** is an indispensable ingredient of the proper Samarkand plov and lamb stew. Crushed **wheat** is a component of khalisa, or haleem, a traditional festive dish that is served only for Navruz across Uzbekistan; here, in Samarkand, it is a daily staple.

There are two large wineries in Samarkand and its environs. **Khovrenko Wine Factory** is in the city itself, a descendant of the distillery founded by the Russian merchant Filatov in the late 19th century. **Bagizagan** grew from one of the wine-collecting depots of the Samarkand winery. Vicinity of the Pamir range and the coolness from the Zeravshan River contribute to a climate of hot days and cool nights, conditions perfect not only for sweet wines, traditional for Uzbekistan, but for good dry wines, too.

Dishes to Try

Samarkand plov is traditionally cooked and served in layers, without stirring, using lamb and beef alike, rice, yellow carrots, chickpeas, raisins, and cumin. As a rule, it is cooked using a blend of cottonseed and flaxseed oils. Speaking about the method of cooking for this plov, people say that it is fried, boiled and steamed to perfection for the rice and tenderness of the meat.

Samarkand flatbreads are probably the best known in Uzbekistan. Dense and hefty, with thick edges and a flat center, they are baked in a tandoor. It stays fresh for a long time, and often tourists take it home as a souvenir.

Khalisa is a typical Samarkand dish of soft-boiled crushed wheat with meat (beef and lamb) cooked for 6–8 hours in a large kozon, occasionally stirred, to reach a creamy consistency with meat practically dissolving in the cereal.

Bamaza noxot is a dish of lamb and chickpeas stewed low and slow; traditionally, it is served in many choyxonas of Samarkand.

Samsa are small beef-filled pasties baked in a tandoor. What makes it special is the special flaky dough and the square shape. The dough is rolled on long tables, folded and kneaded by hand, stretched and folded again, until 20–25 layers are created. The dough is cut into squares and rolled into diamonds to keep the layers, and after baking, these layers resemble the thinnest of paper.

Anzur is a sort of onion growing in the mountains. Pickled anzur is a traditional condiment for the plov in Samarkand. It is harvested in the mountains in spring, cured in brine for 40 days (the brine is changed twice a day) and pickled, just like cucumbers. You can buy jars of pickled anzur in the Siyob Bazaar.

Gura op is another condiment for plov made from juice of unripe grapes cured under the sun for several months. It cuts through the sweetness of the plov, teases the appetite, and breaks down the fats. You can also find it on the markets.

Museum and Tasting Experience

The history of the Samarkand wine factory dates back to 1868, when Dmitry Filatov came to Turkestan from Russia to develop his idea of creating European-style winemaking. He brought dozens of technical varieties of grapes, procured the equipment, trained the workers, and taught the locals how to cultivate the vines; his reward was the gold and silver medals for his wines.

The story goes on with the name of Mikhail Khovrenko, Russian chemist and winemaker, who had started learning his craft in Imperial Russia and in Europe. In 1927, he moved to Uzbekistan and became the Master Winemaker of the "Uzbekvino" Trust. He described the grape varieties of Uzbekistan, expanded the vineyards, and introduced new varieties. In many aspects, he stands behind the system of Uzbek winemaking that underlies the contemporary winemaking industry of the country. The establishment of Uzbek wine industry is the focus of the country's unique **Museum of Winemaking** at the Khovrenko Wine Factory. Your excursion will end with a tasting of at least ten wines crowned with the Samarkand herb liqueur.
+998 90 212 38 20, Mahmud Koshgari Street, 58

Samarkand flaky samsa: golden crisp layers wrapped around a fragrant, spiced filling

Where to Eat: National Cuisine

Siyob Bazaar
There are several markets in the city, but the Siyob Bazaar is of most interest for travelers: it is the biggest, the most ancient, it is located in the old section of Samarkand, not far from the major monuments. This is a gigantic covered space of several hectares selling everything from flatbreads to mousetraps. It is allowed and even encouraged to try things before buying, almost all salespeople speak Russian—and often know a few words in other languages—so bargaining is expected from you. If you are a guest in Samarkand, buy the dried fruit (go for the most wrinkled and unappetizing-looking kuraga or dried apricot, strips of dried melon, and whole walnut kernels), Samarkand flatbreads (they are dense and heavy, but stay good for an amazingly long time), kurt, dried balls of fermented milk, and spices, like cumin, and stamps for flatbreads. The bazaar is closed on Monday, and the most active working hours are from 10 a.m. to 4 p.m.

Deep in the bazaar stands a snow-white building with tall, slender columns: the *Kyzyl (Red) Choyxona*, operating since the Soviet times and beloved by locals and tourists alike. Market workers and city dwellers come here to eat, guides gather their groups, and travelers seek authentic experiences. Order the tandoor-baked samsa, rich lamb shurpa, and fragrant lagman.

Osh Markazi
The only dish they cook there is plov (Samarkand plov, needless to say), the only time they cook it is lunchtime, and yes, it is quite a drive to get here. But it is exactly the place that a traveler is looking for, a place for locals, not for tourists. No fancy interiors to talk about, just the walls, tables, and chairs: people come for the food. The service is fast, and they run out of plov approximately by 12:30, so don't be late. The owner is always present in the dining room.
+998 93 330 21 00, +998 93 348 00 21, Ibn Sina Street, 12

Mahalla Osh
People usually cook and eat plov in the daytime in Samarkand, and some years ago one simply could not get some plov in the evening. But times are changing, and mahalla choyxona opens their kozon of Samarkand plov twice a day, at 11 a.m. and at 6 p.m. Closed on Sundays.
+998 91 558 80 77, Navoiy Shoh Street, 16

Axmadjon Lux Osh
"I have always told I wanted to be an actor. My calling is to surprise people," oshpaz Anvar Mamedov says, inventor of the lux-plov, who made his father, his fellow citizens and guests of the city understand and love his invention. People of Uzbekistan are hardcore conservators in everything about food: following traditions is appreciated, in other words, you cook in the same way your grandfather and your father did. Anvar's father was a well-known oshpaz, he cooked plov on weddings and other important events, but officially, until the collapse of the USSR, he was a handler in a timber yard. In 2000, the family managed to buy a place in one of the mahallas of Samarkand and opened a small oshxona. The restaurant that Anvar has managed since the death of his father cooks only four dishes: Samarkand plov, pelmeni, shurpa, and manti. It is only open during the day.

Kyzyl Choyxona at Siyob Bazaar in Samarkand

The foundation of the lux-plov is the traditional Samarkand plov. All extras are cooked separately: quails stuffed with ground beef, oxtails, qazi, and even octopus. Wait, what? Samarkand has no ocean! "I'm telling you, there is an ocean, and a diver to help me," laughs Anwar, and explains that his "octopus" is beef tendons cooked in a special way.

The father was a staunch opponent of Anvar's culinary experiments, and even rejected deliveries of non-conventional ingredients. He was angry that his son should do everything wrong, and prophesized imminent bankruptcy. In the meantime, Anvar experimented with his extras elsewhere. He convinced his father to get the lux-plov on the menu only to meet a new wave of misunderstanding, this time, from the guests. It was a process of twelve long years... "You know the funny thing in the end?" Anvar is getting close to the most interesting part of the story, and I am as keen to hear it, as I am to try the plov itself. "When things got smoother, he liked it a lot, too. So, whenever I went to cook for a wedding and left my father in the oshxona, he told me about every portion of lux-plov people ordered, and he was proud." Anvar is known as someone who can turn the presentation of well-known plov into a show: he has not forgotten his dream of becoming an actor, and he jokes, he performs, he makes his guests happy.
+998 91 536 99 39, Panjab Mahalla, Firdavsi Street, 161

4 Tanur
I am not even sure if there are people in Samarkand who know the official name of this place: for the locals, it is simply "Samsa in Kokand Street." It seems that one simply finds this street by the smell and smoke from the tandoors and braziers. The samsa here, in my opinion, is the perfect specimen of the dish: small, flaky, crispy outside and soft inside, with fragrant meat. Order some spicy tomato sauce for your samsa, and some suzma and tea to put out the fires in your mouth. Note that they cook samsa only in the daytime; the star of the evening is skewers.
+998 97 396 00 66, Mukumi Street, 107

Furkatovich Café
If you are in the center, you will find equally delicious samsa on the Gagarin Street, in the big Furkatovich Café and, just as in Kokand Street, you can order it to take away. This samsa has two secrets: first, the dough needs to be dense (this is why it is traditionally cooked by men); second, it is baked in the oven, and requires less salt than tandoor-baked samsa. I have seen the sheer amount of effort the cook puts into stretching and folding the layers of dough several meters

If you've already tried Samarkand's famous samsa, it's time to taste another legendary variety! Olot samsa is made with thin, non-layered dough and stuffed with a juicy filling of meat, tomatoes, and bell peppers for extra flavor. This Bukharan specialty can also be found in Samarkand.

Uzbek plov at Axmadjon Lux Osh, accompanied by pickled cherries and anzur onions

long, and I realized: one simply does not try this at home. That's another reason to go to Samarkand!
+998 95 560 88 81, Gagarin Street, 188

Night Khalisa on Limonadka
This is one of those places nobody knows by its official name; the locals navigate by the codeword "night khalisa on Limonadka." Samarkand residents call the Toshokhur area "Limonadka' after its long-gone lemonade factory. The spring hidden in this neighborhood draws crowds of locals collecting water believed to bring trade luck and prosperity.

This café, open since the 1990s, serves khalisa, meat skewers, jyz, and kebabs. The khalisa is what made it famous. In Samarkand, khalisa is usually eaten at night or in the morning. It is made from beef and lamb cooked in a blend of flaxseed and vegetable oil. The meat is fried with bones in a large kozon, mixed with crushed wheat and water, and stirred with a wooden paddle for eight hours. The dish is a thick porridge, where meat and grain blend together. It is traditionally served with beef stewed with chickpeas and carrots.

Suzangaron Mahalla Home restaurant
It is rare to see women behind a choyxona kitchen, but Khayriniso Oriezieva, now in her seventies, has been cooking here for forty years. Samarkand knows her as the maker of arguably the city's most delicious bamaza noxot: tender braised lamb with chickpeas. Meltingly soft meat, plump peas, a bowl of rich shurpa broth, and homemade hasyp: this is what draws people from across the city.
+998 97 931 46 16, 1st Islam Karimov Drive, 11

manti.uz
Legendary manti from Oblakul-bobo that many people consider the epitome of this dish: incredibly thin dough and juicy filling. The café has been around for more than thirty years, and goes in Samarkand by the street name *Mulyon Manti*.
+998 97 913 97 77, Mulyon Street 2, bldg. 44

Chupcha Café
Getting to this café in the Sar-Tepa residential district requires a dedicated trip, and likely some wrong turns, but the reward is worth it. The shurpa I tasted here ranks among the best I have ever had. Even their simple tomato-cucumber salad shines with bright notes of diced Uzbek lemons and fresh cilantro. Don't miss the onion-stuffed patir bread, freshly baked on-site, or the iliq (bone marrow), best enjoyed piping hot, and pai (tendons from large bones).
+998 95 509 44 56

Samarkand
Samarkand is a spacious, beautifully decorated restaurant with a large courtyard that aims to please everyone: tourists come for the food, locals for celebrations and dancing. When it comes to menu variety, value for money, and flavor, it ranks among the city's best. Just be prepared for service that moves at its own contemplative pace. But then again, this is the East!
+998 90 743 04 05, Mahmud Koshgari Street, 54

Platan
A European restaurant with several halls themed in different styles, an inner yard, and a beautiful terrace outside. Extensive menu with national dishes. What I like most is live music, duduk and saxophone. Without doubt, this is one of the best restaurants in the city.
+998 66 233 80 49, Pushkin Street, 2

Karimbek
A spacious restaurant with a terrace overlooking the modern Gagarin Street. Its simple vibes remind me of kebab houses in Isnanbul. People come here for meat and vegetables from the brazier: skewers with larger pieces of meat or kebabs, jyz byz (or simply jyz, braised meat), very simple salad of tomatoes and onions, some flatbread and tea. Karimbek easily attracts companies of locals.
+998 66 237 77 39, Gagarin Street, 194

Juma Mosque in Urgut, a village of Samarkand Region preserving Central Asian Islamic traditions

DECORATIVE AND APPLIED ARTS OF SAMARKAND: *Commercial Charm*

Silk Carpets Factory in Samarkand

A focus on tourism—catering to the tastes of travelers who flock to Uzbekistan and typically begin their journey in Samarkand—has become central to the city's contemporary applied arts scene. Artisans, many representing families with three to five generations of craft tradition, skillfully bridge ancient techniques and modern demand while preserving centuries-old practices.

UNESCO's extensive work in Samarkand during the 2000s **revived ancient crafts** that have since become vital to the city's contemporary artisanal scene. Most notably, the art of **mulberry papermaking** was an experiment that grew into a full-fledged factory. Another success story is **block-printed textiles**, so rare now that even in Tashkent I failed to find a single artisan practicing this once-widespread craft. It turned out that Samarkand was the only place left to go! **Excavations at the Afrasiyab settlement** and the countless artifacts now housed in the city museum serve as the single greatest inspiration for artisans of Samarkand. Nearly every master I spoke to cited Afrasiyab's legacy as their creative foundation: the essential bedrock of their craft.

The Samarkand Region is one of Uzbekistan's few places where **unglazed ceramics** exists, including delicate **clay figurines**. These range from toys to miniature compositions depicting mythical creatures, folk heroes, and everyday scenes, all left intentionally glaze-free. Even larger pieces, like water jugs, follow this archaic tradition, wearing their raw, unglazed finish.

Today, Samarkand is known as a **hub for silk carpet production**, though this was never a traditional Uzbek craft. Both the factory and the nationwide trend for silk weaving trace back to a vision of one determined family.

Suzani embroidery is a craft very important for Samarkand, and one of its centers is the city of **Urgut**, 50 kilometers away. The suzani of Samarkand are easily recognizable by their lavish ornament of flowers and leaves, and the suzani of Urgut are unmistakable with their black circular rosettes contoured with sophisticated spiky patent, and images of teapots and jugs.

Urgut is also famous for its ceramics: the **Ablakulov family** carries on this characteristic style with prevailing terracotta and brown hues and specific green paint runs on the edges of items. This family is the only remaining successors of the Urgut tradition of ceramics.

Samarkand-Bukhara Silk Carpets Factory
The Badghisi family launched handmade silk carpet production three times across their journey: in Turkmenistan,

Afghanistan, and Uzbekistan. Thanks to Hajji Mohammad Ewaz Badghisi, the family patriarch, silk weaving became a tradition in multiple countries and sustained countless households. Affectionately called Hajji Baba in Samarkand, he was born on the Turkmen-Afghan border. His family later moved to Samarkand, then to Afghanistan. In Kabul, then a major hub for village-woven carpets, their workshop pioneered professional silk carpet weaving, training a generation of artisans.

In the early 1990s, the new government of Uzbekistan called on expatriates to return prompting the family to revive their craft for the third time by establishing the Samarkand-Bukhara Silk Carpets factory.

For guests of Samarkand, the Badghisi carpet factory has become as important a point on their list as the monuments of Timur and Ulugbek. The entire process can be seen, from preparation of silk cocoons, spinning of and dyeing of threads to weaving by hand. The guests are treated as guests, not customers or buyers: the owners show them how to see the handmade from machine weaving, see the original work of art from a knockoff. Many guests are lucky enough to shake the founder of the factory by the hand: despite his 100 years of age, he comes to the factory every day.

+998 66 235 22 73, +998 91 525 72 97, Hudjum Street, 12A, silkcarpets.uz

Happy Bird Gallery

Happy Bird occupies two small rooms in the Hunarmand craft center at the very beginning of Islam Karimov Street. In one room there are costumes created by Elena Ladik, the owner, and her team; in the other, a pair of vintage armchairs, a display table with a collection of Uzbek artifacts, and a small burner on which Lena brews her signature cinnamon coffee for guests in a copper cezve. The dresses, coats, robes, and suits by Happy Bird are works of haute couture, garments infused with the highest degree of handcrafted labor. Each piece combines multiple techniques: Elena's creative style is highly distinctive. She often dyes the fabrics herself, meticulously designs the finishing touches, and brings in specialists for every stage of production. Some make the block printing, some spin the trimmings, and artisans from different regions do the embroidery. Footwear, headwear, and leather goods are also crafted as one-of-a-kind pieces by the best of the best artisans from across the country. Happy Bird's ensembles incorporate arts from different regions of Uzbekistan. Every dress or coat is like a unique journey through the country. The second showroom of Happy Bird is located in the **Silk Road Samarkand** Complex.

+998 93 720 42 15, Islam Karimov Street, 43A

Sharif Azimov Ceramics Studio

Sharif Tursunovich Azimov is one of the most famous Samarkand potters, a member of the Uzbekistan Academy of Fine Arts and a disciple of Usto Umar Jurakulov, founder of the Samarkand school of ceramics. Jurakulov's studio was the starting ground for many brilliant potters of Samarkand, but in the 1990s and early 2000s, the same school of ceramics was only spoken of as a history of the past. At the time, Sharif Azimov worked in New York, and for seven years, the studio of the Uzbek master Azimov had been operating in Queens. Sharif speaks thus about his return, "I believed that Uzbekistan needed me."

Clay and glaze are brought to Sharif from across the country, and some items are painted by modern artists in Tashkent. Some of his ideas even come from

Happy Bird Gallery by Elena Ladik

Processing mulberry bark using ancient methods to produce Samarkand's famed handmade paper at the Meros workshop

technical failures or accidents during the process. If you want to buy one of his jugs, you will need to visit his studio personally, and plan quite some time for the visit. The master will put his heart and soul in telling the story of each of his items.
+998 66 236 02 14, +998 90 250 55 72, Tamhid Street, 2nd Drive/22

Meros Mulberry Paper Factory
Zarif Mukhtorov was looking for the secret of manufacturing of Samarkand paper for five long years. It was known to be robust, smooth, and expensive; and that caravans were carrying it to Baghdad, Damascus, and Cordoba. Only one bit was missing, the material. Japanese specialists helped create the formulation, but the main ingredient, the main thing was of Zarif's

own insight: the secret of the paper of Samarkand was mulberry, trees and groves to be found everywhere in Uzbekistan.

Unlike Japanese, Korean or Chinese paper, one can write on paper from Samarkand on both sides. Traditionally, hard-point instruments were used, like quills; however, soft brushes were used in Asia. Samarkand paper is polished with shells or semi-precious stones giving it the gloss, smoothness and strength. Such paper will last for some 300–400 years.

At the factory, you can witness the entire production process: how branches are soaked, how they are treated, how water-powered mallets work to soften the fibers, and how swiftly the hands of the polishers move with pieces of onyx. Everything here is done just as it was ten centuries ago.
+998 90 224 34 96, sammeros_68@yahoo.com

Ilkhom Bobomurodov Ceramics Studio
Ilkhom Bobomurodov is a hereditary potter and successor to the legacy of the renowned Samarkand master Umar Jurakulov. Like Jurakulov, who was not merely a ceramist but also a researcher deeply versed in the intricacies of Samarkand ceramics, its distinctive features, and historical periods, Ilkhom cites ancient Afrasiyab pottery as his primary source of inspiration.
Ilkhom and his son Mehroj work on both larger pieces, such as plates, lagans, and ceramic panels, as well as smaller items like handcrafted dragon figurines. These dragons are not products of the masters' imagination but rather a legacy of Afrasiyab, where excavations uncovered figurines of mythical animals. They also represent a continuation of the tradition revived by Umar Jurakulov. It was he who, back in the 1960s, began crafting clay toys again, pieces that bear the imprint of both the artist's hands and soul. The Bobomurodovs' workshop is also located in Konigil, near the Meros paper factory.
+998 90 601 95 64, +998 97 921 75 71

Vladimir Akhatbekov's block printing
Block printing on fabrics with stamps, or *chitgarlik*, was a craft widely spread across Uzbekistan. The master block printers worked in the Fergana Valley, Tashkent, Bukhara, Khorezm, and Samarkand. "There were old masters, but they have already passed away," Usto Vladimir Akhatbekov says, succinctly describing the situation.
Block printing is the art that Vladimir practices in spite of everything. Finding the formulation for the paint alone is not enough: one needs to find a way to make it durable. Then, one needs to find the fabrics, not the regular cotton and calico, but fabrics with a rich structure, where the print becomes raised. Unfortunately, they do not produce them in Uzbekistan anymore, and Vladimir buys old silk shawls and uses them as substrate. Another problem is the stamps, or *kolybs*. Vladimir's collection of over a hundred patterns is a result of careful piece-by-piece searching. These stamps are meticulously made by hand, with attention to minute detail, crafted in a manner entirely different from that used by wood carvers. Of course, they can be made on a machine... but it is important to keep the ancient technique original and completely handcrafted.
+998 90 286 48 11, Gurugli Street, Lock 3, bldg. 5

At Vladimir Akhatbekov's workshop—a handcrafted wooden block for traditional Uzbek fabric printing

Potter Ilkhom Bobomurodov in his studio

Abdujalil Ergashov
Four decades in the profession, Abdujalil Ergashov has been teaching Arabic and calligraphy. Calligraphers have a lot to do in Uzbekistan: Abdujalil works on the restoration of historic sites, prepares sketches for new mosques, and teaches calligraphy to tourists in his workshop, located in one of the cells of the Ulugbek Madrasah. Spend an hour or an hour and a half here, and you will feel the ink glide onto the silky paper as delicate Arabic script flows from your pen.
+998 97 916 69 09
jalil.ergashov.1960@gmail.com

Bobir Sharipov
Bobir Sharipov's small workshop in the Sherdor Madrasah is a true museum of Uzbek folk musical culture. From two-

Bobir Sharipov, expert musician and master tuner

stringed instruments to those with 75 strings, Bobir can play them all. A whole team works on every instrument: one crafts the neck (usually made of apricot wood), another carves the headstock (mulberry wood), while others handle bone or mother-of-pearl inlays or adorn the instrument with leather. As for Bobir himself, he is the master tuner, who sets the frets and brings the instrument to life with sound.
+998 91 541 82 92, bobirsharipov@yandex.ru

Fatima Gulyamova
Fatima Gulyamova's shop in Samarkand is one of my favorites. Located on the pedestrian Karimov Street, on the right side when heading from Registan towards Siyob Bazaar, this small showroom reflects Fatima's journey from an economist to a passionate seamstress and designer. What stands out is the impeccable finishing and contemporary approach to designs: whether dresses, coats, or bags, most pieces crafted by Fatima, her sisters, and apprentices transcend local trends, making them wearable far beyond Uzbekistan.
+998 90 919 71 99, Islam Karimov Street, 43

Gulom Isaev
Gulom Isaev is the son of the renowned Urgut embroiderer Mavlyuda Hamdamova. He manages a shop, entirely dedicated to hand embroidery, in the Hunarmand craft center. His family hails from the kishlak of Gus in the Urgut District, where over time, a true suzani embroidery hub formed around Mavlyuda, her fellow

Suzanis works at Gulom Isaev shop

embroiderers, students, and family members. The craft, whose secrets Mavlyuda inherited (as is customary in Uzbekistan) from her grandmother, thrives partly due to Gulom's organizational skills and leadership. In the shop, you can purchase exquisitely delicate suzani works, observe the embroidery process, and learn about the symbolism of the patterns. If you left the country but did not have time to buy the piece you liked, Gulom can arrange delivery for you.
+998 90 743 82 42, Islam Karimov Street, 43A

Eternal City Historical and Ethnographic Park
The Eternal City Historical and Ethnographic Park is a part of the multifunctional Silk Road Samarkand Complex, built outside Samarkand along the rowing canal, the only one of its kind in Central Asia. Since the opening of the complex, visitors can now take Dubai-style boat rides along the canal and admire the singing fountains. The "Eternal City" is a utopian architectural fantasy of an ideal Uzbek town: clean, beautiful, and entirely uninhabited. The real reason to visit is not the postmodern architecture but the chance to explore the craft traditions of the entire country. Be sure to stop by the workshops of the Rishtan potter Alisher Nazirov and Shahrisabz embroiderer Saodat Nizamova.

SUBURBS OF SAMARKAND

Kitab Pass Market
between Samarkand
and Shahrisabz

In many ways, the traditions of Samarkand embroidery in the 20th century, when the increasingly industrialized city saw fewer and fewer embroiderers, were preserved and advanced in Urgut. Here, in this rural area near the Tajikistan border, surrounded by mountains, life continues to follow rhythms established centuries ago. As a result, the appreciation for handcraft, particularly embroidery, an essential part of bridal dowries, remained strong. Even in modern Urgut works, the dominant compositions are those that took shape in Samarkand before the early 20th century. When you look at contemporary suzanis from Urgut, you are seeing the artistic embroidery of Samarkand from a century and a half ago.

Urgut: Ceramics, Suzani, Chinaras
Urgut suzanis stand out with their nearly suprematist compositions, featuring large central rosettes in deep burgundy or black. Some pieces employ background-free embroidery, where nearly the entire fabric is densely covered with meticulous stitching. Every motif carries protective symbolism, many representing fruitfulness and the continuity of life. The distinctive jugs and teapots embroidered on Urgut suzanis likewise embody the folk concepts of fertility, serving as hallmark motifs on pieces created for newlyweds.

In this part of the country, Urgut is a capital of suzani of sorts, the region where needle-and-thread pictorial art is known almost in every household. One of the best places to carefully examine suzanis and, after some bargaining, purchase them is the grand **Urgut Bazaar**. This colossal clothing market, the largest in Samarkand Province, draws locals shopping for household necessities. Tucked away in the market's outskirts are rows of pavilions specializing in suzani. One of my frequent stops is *Shokhida Ziyaeva's shop* (*+998 97 913 37 97*), a veritable treasure trove of old and new Uzbek and Tajik embroideries, vintage chapans (including those made of Chinese silk), Afghan silver jewelry inlaid with semiprecious stones, and embroidered skullcaps. Naturally, prices here are a bargain, compared to both Samarkand and, especially, Tashkent.

Another reason to come to Urgut is the *workshop of the Ablakulov potters' dynasty* (*+998 91 547 62 83, Hunarmandlar Street, 82*), the only family business to preserve the traditions of the Urgut ceramics style. The family patriarch, Numon Ablakulov, a potter renowned in Uzbekistan and beyond, is a cavalier of the Award for the Merits to the Fatherland. The tradition of handing over the craftsmanship secrets from father to son, from grandfather to grandson has continued in the family since the 17th century.

The ceramics of Urgut, as well as suzani, are branches of popular and not urban or palace traditions. It never uses brushwork. Urgut ceramics are recognized by the reddish and ochre hues and characteristic runs of green paint on the edges of pieces, and

At Bagizagan Wine Estate

somewhat archaic embossed ornaments. All pieces of the Ablakulov family are kilometer zero products: the clay, the vegetal components making the mixture strong, and the glazes, are all local. I love visiting Numon-aka: it is a chance to witness the entire pottery process unfold, to see the shapeless lump of clay transforming into a graceful jug or phial in the hands of the master, and an opportunity to try the potter's wheel myself. The Ablakulov family radiates hospitality: where else could you savor authentic Urgut plov and delicate rose-shaped samsa, lovingly prepared by the women of the household?

Another good reason to visit Urgut is the possibility to enter the inside of the millennial chinar tree in the **Chor Chinor** Complex. In the Uzbek language, *chor* means "four," but there are more gigantic trees here. The legend has it that an Arabic Sheikh planted the four chinar trees here in the 9th century, during the Arabic conquest of Central Asia. The Sheikh later became the ruler of Urgut and was then buried by the trees he had planted, and the place itself became sacred ground where a mausoleum, a madrasah and a mosque were built. The mosque is open to this day.

Bagizagan
First Choice
Bagizagan is the brand of some of the most popular and widely available wines of Uzbekistan. Almost everywhere you go, any restaurant anywhere in the country, Bagizagan will be the first choice on the menu. The winery is just a thirthy-minute drive from Samarkand. It was founded in the 1990s on the basis of a wine collecting depot of the Khovrenko Samarkand Wine Factory. This place is very hospitable. Guests are invited to harvest festivals and tasting events organized in cellars decorated with stone and wood. The best wines come under the name Bagizagan Select (be sure to try the Nargis, rose semi-sweet wine from Pinot Noir grapes) and under the brand Peri (especially Chardonnays, from a grape uncommon in Uzbekistan). The other tasting room of the winery is in Samarkand.
+998 66 664 41 42, +998 91 525 48 04, Samarkand Branch, Beruniy Street, 65

HOTELS OF SAMARKAND

The courtyard of
L'Argamak Hotel

Hilton Samarkand Regency
A true five-star hotel that Samarkand lacked. Located on the territory of the Silk Road Samarkand Complex, it boasts views of the rowing canal and the "Eternal City." The open swimming pool and sunbathing terrace add to the advantages of the hotel.
+998 55 705 70 10, Konigil District

Zarafshon Parkside
This hotel occupies an elegant historic building that once housed one of Samarkand's first lodgings. Located in the city's colonial district, it is just a fifteen-minute walk to Gur-e-Amir. Its tranquil inner courtyard features a finely tended garden and an outdoor pool. Note that alcohol is prohibited here reflecting one of the newer trends in hospitality.
+998 99 503 00 04, Abdurahman Jomiy Street, 65

Khan Hotel
A new hotel owned by one of the country's oldest tour operators, this property is located directly opposite the Shah-i-Zinda necropolis. Its spacious European-style rooms surround a quaint courtyard pool. The Bibi-Khanym Mosque, Siyob Bazaar, and Registan Square are literally few steps away.
+998 55 705 70 71, Umar Jurakulov Street, 48

Bibi Khanum
The hotel's prime location adjacent to Bibi-Khanym Mosque provides walking access to major landmarks. Its interior courtyard and second-floor balcony (accessible from rooms) offer exceptional views of Samarkand's signature blue-domed architecture, arguably, one of the city's most breathtaking hotel vistas. Note that vehicle access to the property is limited.
+998 93 355 88 00, Tashkent Street, 10

L'Argamak
A small Franco-Uzbek boutique hotel located near the Gur-e-Amir Mausoleum, with a flower-covered inner terrace and rooms decorated in European style with local touches.
+998 66 239 11 01, Sultan Muhammad Street, 4

Platan
A 12-room boutique hotel with a beautiful courtyard is located in the colonial part of Samarkand not far from the Platan restaurant, owned by the same proprietors. European style with Uzbek nuances in the interiors. It is one of the best hotels in the city, to my taste.
+998 94 187 77 77, Mironshokh Mirzo Street, 13

Rabat Boutique Hotel
This hotel is nestled in a Jewish mahalla (a traditional residential quarter) and is housed in a historic Bukharan Jewish home that has preserved all its authentic charm. It is more than just an accommodation; it feels like visiting long-lost friends.
+998 97 918 08 45, Bukhara Street, 26

Kosh Havuz Boutique Hotel
A new boutique hotel at the crossroads of the tourist center and traditional residential neighborhoods, just minutes away on foot from major attractions. The hotel is reminiscent of Moroccan riads: intricate wood carvings, mosaic detailing, and a breathtaking inner courtyard.
+99855 702 77 70, Kosh Havuz Street, 40

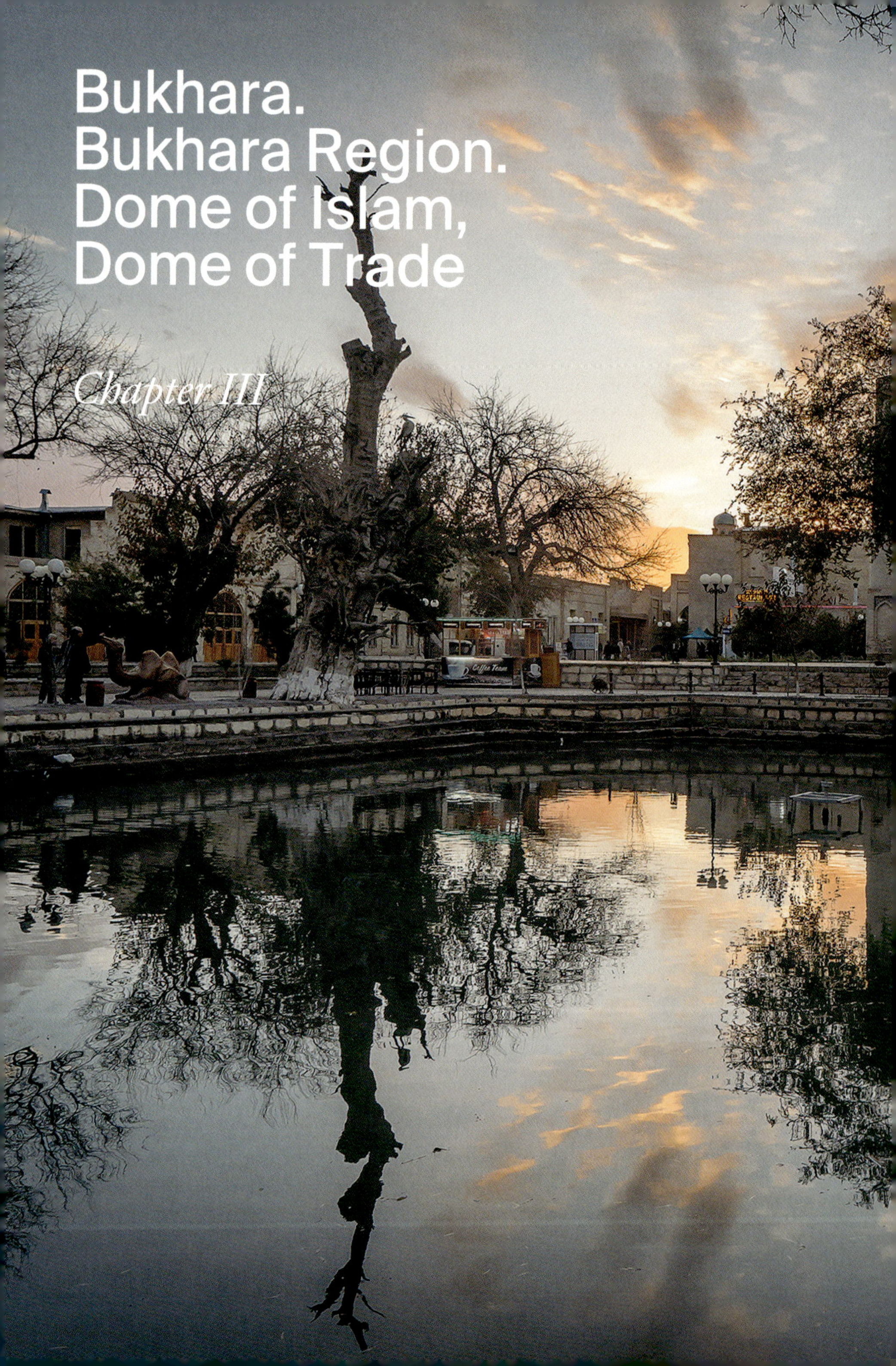

Bukhara. Bukhara Region. Dome of Islam, Dome of Trade

Chapter III

The Uzbeks know: everywhere in the world, the light shines from above, but only here, in Bukhara, it goes from below, from the ground.

Tea&Coffee

The place is considered sacred, *Bukhoroi Sharif.* The name is related to the religious value of Bukhara for the Islamic world. In the 8th century, it became the first regional Islamic center, and to this day it plays an important role. Muhammad al-Bukhari, one of the most famous and revered collectors of hadith, or reports of the saying and deeds of the Prophet, was born and lived in Bukhara. Not far from it, in Gijduvan, lies the tomb of the Sufi saint Abdulhalik Gijduvani. Those who shape the spiritual life of Muslims in Russia and neighboring countries studied and continue to study at the Mir-i Arab Madrasah in Bukhara, still the most prestigious Islamic school in the post-Soviet territories. Founded in the 16th century, this madrasah never ceased its educational activities, even during Soviet times.

Bukhara was an important hub on the Great Silk Road, and throughout its history, it remained not only a sacred city, not merely a place where philosophers, scholars and poets lived and worked, but also a center of thriving commerce. Here, the road intersections were covered with domes to ensure protection from heat or rain. These domes have survived to this day, and beneath them, just as in times past, one can hear the calls of vendors, the clanging of tools on copperware, the jingling of doira tambourines, and see the glimmer of jewelry.

What makes trade in Uzbekistan unique is its personal nature: you are buying something directly from an artisan or their family, in most cases. Tourism has an ill repute of irreversibly altering its destinations; however, in Uzbekistan this has not yet occurred. On the contrary, tourist demand encouraged the revival of crafts and family workshops, where you can meet artisans in the third, fifth, or even in the seventh generation. In my mind, Bukhara is the best place for buying things, slow rambling in the streets, talking to salespeople and, of course, bargaining. As you plan your time here, save at least half a day to walk around the city, to look into every single shop you like and to see the masters working. Almost every such shop will be a tiny museum.

Toki-Sarrofon Trading Dome in Bukhara

A BIT OF HISTORY

Capital of Persian Culture and Center of International Trade

Samanid Mausoleum
in Bukhara

One of defining characteristics of Bukhara is that the city has developed within the same territory since its founding and has preserved its urban structure virtually unchanged to this day. Understanding this layout provides the key to understanding Bukhara and makes it far more accessible to perceive than Samarkand, which now has two distinct centers.

No one can tell when Bukhara was founded, exactly. Its age is believed to be over 2,500 years. The cultural stratigraphy here is remarkably deep, exceeding 20 meters, with monuments dating from the 9th to 20th centuries. The Islamization process began in the 8th century. Visitors will see the most ancient mosque of the city, the **Magoki-Attari Mosque**, standing on the site that housed a Zoroastrian Fire Temple prior to the Arab conquest, and earlier still, a Buddhist monastery.

The **Samanid Mausoleum**, a structure of pale-yellow brick with astonishing carving, almost lace-like decoration, dates back to the late 9th century, when Bukhara was the capital of the Samanid Empire, the last Persian dynasty in Central Asia. It was at that time that the city became the cultural capital of the region. The time of the Samanid rule was the time of bloom of the new Persian language and literature, as well as global spread of the Islam, in which Bukhara played a key role. Scientists, poets and theosophists gravitated to the city, and all the activities of Samanids, who ruled until the year 999, were focused on strengthening Islam as a religion of peace, enlightenment, and cultural diversity. The system of madrasahs, educational establishments that taught Quran and hadiths, or stories of the Prophet, was developed at the time of the Samanids.

Bukhara was also an important trade hub: horses and glass were brought to China, and weapons and jewels, to Europe. Samanid coins are still found in places as Asia, Europe and Russia, quite far from Bukhara. The arts and crafts that originated in this period became the foundations of applied techniques used in Usbekistan to this day. This was the New Persian Renaissance.

The urban structure of today's Bukhara is also the legacy of the Samanids. The heart of the city was the **Ark** citadel, where the ruler and his court lived. Outside the citadel, there was the *shahristan*, the district of governmental institutions, madrasahs, artisans' workshops, and living quarters. The shahristan was divided into *mahallas*, or districts, where groups of craftsmen lived (blacksmiths, weavers, and so on), or national diaspores. Since ancient times, those were Jewish diaspores.

Today, their homes are occupied with hotels and restaurants carefully preserving the traditional decorations, and synagogues are still open for worshippers. The mahallas were self-governed and to this day remain an important form of organization of public life in the neighborhoods. Everything outside the shahristan was the *rabad*, or workers' districts.

Water was the most important thing in the organization and the history of Bukhara. Its preservation and use for irrigation in the dry climate was a priority: hence the numerous ponds and reservoirs (local name: *hauz* or *havuz*) by the main madrasahs and mosques. Many of them were filled with earth in the Soviet period, but the water reservoirs near the **Nadir Divanbegi Madrasah** and the **Bolo-Hauz Mosque** remain to this day. Like in the ancient times, the Shahrud canal flows across the entire city. Two **hammams** are still in operation (one for men, another for women) and welcome guests, both local and visiting. The **Chashma-Ayub Mausoleum** has a link with the saint spring and the legend of Ayub (Job), today the museum of the history of water supply in Bukhara.

In 1220, Bukhara was conquered and devastated by Genghis Khan. The symbol of the city, the **Kalyan minaret**, built in 1127 year, is one of the structures that survived the conquest. With Timur's rise to power and the establishment of the Timurid state a century and a half later, Bukhara became part of his empire. The pendulum swung the other way in the late Middle Ages under the Shaybanids; now, Samarkand became the second city of the Bukhara Khanate, later the Bukhara Emirate. This was a period of revival, but a local one, without influence on the Iranian or Persian world. The 16th–18th centuries marked a time of economic and cultural growth for the city, an era that shaped the monuments that still define the appearance of the present-day Bukhara: the **Lyab-i Hauz ensemble**, the **Mir-i Arab Madrasah**, and the **Abdulaziz Khan Madrasah** all date from this period.

From 1868 to 1917, the Bukhara Emirate was under the Russian protectorate. The Emirs enjoyed a lot of respect: the last Emir of Bukhara, Said Alim-Khan, was educated in St. Petersburg, owned summer houses and palaces across the Russian Empire, provided financial aid to construct the St. Petersburg Cathedral Mosque, and was expecting a guest visit from Emperor Nicholas II. His **summer palace Sitorai Mohi Xosa**, located off the center of Bukhara, is a curious specimen of Western and Eastern architectural accents coming together.

The Emirate gained independence following the fall of the Russian Empire, but in 1920, the well-prepared and armed Red Army commanded by Mikhail Frunze stormed the city, bombing and severely damaging the Ark Citadel. The Emir fled to Afghanistan, allegedly burying immense treasures somewhere along the way, and died over twenty years later in Afghanistan, blind and forgotten by all. By November 1924, Bukhara had become part of the Uzbek SSR. As early as 1922, the Bukhara Museum Preserve was established. Nearly a century later, Bukhara remains a living museum city.

The façade of the Abdulaziz Khan Madrasah in Bukhara

Sitorai Mohi Xosa Palace, near Bukhara

Bukhara: Highlights

–**Museum of Fine Arts** is within walking distance from Lyab-i Hauz, in a historical building of 1912, where merchant Savva Morozov's shop once was. The gem of its collections are the pictures of Pavel Benkov, an artist who loved Bukhara and captured it so full of light in many of his works, as well as paintings of Mikhail Kurzin, Alexander Volkov, Alexander Nikolaev, and other artists who stood at the outsets of the Uzbek school of painting.
+998 65 224 49 48, Naqshbandi Street, 41

–**Abdulaziz Khan Madrasah** is one of the most spectacular madrasahs of Uzbekistan dating back to the late 17th century with absolutely unique decorations. Do not let the multi-colored lavishly ornate portal detain you: enter and see how the monuments had looked before the restoration, their beauty is worth your attention.

–**Khalif Niyozquli Madrasah**, referred to as the Chor Minor, is recognized by its four towers resembling minarets. This amazing entrance portal is all that remains from the madrasah. Several antique dealers are open close by.

–**Palace of the Emir of Bukhara in Kagan**. If you leave Bukhara by train, come to the train station in advance, because just a few hundred meters from it there is a palace of breathtaking beauty designed for the Emir of Bukhara by Alexei Benois. This eclectic structure with sophisticated decorations now houses different official organizations, but do not let that stop you: simply ask some of the keepers or employees to show you around the interiors, and you will see that Uzbekistan does not dismiss the requests of its guests.

Bukhara: A Schedule

Day 1
A full day in the Bukhara Old City. Lyab-i Hauz Complex, trade domes, Abdulaziz Khan Madrasah, Mir-i Arab Complex. Lunch. Ark Citadel, Bolo-Hauz Mosque, Samanid Mausoleum. Dinner.

Day 2
Visit to the Akbar House Collection Gallery. Drive to the summer palace Sitorai Mohi Xosa of the Emirs of Bukhara. Drive to Gijduvan (40 minutes). Excursion and lunch at the Narzullaevs' studio. Return to Bukhara. Dinner in Bukhara.

Abraham Ishakov, a Bukharian Jewish community elder, at the historic synagogue by the Lyab-i Hauz Complex

CUISINE AND WINEMAKING OF BUKHARA:

Deconstructed Plov and Best Meat Skewers of Uzbekistan

Spices for sale at Silk Road Tea House in Bukhara

One of the most important features of culinary traditions of Bukhara is the very strong Persian influence. For example, the plov of Bukhara is cooked in a manner that is not followed elsewhere in Uzbekistan, moreover, nowhere in Central Asia. The fact that ingredients for the oshi sofi, or the wedding plov, are cooked separately is the direct legacy of the culture of Middle Asia and a unique example where the ancient tradition was preserved.

The deep synergy of **Persian and Jewish traditions** is another crucial gastronomic feature of Bukhara. Being quite large some fifty years ago, the Jewish community of Bukhara has now decreased to a minimum: once the borders were open, almost everybody who could leave, did so. The festival oshi sofi plov, cooked in Uzbek families in Bukhara as a special event or wedding dish, was also cooked in families of Bukhara Jews with the only difference that the latter added chickpeas for their magical significance. The indigenous Uzbek and Tajik people and Bukhara Jews alike added raisins to the plov. This is the influence of cultural traditions of the ancient Iranian world that was the origin of the plov itself and the rites it accompanied.

Bukhara and its suburbs lie within desert and semi-desert zones. Traditionally, locals raise not the Hissar lambs with their massive fat tails and thin subcutaneous fat layer adapted to mountainous conditions (as seen in Surxondaryo, for instance), but rather the **Karakul sheep**: hardy, undemanding animals accustomed to extreme temperature fluctuations typical of desert pastures. These are sheep that can drink salty water and feed on thorns, sheep that have never seen alpine meadows with their high-mountain grasses. The meat is different, too: "The meat is salty, and the fish is sweet," say the locals about their local cuisine.

Fishing in the desert is not a joke for the Bukhara Region. The great Lake Tudakul has a fishery cultivating catfish, bream, and wild carp. So, fish is a common dish, usually, fried in oil or braised over an open fire.

The vicinity of Tajikistan and Turkmenistan is another important factor influencing the gastronomic landscape of the city. There are numerous similarities and coincidences, e.g., kaish, or boiled dough with garnishes, that Tajiks and Turkmens also have. Bukhara is known for the intertwining of Tajik and Turkmen fate.

Gijduvan kebab represents Uzbekistan's most powerful local culinary trend that has spread nationwide. It is difficult to say why this small town 40 km from Bukhara became the birthplace of what is arguably Uzbekistan's most

Bolo-Hauz Mosque in Bukhara

famous variety of ground (or chopped) kebab. Firstly, the kebabs here are truly exceptional, and, secondly, locals have mastered the technique of keeping them from falling off the skewers into the fire.

Bukhara may find its way on the wine lover's Uzbekistan itinerary, above all, because of the **Shohrud Winery** (*+998 90 299 41 46: winery, +998 91 445 05 57: tasting room in the old city, Nogai Caravanserai, Naqshbandi Street, 195*), the only winery in the region. Besides, the winemaker family of Jamal Akhrorov and Lutfia Achilova and their daughter Dilnoza put great effort in making good quality wines, and making tasting experience possible both in the historical center and at the winery.

Bukhara: Dishes to Try

Oshi sofi is the festive plov of Bukhara; the rice, the mat and the vegetables for it are cooked separately. Traditional oshi sofi is cooked in copper pots, for Bukhara has always been one of the main coppersmith centers of Uzbekistan, and still remains.

Barracha is a seasonal spring-only dish of meat of very young freshly slaughtered lambs.

Waguri is a dish of oil-fried lamb entrails served with onions.

Gijduvan kebab is chopped lamb kebab made without the addition of bread or other thickening components. Its secret is the multiple freezing of the ground meat.

Alat samsa is baked in an oven from regular (not layered) dough; it bears its name after the town of Alat in Bukhara Region.

Kaish is the closest relative of Kazakh beshbarmak and Uzbek shilpildoq, but with Turkmen and Tajik roots: boiled pieces of dough served with a garnish of vegetables, beans and tomatoes, sometimes with added meat.

Bukhara kaymak is a dairy product found exclusively in Bukhara. It consists of the cream skimmed from heated milk. The secret lies in the multi-stage process: the milk is heated, the cream is skimmed, cooled, then reheated and skimmed again. The kaymak with a hot flatbread and tea makes the perfect breakfast in Bukhara.

Holvaytar is liquid halva made from flour, a homemade dessert resembling toffee.

On Uzbek Entrepreneurship, Jewish Mahalla, and the Market Visited by the Emir Himself

Tourism sustains Bukhara today. The city's compact and exceptionally preserved historic center, its large centrally located Jewish quarter whose owners of ornately decorated homes gradually left the country, enabling their former properties to be converted into hotels and restaurants combined with the entrepreneurial spirit of locals have shaped the Bukhara we see today. To no small extent, this is the achievement of Rustam and Zukhra, owners of the **As-Salam Hotel** (*+998 90 710 71 17, Naqshbandi Street, 116*). This hotel was my first stay in Bukhara when I arrived in the country as a tourist. Since then, I return here time and again, feeling like a guest of a large, close-knit family that preserves the traditions of old Bukhara itself.
Rustam and Zukhra grew up and spent their entire lives in this very corner of Bukhara. They witnessed the city transform from an old, dilapidated town

where water and electricity were rationed into Uzbekistan's most harmonious city, impossible not to love at first sight. Back in the 1990s, the family invested their shuttle-trade earnings into real estate. Step by step, they turned a small guesthouse into a boutique hotel. Rustam and Zukhra recall sleeping in their car parked outside because tourists took every bed in the hotel and the tiny guesthouse. Today, the family owns several hotels in Bukhara, with nearly all their close relatives involved in the business.

The neighborhood where Zukhra and Rustam grew up and opened their hotel borders the Jewish quarter. One of the synagogues is just a two-minute walk away, located right next to Lyab-i Hauz. Local lore recounts that Nadir Divan-Begi, the vizier of one of Bukhara's khans (after whom the entire Lyab-i Hauz ensemble is named), was planning this construction project in the 16th century and discovered an elderly Jewish woman's house standing precisely where the reservoir was to be built. She refused to leave—at any price. The story has it that the Khan forbade evicting her by force. Yet the eastern cunning, combined with a series of carefully orchestrated disruptions, eventually compelled the homeowner to negotiate with the vizier. The affair concluded with her being granted the land to build Bukhara's first synagogue in immediate proximity to Lyab-i Hauz.

In Bukhara, the Jewish community was quite large. Apart from fabric dyeing (in the local dialect, the expression "to go to the Jew" meant "to have one's fabrics dyed" for a long time), it was busy with winemaking, and there is a story that the Emir's court used to buy this wine through an intermediary. Jews paid higher taxes and had some restrictions when it came to horse-riding outside their quarters, or to the height of buildings, but the situation is generally described as positive both by historians and people who had tales of old Bukhara recounted by their grandmothers and grandfathers. After the Russian conquest of Central Asia, the Jews of Bukhara controlled nearly all trade between the regions. By the early 20th century, Bukhara had three distinct Jewish quarters, and these had no shortage of affluent homes.

The Jewish mahalla near Lyab-i Hauz was fortunate: it remained largely undamaged by Frunze's army, which bombed the city in 1920 while attempting to banish the last emir. The Soviet era also passed without significant harm to the district, with no five-story apartment blocks and no highways constructed here. Since the early 1990s, this mahalla, like Bukhara's entire historic center, has been under UNESCO protection. Consequently, the new owners of old, ornately decorated Jewish houses, now being converted into hotels and restaurants, must conduct any renovations under strict supervision. These historic Jewish homes represent the most valuable real estate on the property market of Bukhara.

One early morning, right after the morning prayer, Rustam and I went to the Green Bazaar. I had visited Bukhara many times, but it was only the day before that I learned about this market deep inside the mahalla: the way to the second, or farther, synagogue of Bukhara took me through it. The day before Emmanuel Elnatanov, one of the leaders of the city's Jewish community, showed me this synagogue built over two hundred years ago. In the Soviet times, it housed different organizations, but as early as in the 1990s the building was handed over to the worshippers and restored. This is a place for everyone, and Rustam (we went to buy some cottage cheese for his grandchildren) recalls a story from his grandmother: she had seen here the last Emir of Bukhara, who was partial to the traditional Bukhara kaymak. Emmanuel tells me that the now small Jewish community orders bread at the local bakery. The market is abuzz with people (it is just past sunrise!), sellers and buyers exchange greetings, and I understand: these people have known each other well for a long time. Though renovated in recent years, the market is still the corner of Bukhara that brings together different people, times, and traditions.

If you stop by the synagogue at the Lyab-i Hauz—its doors are always open for guests—you are likely to meet Abraham Ishakov. He will tell you that, if he had two lives, he would have spent one in Israel. But he only has one, and it goes on here, in Bukhara: "They're all gone, and I remained," he says about the state of the community. It is hard to gather the *minyan* of ten men, required for some prayers.

Bazaars of Bukhara

Markaziy Bazaar
Bukhara's largest market spans several large pavilions. Spices and bread, vegetables and fruit, meat and dairy products are allocated to different sections. While this market has a reputation for being less touristy than the Siyob Bazaar of Samarkand, the difference isn't so stark (forgive me, Samarkandis). If you missed visiting the bazaar in Samarkand, you can make up for it in Bukhara. One thing I always buy here is herbal tea. Ask anyone in the spice-and-bread pavilion to point you to the tea seller's stall... and tell them, I sent you.

Green Bazaar
Located in the Jewish mahalla in the historical center of Bukhara, this bazaar is only open early in the morning to cater the dwellers of nearby districts. Come at 6 or 6:30 in the morning, and stand in the first queue to buy some fresh Bukhara kaymak.

Where to Eat: National Cuisine

Minzifa
Offering a nice view of the center of Bukhara, this restaurant features many vegetarian options on the menu: some traditional Uzbek dishes are made only with vegetables.
+998 93 960 23 26, Khoja Rushnoyi Street, 6

Old House
Old House operates in one of the historic Jewish homes, managed by Sharif Sharipov, owner of Old Bukhara. This museum-like restaurant offers an intimate setting with a painted ayvan (terrace) and lavishly decorated living room, hidden behind thick walls from the tourist bustle of Bukhara. The menu features classic Uzbek cuisine, including all the highlights of regional national dishes. Note: reservations only.
+998 90 929 99 09, +998 90 185 70 77, Sarafon Street, 5

Old Bukhara
The building of Old Bukhara is a true particle of the ancient city, inherited by the owner, Sharif Sharipov, from his grandmother. Sharif's great-grandfather

was the right-hand man of the Emir of Bukhara; his grandfather was also one of the inner circle and had several shops in the city.

As a restaurant, Old Bukhara used to seat 120 people, today it hosts 330 people at a time, and there may be several seatings in an evening during the high season. This is ample business for a small city! Here, at Old Bukhara, they make the ideal Alat samsa with thin crust and juicy filling, and the absolutely amazing shakarob salad with peeled sweet tomatoes and purple basil, or rayhon. I believe it to be the best in the world! Delicious lamb. Excellent tea with lemon and sugar: one might think, brewing tea is no rocket science... and yet.
+998 90 185 70 77, Samarkand Street, 3

Joy Chaikhana Lounge
Homemade Uzbek food, live music and hookah inside an old madrasah. The restaurant is just steps away from the monument to Khoja Nasreddin, by the Lyab-i Hauz.
+998 88 183 02 00, Sarafon Street, 2

Zaytoon
Middle-Eastern cuisine from Shuhrat Ishankulov, a chef with international experience. No manti and plov on the menu, but you can try falafel, tabbouleh, excellent steaks and delicious flatbreads.
+998 90 416 15 15, Zulfiya Street, 11

Saffron
A restaurant with a terrace and a panoramic view of Bukhara in the Mercure Bukhara Old Town Hotel offers Uzbek cuisine with some international accents.
+998 88 852 05 00, Samarkand Street, 206

Sazanchik
A simple café off the city center, seldom visited by tourists but offering excellent fried fish.
+998 90 711 38 83, Kayum Murtazaev Street, 6/3

The Plov
The only dish of this place is the Bukhara plov, the original, cooked in a copper kozon only at lunch time (11:30 a.m. –3 p.m.), open weekly. Plan for a sevent-to-ten-minute taxi drive from the center. *Essential reference point for drivers: Dunyo Tekstil shop.*
+998 93 960 25 55, Abu Ali Ibn Sina Avenue, 8/1

Olim ota
This spot is not in the center either, and tourists seldom find it, but locals know that Olim Ota serves the most authentic, lean festive oshi sofi plov: fluffy rice, sweet carrots, tender meat (and of course, chickpeas and raisins). Arrive by 12 a.m. to watch them serve it straight from the massive copper kozon.
+998 93 969 98 89, +998 91 442 39 55, Gazli Highway, 160

Chor Bakr Choyxona
This simple teahouse outside the city center by the Chor Bakr necropolis is the best meat café in Bukhara frequented and loved by the locals. Find a table on the vine-covered terrace and order bone-in lamb and warm homemade flatbreads, salad of juicy tomatoes and tea. It may well happen that you will be the only tourist in the restaurant.
+998 65 545 34 04

Traditional tea service with sweets at Bukhara's Silk Road Tea House

Tea and Coffee

Silk Road Tea House
Probably, the most famous teahouse in Bukhara. The family of its owner, Mirfayz Ubaidov, has traded spices for centuries. Sitting here with a bowl of ginger tea amid the antiques collected by the family, it's easy to imagine the caravans laden with exotic spices from Iran, China, and India crossing mountains and deserts. Mirfayz himself is the go-to person for custom spice blends and herbal tea recipes. The spice mixes made in the Silk Road are used in the spa procedures in the men's and women's hammams of Bukhara. You can try the tea with ginger, saffron and spice mix, and coffee brewed in a cezve, with cardamom or cinnamon. Assorted Oriental sweets will be served for tea and coffee, including probably the best halva in Bukhara. Of course, you can buy the teas and spices in exquisite packages as well.
+998 93 383 40 34

The Kebab Capital of Uzbekistan
Almost everyone in Uzbekistan knows this for a fact: in Gijduvan, 50 km away from Bukhara, they make excellent shashlyk. Many would even agree that these are the reference kebabs. Gijduvan is the kebab capital of the country. The very term *Gijduvan shashlyk* may be the first on the list of Uzbekistan's denominations of protected origin, and Gijduvan itself, the *appellation* of kebabs. I have heard countless debates about which city makes the best plov, but never about where to find the best shashlyk. One might say Uzbeks are united on this matter, even those who

Khairullo Mukhamedov with his son, masters of Gijduvan kebab

have never visited Gijduvan. (Of course, there are some voices from Tashkent, accustomed to considering shashlyk from the nearby So'qoq as the finest.)

It seems that there must be some secret ingredient to explain the fame and glory of Gijduvan kebabs. Is it the marinade for the meat? Is it margination time? Or something added to keep the meat from falling off the skewer? Surprisingly, they do not add anything special other than meat, fat, onion, salt, black pepper, and cumin. The meat-grinder, however, is an indispensable tool.

White Hall decorated with ganch carving at Sitorai Mohi Xosa Palace

DECORATIVE AND APPLIED ARTS OF BUKHARA:

Under the Persian Influence

Akbar House Collection Gallery in Bukhara

Persian influence can still be seen in the gastronomy and the decorative and applied arts of Bukhara and the region. Many arts and crafts, characteristic for the region, are rooted in Iranian traditions.

Bukhara stands as one of Uzbekistan's most important centers for **artistic copperwork.** The craft of intricate, low-relief chasing that lived through several periods of decline and revival over the past century is now undergoing renewed vitality. In recent decades, tourist demand has shaped a new style: meticulously executed patterns now enhanced with vivid, eye-catching colored enamels.
Gold embroidery, or *zardozi*, also comes from Persia. Until the Soviet era, Bukhara remained a capital city, home to many noble families that commissioned the finest artistic talent of the region. Like in Persia, gold-thread embroidery here persisted as a traditional men's craft. It was revived in the 1920s and managed to survive the collapse of the planned economy to re-emerge later in small private ateliers.

The Bukhara school of **book miniature**, most influential in the country, also experienced a strong Persian influence. An important center of religion and literacy, Bukhara was the place where some of the most talented artists and calligraphers worked designing the books for the most demanding clients. Highly decorative miniatures, full of deep meaning executed on mulberry paper and put in a frame, are an excellent original buy.

Suzanis from this part of the country are also some of the most beautiful in Uzbekistan. Embroidery has always been a prosperous craft in Bukhara and Nurata, part of the Bukhara Emirate. Specialists tend to unite the embroidery from Nurata and Bukhara into one type that implements some motifs borrowed from Iranian ornament art. Pieces from Bukhara and Nurata are recognizable for their rich colors, minute embroidered ornaments and sophisticated composition. Like many other arts and crafts of Uzbekistan, suzani is sustained from the tourist demand. The embroidery made in Nurata, a large town in the Navoiy Region that lies outside tourist routes, is sold across Uzbekistan, but most of it is sold in Bukhara. The interest of today's buyers resulted in the emergence of fully embroidered items of clothing (gowns and jackets) that had never been traditional.

Bukhara region is the home to one of the **most interesting schools of ceramics**

in Uzbekistan, the Gijdunav school. Located near Bukhara, on a route from Samarkand, Gijduvan became an important tourist destination thanks to the effort of the family of Narzullaev, hereditary ceramists. Earlier, in the Soviet time, this family literally saved the traditions of the Gijduvan ceramics.

Bukhara region maintains the now-rare tradition of crafting **small molded whistle-toys** (khushtak) that date back to Zoroastrian times. In Central Asia, this tradition persists in the Fergana Valley, Tajikistan, and in the places near Vobkent, close to Gijduvan. By the way, Nurata embroidery features schematic depictions of these toys.

Iskandar Hakimov Puppet Workshop
One of pioneers of tourist business in Uzbekistan, Iskandar Hakimov, wanted to show Uzbek customs and rituals to guests without hiring professional actors, hence the idea of using puppet performances, and their first characters were rod-puppets.

One day, a girl visiting from Japan recognized her own living image in one of the puppets and said she was not willing to part with it. Iskandar was left with nothing else but to surrender the puppet to the girl and ask the head artist of the theater to make a replica of that puppet, as soon as possible. It became clear that selling the puppets could become one of the ways to sustain the theater that had never had any support from the state. At some point, he even had to decide what was more important, the performances or the trade. This was how the workshop with a store appeared and became a tourist attraction of Bukhara.

After all, Iskandar himself had to learn to make the puppets: head of papier mâché, soft hands of fabric, and costumes of national garments. The master decided to focus on hand puppets with a rod inside once he saw how easy it was for children to control them: in their hands, the puppets were almost dancing! And so it happened that a dance to the accompaniment of merry music became the performance that every guest of the workshop would see: the puppet becomes alive in the master's hands and behaves like a true Oriental beauty, shrugging and turning her face away coquettishly.
+998 90 514 44 22, Sarafon Street, 2

Men's Craft
"Traditionally, gold embroidery was an exclusively men's craft," explains Bakhshillo Jumaev, a fifth-generation gold-embroiderer. Both his father and grandfather practiced the art. During the reign of the last Emir of Bukhara, Bakhshillo's grandfather owned one of thirty gold-embroidery workshops in the city. Imagine, one of thirty, not counting the three workshops maintained at the court of the Emir, each employing 30 to 40 artisans.

When the regime changed, Bakhshillo's grandfather became a shoemaker. As Bakhshillo recalls from his mother's stories, authorities came to confiscate their property seven times. "The last time, my family was left just wearing their clothes," recounts he explaining how his grandfather nevertheless managed to preserve the materials for gold embroidery. Thanks to this courage, the ancient craft tradition continued in the Jumaev family.

The person who saved the art of gold embroidery of Bukhara was the star of

Uzbek dance and song Tamara Khanum. In 1925, she went to the International Exhibition in Paris to represent Uzbekistan. She needed costumes, such costumes as to make the entire Paris gasp. Her garments were embroidered in Bukhara, and this was the first time in the 20th century that the ancient craft rose from the ashes.

In the 1930s, the first gold-embroidery artels appeared, and, in 1939, the Bukhara Gold Embroidery Factory was established. Then came the war, and the women remaining in the city had to take up needles and work for military needs. "After the war, we had to revive the craft again," Bakhshillo says, "Some masters returned, while others disappeared." Throughout the Soviet era, the factory produced clothing and interior items, and large pieces with ideological motifs. By the time Bakhshillo came to the factory as the head artists in the late 1970s, it had employed 1,500 people. "How about today?" I asked. "Fifteen," he says. Women started embroidering with gold in the Soviet period, when the craft had been industrialized. No longer they had to kneel on a *kurpacha* mat thrown on the cold floor; they were working in warm workshops, and their material was placed on a special frame of a machine in front of them.

Today, Bakhshillo and his family own Bukhara's most famous gold embroidery workshop. "We create unique items and we know for sure that they will find their customer," he says pointing at a glass cabinet containing a man's robe fully stitched with gold. Weighing over 15 kilograms, it is fully covered with eighteen different kinds of stitches. Each robe like this one takes six months of work of five people: each of the sleeves, each of the two frontal parts and the back are works of different masters. Each square centimeter of fabric is covered with some sixty stitches. Back in the day, they used to work with velvet sent from Moscow. Earlier still, during the Emirate, with local velvet from Bukhara, or *bakhmal*, but it is no longer manufactured here. All raw materials today are imported, but the skill and talent are local. The thread for the gold embroidery contains real gold, today up to 7 percent, but in the past the thread had up to 30 percent gold. In the old days, threads were also manufactured in Bukhara, and gold stitching was a craft fringing together the local jewelers and embroiderers.

Bakhshillo and Mukkadas Jumaev in their workshop in Bukhara

Gold embroidery, known by the local name *zardozi*, is still in demand. Lavish weddings are incomplete without gold-embroidered garments: even modest households spare no expense for these celebrations. Museums and private collectors are major buyers as well. "Ideally, one should master three skills," explains Bakhshillo, "To be an ornament designer, to know how to cut templates, and, of course, to master the stitching." Only by possessing all of these can one become a true master artisan.
+998 91 415 52 43, Hakikat Street, 43, sovga.world@mail.ru

Davlat Toshev Miniature Workshop
Davlat Toshev, one of the most renowned artists of the country, turned a decrepit old caravanserai in the center of Bukhara into an artist's studio, where gifted children and children with special needs learn free of charge.

Bukhara has the most influential tradition of book miniature in Uzbekistan, a craft inherited from Persia. An important religious center, the city was one of the main site of book writing, and illustrators of medieval volumes always had to work here. The Bukhara school reached its peak in the 15th century attracting the world's best artists and calligraphers. It formed its new style: in contrast to the eye-catching bright colors of Iranian miniature, Bukhara artists used subdued tones. The books were adorned with miniatures only for the very rich of customers, and sometimes, pages in the books were left blank until the time when the manuscript found its way into the hands of a person capable of paying for the job. Every illustration is a veritable universe, a self-contained system with a definite hierarchy and extensive symbolism without a single random element.

Every piece by Davlat Toshev is more than just exquisitely crafted drawings executed with fine tools on smooth silk paper. Each of them tells a story of the world, its understanding, and divine forces. Davlat learned to draw from his brother, who was taught by their uncle. It was Davlat's father, though, who instilled in him a love for miniature art. In the Soviet times, he concealed publications containing samples of ancient miniatures and books on Sufism in numerous hidden compartments of their house, and the family only discovered many of them after his death.
+998 90 715 37 86, Arabon Street, 10

Kasimov Metal Craft Workshop
The workshop of Kasimov family of metal chasers occupies one of the cells in the ancient Nadir Divanbegi Madrasah. Tahir Kasimov, the head of the family, is a student of the famous Usto Salimjon Hamidov, founder of the Bukhara school. Tahir-aka not only worked on restoration and continuation of the craft, having trained over a hundred masters, but invented a new method of applying the ornament with tiniest points.
Metal chasing is meticulous handiwork, and ornaments are applied to a copper or brass piece in several stages resulting in two or three layers of varying depth. The tools of the trade are outwardly simple and have not changed over time, the main tool being the chisel (*kalyam*). At first, the master will prepare a sketch on thin dense paper, then, carry it over to the metal carefully aligning it against the center, and only then will start working on the ornament. An essential skill is to hold the tool at the same angle: even a minute change in the inclination

will change the pattern. It is at least a year from the moment a student takes a pencil and homemade worksheets to copy the basic elements to their first exam in drawing. One needs to know the patterns by heart, to understand their logic, and to see their beauty.

Traditional metalwork of Bukhara is restrained in color yet exceptionally refined in its ornamentation. The patterns engraved on brass or copper are accentuated with blackening. Today, in response to tourist expectations shaped by the vivid aesthetics of Uzbekistan, Bukhara's artisans enhance their pieces with colored enamel.
+998 90 636 33 99, +998 90 636 59 95, Hakikat Street, 29, metalcraft-bukhara.com

Jurabek Sidikov
Jurabek works with brass and copper chasing combining traditional Persian art with elements of miniature, enamel, and calligraphy.
+998 90 298 87 33, Sayfiddin Caravanserai

Ikramov Brothers' Smithy
A complex family tree on the wall of the workshop by the third trade dome, Toqi Zargaron, proves that the blacksmith craft has a long tradition in the Ikramov family. The smithy produces Damascus steel knives, for household and hunting, and national sabers. The most popular souvenirs are miniature foldable knives to peel and cut fruit and vegetables, and delicately curved scissors in the shape of a stork. This unusual shape is the result of interaction between two traditional crafts of Bukhara, blacksmith's and gold embroiderer's crafts, because the sharp and handy scissors are indispensable for cutting even the most complicated ornaments. The stork is one of the symbols of Bukhara, hence the exquisite shape of the tool.
+998 93 383 07 70, +998 90 510 07 70, bukharaknife@mail.ru, Hakikat Street, 6

Akbar House Collection
Several rooms of the gallery near the Lyab-i Hauz are crammed with ancient silk chapans, century-old Uzbek fabrics, antique carpets, tableware, household and decorative items... Akbar Hakimov worked on his collection all his life, following the steps of his grandfather. Today, it is truly worth a museum exhibition! Akbar and his wife Mastura welcome their guests in a lavishly decorated living room of an old Jewish home that they had carefully restored. A visit here is a chance to learn more about the arts and culture, gastronomy and rites of Bukhara from the people who are fascinated with the heritage of the city.
+998 91 405 32 32, Babakhanov Street, 1 akbar_house@yahoo.com

Abdulvakhid Bukhoriy Karimov
Some think that the white and blue colors unite the Khorezm and Fergana ceramics and oppose them to the ochre and brown tinge of Bukhara and Samarkand schools. In reality, azure was the color of preference of all large developed cities that witnessed the pieces from the Timurid period, whereas centers of ceramics of more remote areas worked in a warmer spectrum of fallen leaves. The larger cities were the first to lose their tradition of azure ceramics due to import of factory-made earthenware, but the artisanal workshops continued in the traditional ochreous colors. The archeologists know the blue ceramics of Bukhara from the 18th–19th centuries, and Abdulvakhid Karimov, potter and scholar, carries on with this tradition. He learned from Alisher Nazrullaev

Traditional Uzbek fabrics at Feruza Akhrarova's store in Bukhara

and Kubaro Babaeva, participated in numerous archeological expeditions. Holding ancient shards in his hands, he tried to understand how the old masters prepared the pigments, and how they painted the ceramic pieces. In his quest for the answers, he gathered literature, and, supported by UNESCO, succeeded in reviving that legendary azure-colored ceramics.
+998 90 934 83 71, Mirzo Fayoz Street, 13

Numon Samiev
For centuries, Bukhara has been famous for its furs. Dressing of karakulcha and karakul pelts remains one of the region's most vital trades. While fur coats, jackets, and hats are sold throughout the city, one of the finest workshops lies hidden in backstreets far from tourist centers. I personally visit and bring my guests to the Samiev family, who have specialized in karakul dressing and tailoring for decades. The atelier also takes custom orders, delivering speed and quality.
+998 91 413 00 12, Kokuli Kalon Street, 22

Feruza Akhrarova
Full of traditional Uzbek fabrics from floor to ceiling, Feruza Akhrarova's shop is the best in Bukhara. It offers a wide selection of fabrics (silk, silk and cotton blends) and ready-made clothes, dresses, gowns, decorative accessories, such as scarves and makeup bags. Feruza has a big team of seamstresses, who can craft a new attire from the material of your choice overnight.
+998 65 224 15 70, +998 91 413 97 37, Naqshbandi Street, near the Second Covered Bazaar

On the streets of Bukhara

Sanjar Nazarov
Sanjar Nazarov's vibrant shop beneath the third covered bazaar (Toqi Zargaron) is instantly recognizable by its rainbow of embroidered robes and stacks of impeccably finished suzanis. Sanjar represents the third generation of his family specializing in traditional embroidery of Bukhara. You will find embroidered pillowcases, delicately crafted bedspreads, fully stitched boots and bags, jackets and robes adorned with diverse patterns. The artisan will gladly share insights about the traditions of the Bukhara and Nurata schools.
+998 93 454 55 25, +998 93 383 19 61, Hakikat Street, Third Covered Bazaar

The Jewellery Workshop
Located between the Omar Khayyam Hotel and the gold embroidery workshop of Bakshillo Jumaev, this store is one of my absolute favorites in the entire country. The items here are laconic and provide a pleasant contrast to the majority of ethnically styled bijouterie that you will see in Uzbekistan.
+998 97 301 00 07, Hakikat Street, 47

Sabina Burkhanova
Sabina Burkhanova founded Bukhara Silk Carpets in 2010; however, her workshop weaves carpets of both silk and wool.
+998 905134824, Khoja Nurobod Street

Pavillon Kalon
A boutique and art space entirely dedicated to Uzbek applied arts. Inside, you will find a curated selection of Uzbekistan's finest brands, artisan ceramics, jewelry, and a breathtaking view of the Kalyan minaret.
t.me/pavillon_kalon

SUBURBS OF BUKHARA

Olimjon Narzullaev, master of the Gijduvan pottery tradition

Gijduvan
To Have, and to Have it Done

It was a miracle that kept Gijduvan ceramics alive in the turbulent 20th century. In the times of the Emirate, Gijduvan, located 50 kilometers away from Bukhara, had several dozen ceramic workshops. In the 1960s, the last one, belonging to the ceramist Ibadulla Narzullaev, was demolished. Ibadulla's grandson, Olimjon Narzullaev, recalls: "Grandfather used to say that firing was the most complicated, the process lasted for three days. It was a good thing that our ceramics factory covered him." For more than ten years, Olimjon's grandfather tried to convince the authorities to give him some land for his own workshop: he could not bear the thought of abandoning the craft that his family carried on for over two centuries. The workshop did appear thanks to Konstantin Simonov: the poet and the potter met at a health resort in Namangan. Sometime later, during a working visit to Bukhara, Konstantin Simonov stopped at Gijduvan. He was so impressed by the local tradition of ceramic art and by the zeal of Ibadulla that he managed to persuade the officials in Moscow to help this tradition to carry on. Ibadulla and his son Alisher were admitted to the Union of Artists of the USSR, and a place was allocated for their workshop.
Thanks to Konstantin Simonov, Moscow knew and appreciated the talent of Narzullaev family. When you visit the State Museum of Oriental Art in Moscow, you will see the Gijduvan lagans in its glass cabinets. Sometimes, this style of ceramics is called *wild* for its vivid natural colors and original ornaments, each of them local, invented or developed by Ibadulla based on ancient pieces without a single foreign or borrowed motif. "Gijduvan ceramics is not about smoothness," they say to each guest of the workshop.

The Gijduvan Ceramics Center, where we speak with Olimjon, was organized recently: the state allocated the land, recognizing that traditional crafts attract tourists (and money). From the outset, everything was built big to accommodate crowds: the site was chosen outside the old city for tourist bus access, housing both a Gijduvan ceramics museum and a meticulously designed demonstration of the full production process. Dining halls and shaded terraces spare the guests the effort to go elsewhere for the famous Gijduvan shashlik, especially since Olimjon himself is married to the daughter of Hayrullo Mukhamedov, master kebab chef of Gijduvan. "If you have no skill, you have nothing," goes the Narzullaev family saying.

As far as the manufacturing is concerned, the family strictly follows the old traditions that shun mass production. Here, in the largest center of Uzbek ceramics, everything is done in the same way as they did a century or two ago: only by hand. Even the grindstone milling the glaze components is not motorized: a donkey keeps turning it.

The *Narzullaev home* upholds the tradition of embroidery to this day, and the women of the family keep it alive. Guests from all over the world buy ceramics and suzani. "We are grateful to our grandfather: he did not stop, neither did he want to," Olimjon says. Gratitude

is the feeling that every guest takes away with them on leaving.
+998 65 572 24 12, Gijduvan, Navoiy Street, 45, Kimsan Street, 55, ceramicsuz.narod.ru

Vobkent: A Minaret Gambled Away and Zoroastrian Toys

As you travel from Bukhara to Gijduvan, make a short stop in Vobkent near the minaret of Vobkent. It does look familiar, does it not? It is for a reason that they call it the little brother of the Kalyan minaret of Bukhara! Similar to the Bukhara structure, the Vobkent Minaret was built before the Mongolian conquest and survived the ordeal. Once upon a time, says a local legend, the local mullahs lost their minaret while playing dice with their neighbors from Shirin. The game was so intense and the gamblers so carried away, that they bet the beautiful minaret, no less. However hard the winners tried to cut down the tower and take it home to Shirin, they failed. Look closely, and you might find the traces of that struggle at the foot of the minaret.

Vobkent District is known as one of the few places of Uzbekistan that still has the tradition of making whistles (*khushtaks*) in the shape of mythical animals. This tradition has Zoroastrian roots. Mothers used to make such toys from clay for their children to give for the holiday of Navruz, the spring equinox symbolizing the beginning of a new year. It was believed that the whistle would call the rain and make the year successful and rich of harvest. The last mistress of this craft was Kubaro Babaeva. I was lucky to have visited Kubaro-opa, when she was past her eighties. All her life she worked as a tractor driver, but when she retired, she began making the whistles, taking on the tradition from her mother and aunt. In her youth, she wanted to take the place at the potter's wheel, but, as a woman, she could not get into the traditional men's profession. After her death, Abdulvakhid Karimov and the Narzullaev family maintain the tradition of Vobkent toys.

Sentob and Nuratau Mountains

The small kishlak of Sentob (also known as Sentab) lies between the Lake Aydarkul and Nuratau mountains, or, it sticks to the mountain slopes, with shining white walls of houses and bright blue frames of windows and doors, and blue pillars supporting the roofs of terraces. The road here is very long and rather bumpy, but on your way, you will drive past Faris (believed to be named after a certain Paris), and if you are really lucky, in spring you may see girls picking kovul, or wild capers, their hair in long braids. You will see herds of Karakul sheep famous for their furs. Far away, you will see the shimmering water of the Lake Aydarkul and marvel at its size. Only experienced and confident drivers may drive to the kishlak: the paved road suddenly turns into a dirt road jammed between the mountain slope and a precipice above a stream. My driver, however, brought me into the waiting arms of Shodiboi and Mutabar Boboev, owners of one of guest houses of Sentob. As we were driving, a boy called us: he understood that the only reason why a jeep could get here was that a foreigner would be inside, so he started advertising one of local guesthouses in English. Thus, in the remote locality of Sentob, without any initiative of assistance from the government, a tourist cluster

Vobkent Minaret

A view from Sentob

organized by itself. I should confess, I can hardly imagine how they delivered furniture and construction materials.

The road ends at the Mutabar House (the owner, Shodiboi, named it after his wife). The tourists can enjoy everything that is only possible in such a remote spot: a bar decorated with local stone, a swimming pool on the slope above the mountain stream, and a fountain. This Tajik kishlak (with clear influence of Bukhara) is the native soil of Shodiboi and Mutabar, and the house, around which the guest facilities grew, is the home of their family. Shodiboi tells they have quite a lot of foreign tourists, French, British, and German, and asks us to tell our travelers about Sentob.

Typically, travelers stay in Sentob for two to three days in spring and summer. They embark on long hikes through the surrounding areas rich in petroglyphs, remnants of Zoroastrian sanctuaries, and mountain lakes; they bake tandoor flatbread and ride donkeys, of course, they sample local cuisine. It is a retreat from the noise of big cities, a chance to breathe fresh air and immerse in rural life. Surely worth a visit!
Mutabar Guest House: +998 99 756 61 01, Sentob Village, Balandiumar Street, 12

Lake Aydarkul

This is the famous Uzbek riviere, a wonder of nature and human labor, a freshwater lake in the midst of steppes. Lake Aydarkul appeared on the map of Uzbekistan in the late 1960s due to abnormally high waters of the Syr Darya. In the recent years, the lake became a popular recreation site. Tourists can taste the nomad life and spend the night in yurt camps, listen to the songs of akyns, and marvel the stars. The best campsite managers (*+998 94 372 44 55,* Vakhid; *+998 97 929 99 22*, Yulia) have new motorboats on the lake and well-tended beaches. Fishing is a popular pastime, as well as swimming (in spring): there is some clay in the shallow water, but cool and clear water is just a few strokes away.

One of the yurt camps near Lake Aydarkul

HOTELS OF BUKHARA

The courtyard of Lyabi House Hotel

Malika Bukhara
Located in the city center, Hotel Malika Bukhara, from a well-known local chain, maintains a solid four-star standard. It features spacious European-style rooms, an ATM in the lobby, a compact fitness center, and a sauna.
+998 65 224 62 56, Gaukushan Street, 25

As-Salam
A boutique hotel in the national style, featuring spacious, ornately decorated rooms and a lavish buffet breakfast with freshly prepared homemade hot dishes. The nearby Fatima and Anor hotels belong to the same family.
+998 90 710 71 17, Baha-ud-Din Naqshband Street, 116

Lyabi House
I appreciate the blend of European-style understated room decor and the national motifs of the breakfast terrace, once part of a wealthy Jewish family's home, around which the hotel gradually expanded.
+998 65 224 24 84, +998 65 224 59 47, N. Khusainov Street, 7

Wyndham Bukhara
A modern four-star hotel located a short distance from the city center. Stylish decor devoid of Eastern motifs, a large outdoor pool, and rooms of all categories and sizes, including vast suites.
+998 55 305 00 00, Alisher Navoiy Street, 8

Mercure Bukhara Old Town
A chain hotel designed in the local style close to the old section of Bukhara. The architects managed to blend Oriental flavors with international standards.
+998 55 305 07 07, Samarkand Street, 206

Khorezm and Karakalpak Region. Azure and Clay

Chapter IV

Khorezm is a vast territory that the ancient Arabs called the land of a thousand fortresses, one of the most ancient historical and cultural regions of Central Asia, a historical area with the center in the lower reaches of the Amu Darya.

Madrasah of Muhammad Ali-khan in Khiva

These lands are occupied by two regions of Turkmenistan, Khorezm Region of Uzbekistan with the capital city of Urgench, and the autonomous republic of Karakalpakstan with the capital in Nukus. The desert of Kyzyl Kum separates it from the rest of Uzbekistan. This land gives the travelers a wonderful feeling of being trailblazers, not a very common thing in today's world. The effort it takes to get here surely makes the impressions stronger.

Descendants of the ancient civilization of Central Asia, Khwarasmians identify as representatives of a separate nationality. Historian Sergey Tolstov, an almost cult figure here, in the salty lands of ancient Transoxania (he was the one who discovered the Khwarasmian civilization in the first half of 20th century), wrote that the Khwarasmians were rather related to Georgians and Dagestani, judging by the language. The 20th century encyclopedist Al-Biruni believed Khwarasmians to be a branch of the Persian (Iranian) tree. Here, people share a firm conviction that first came the Khwarasmians and, only then, Uzbeks and Tajiks.

Things are simpler and more complicated at the same time for the Karakalpaks and Karakalpakstan. This is a unique ethnicity historically positioned between Uzbekistan and Kazakhstan, together with their language, culture, and cuisine that found many borrowings and common traits with peoples and tribes that lived nearby throughout their history. They are neither Uzbek Kazakhs nor Kazakh Uzbeks: they are people who keep their language, traditions and household customs no matter how scattered they have been. The Republic of Karakalpakstan is an autonomous republic within Uzbekistan, and the status raises numerous questions. One thing is for certain: the Karakalpak history and culture, as well as the region itself, are just an extra added to Uzbekistan in the eyes of tourists, although it deserves special in-depth studying. The catastrophe of the Aral Sea is the only thing that people at least heard about, and this is the main tourist attraction of the republic. The shallowed sea has become the region's prime tourist brand, yet Karakalpakstan has lots of living things to show. Connoisseurs of art will not miss the museum created by Igor Savitsky and, once there, will not be indifferent to the charm of the carefully curated collection of ancient Karakalpak pieces that became its core.

A BIT OF HISTORY

Cradle of Zoroastrianism, Miracle Well and No Man's Land

Kalta Minor Minaret
in Khiva

The Amu Darya, river flowing across Khorezm, is one of the most turbid and silty rivers in the world; its waters have always carried plenty of clay that became the major construction material here. Shoveled layer by layer, clay becomes incredibly tough. The fortress walls built in this manner and surrounded with a mote were designed in such a way that made it impossible to climb them. The cities of Khwarasm became hard-to-conquer coveted prizes.
Across the territory of ancient country one can still find the ruins of strongholds connected in a chain. Some of the most famous of them are **Toprak-Kala** and **Ayaz-Kala**, and the former is believed to have been the capital of the Khwarasmian state in the antique period, abandoned in the late 5th century. Well-fortified settlements with powerful walls and richly decorated palaces, complex urban infrastructure and developed irrigation system testify to the might and power of ancient Khwarasm. The life of Sergey Tolstov and the largest archeological expedition in the history of the USSR were dedicated to the search for these fortresses and unlocking of secrets of the ancient state. The expedition set out in 1937; its excavations discovered and studies a great number of archeological monuments spanning the period from the Stone Age to the late Middle Ages. Almost all of our knowledge of history and culture of ancient Khwarasm is credited to Sergey Tolstov.

He believed that the Khwarasmian civilization established in 7th–8th centuries BCE and related the advent and strengthening of the state in this territory with the expansion of irrigation farming. The monuments of ancient Khwarasm were designed and erected by prominent scientists of the time! Tolstov also suggested that it was the lower reach of the Amy Darya that was the birthplace of Zoroastrianism, not Iran and the environs of Termez. **Gyaur-Kala** in the Xojeli district, near Nukus, the second biggest city of the ancient Khwarasm, is now part of an extensive complex of antique and medieval monuments commonly referred to as **Mizdakhan**. For a long time, Gyaur-Kala remained the center of Zoroastrianism on the territory of Khwarasm, already occupied by followers of Islam.

For centuries, the ancient Khwarasm accumulated the best of the Persian, Greek and Macedonia, and Sarmat cultures creating a landscape of its own, unlike any other. The Khwarasm-shah Empire that had existed until the Genghis Khan's invasion, covered not only the territories of present-day Uzbekistan and Turkmenistan, but included the Iranian Isfahan, Balkh, and Nishapur. In the second half of 16th century, Khorezm became part of Timur's Empire. The great warlord and constructor was overwhelmed by the talent and skill of Khorezmian architects. There is proof that Khorezmians built the Chashma-Ayub Mausoleum in Bukhara and worked on Timur's grandioso project, the Ak Saray Palace in Shahrisabz.

The year 1511 is considered the year the Khiva Khanate was founded (name of the Khorezmian state of the period in Russian historiography). The river changed its bed and moved from the old capital, Gurganj (present-day Konye-Urgench in Turkmenistan), forcing people to look for a new place for the capital. This place was Khiva.

A traditional story has it that **Khiva** was founded around a well, the source of water, in the center. "Hey, wah!"—such nice and fresh water!—cried the merchants driving their caravans along the Silk Road after trying the water with a pleasant salty taste. The well **Kheivak** is still in the center of the Old Town. Another story relates the well with Shem, son of the biblical Noah. It is difficult to tell the exact age of the city, but it is believed to be more than two and a half thousand years.

In the second half of 18th century, Khiva began transforming into the city we know today. The **Juma Mosque** with its 200 carved columns, most ancient of which were allegedly brought from the medieval capital of Khorezm, Kyat, acquired its present-day exterior. This is a period of progress, the era when the majority of monuments now giving the city its signature skyline was constructed. The 19th century witnessed the building of the **Mausoleum of Said Alauddin**, a revered Sufi Sheikh, of the imposing **Mausoleum of Pahlavan Mahmud**, patron of the city, and enormous **Kalta Minor Minaret**, fully decorated with ceramic tiles, the **Tosh Hovli Palace**... It seems that Khiva stood still in the 19th century. Dozens of madrasahs, the landmarks of Khiva, were also built in this period.
The Khiva we see today remains more or less as it was under the last Khivan Khans. Its core, the old (or inner) town where the Khan resided with his court, clergy, merchants, and the wealthiest citizens is called **Ichan Qala**. This part of the city is now an architectural preserve and Uzbekistan's first UNESCO World Heritage Site.

The nomadic Karakalpaks were under the Bukhara Khanate and the Khivian Khanate at times, but for a short period of 18th century that turned out to be a dire time after the invasion of the Dzhungars who had split the nation in two, they succeeded in setting up the Karakalpak Khanate. Karakalpaks had strong resentment against Khiva. They remained in their territories after the Dzhungar attacks without having left for Tashkent or Fergana. The people in these territories did not consider the Khivian Khan legitimate as not descending from Genghis Khan, they were outraged at the dues payable to the center, and were generally inclined towards Russia. At least, this is the vision of Alexei Butakov, who headed the first exhibition of the Aral Sea Region in the mid-19th century, an area of crucial importance for Russia in taking over the Central Asia, the region, where geopolitical interests of Russia, Persia and Great Britain clashed.

As part of the Khivian Khanate, the Kapakalpakians got under the protectorate of the Russian Empire in the second half of 19th century and became part of the Soviet state in 1918. In 1936, the Karakalpak Autonomous Soviet Socialist Republic with its capital in Nukus became part of the Uzbek SSR. Under Stalin, this region, almost the end of the Soviet world, received great number of deportees: in early 1980s, representatives of thirty-three ethnicities lived in the Moynaq District alone. However, the first exiles came here as early as in 19th century. They were the Old Believer Cossacks, relocated here by Alexander II.

In 1992, the Karakalpakstan Republic was founded, and in 1993 the decree of affiliation as part of Uzbekistan was ratified. In the Soviet period, the territory of Karakalpakstan, especially

In the Mizdakhan necropolis, near Nukus

Ichan Qala, Khiva's inner city

the areas around Aral, were classified: numerous military bases, chemical proving grounds and test sites… Even the tourist groups reaching as far as Khiva never got here. The silence that enveloped the republic, its hard-to-reach location, rumors of chemical and nuclear tests, and a world-class museum of fine arts that appeared in Nukus out of the blue, all glorified this destination and depicted Karakalpakstan as a tormented and abandoned land still full of life.

Khorezm and Karalpakstan: Highlights

–**Museum of Applied Art and Household of Khorezm is inside the Kazi-Kalyan Madrasah of Khiva**. It houses a collection of items mad by local artisans: ceramics, jewelry, carpets, metalwork and carved pieces. The go-to place to draw inspiration from regional art.

–**Nurullaboy Saroyi Palace** is the summer palace of Khivian khans built at the turn of 19th and 20th centuries. Similar to the summer palace of the Bukhara Emir, the Sitorai Mohi Xosa, it blends Oriental and European architectural approaches. The palace is perfectly restored and houses a nicely curated museum focusing, among other things, on decorative and applied arts of Khorezm. It is located just fifteen-minute walking from Ichan Qala.
+998 97 526 62 42, Khiva, Najmiddin Kubro Street, 43

–**Memorial house of Azad Sultanov**, art historian and collector who dedicated years to preservation of objects of Khorezm decorative and applied arts.
+998 93 343 44 77, Urgench, Istiklal Street, 10

One of the courtyards of the Toshhovli Palace in Khiva

–**Contemporary Art Museum of Uzbekistan** is a small museum in Urgench showcasing a collection of works of contemporary Khorezm artists. *+998 62 228 46 90, +998 62 228 46 89, Urgench, Uzbekistan Street, 21, camuz.uz*

–**Museum of Local History of the Karakalpakstan Republic** has an excellent collection of ethnographic curiosities revealing the history of the republic. *+998 61 222 30 21, Nukus, Sabir Kamalov Street, 24*

Khorezm and Karakalpakstan: A Schedule

Day 1
Full day in Khiva inside Ichan Qala. Muhammad Amin-Khan Madrasah, Kalta Minor Minaret, Juma Mosque, Tosh Hovli Palace. Lunch. Continuation of the city tour including the Konya Ark Complex, Islam Khoja Madrasah and Minaret, Pahlavan Mahmoud Mausoleum. Dinner.

Day 2
Excursion out of the city: Nurullaboy Palace (15 minutes from Ichan Qala). Transfer to Nukus (3.5–4 hours) with a stop at Ayaz Kala fortress. Dinner in Nukus.

Day 3
Excursion out of the city: Mizdakhan necropolis (30 minutes from Nukus). Lunch in Nukus. Visit to Savitsky Museum. Dinner.

CUISINE OF KHOREZM AND KARAKALPAKSTAN:
Melons and Flatbreads

Flatbread crafted by hand in Khiva

Even in gastronomy, the proud people of Khorezm emphasize their difference from the rest of Uzbekistan. They say the local version of the national cuisine is one of the leanest and healthiest, as much as the terms may be applied to a diet where flour, rice, meat and oil are the main ingredients. Beef is used more than elsewhere in the country, and cottonseed oil is used with less animal fats.

Khorezm and Karakalpak cuisine is **very modest on seasonings and spices**. Salt, black and red pepper—again, in very modest quantities—comprise their entire set.

The greater part of **rice** grown in Uzbekistan comes from the territory of Khorezm and Karakalpakstan. In any bazaar in Uzbekistan the **Khorezm rice**, known here as lazer, is one of the best and most expensive. This soft, low-starch long-grain rice variety keeps its shape without swelling in the process of cooking. It is used across the country for the various types of plov.

Flatbreads are another feature of Khorezm cuisine: large, thin, decorated with stamps and baked in tandoor to a crispy crust with soft dough will be served in a good restaurant or at home. Flatbreads from wheat flour are also cooked flat in Karakalpakstan.

Wheat was a rare ingredient for the karakalpaks with their nomadic or semi-nomadic lifestyle. They had to change their places of residence depending on the availability of water, hence their other reference, *nomadic farmers*.

The modern Karakalpak cuisine uses alternatives to **wheat flour** more than elsewhere in Uzbekistan: most common substitutes are sorghum (joughara) and millet. Flatbreads are made from these cereals, sometimes, pumpkin is added.

Living relatively close to the river, the Khorezmians and the Karakalpaks had a lot of **fish** in their diet. Ancient dwellers of Khorezm were referred to as *mahi hor khorezmi,* or "fish-eaters" by their neighbors from Iran and Horasan. Fish is either cooked on open fire or fried in oil, but sometimes, when people go on picnics, they put it in a crust of clay and bake it in ashes to keep the fish soft and juicy. In Karakalpakstan, one can try the traditional dish of the Aral Region, karma, thick cereal with catfish.

Melons and pumpkins are cultivated in abundance thanks to the vicinity of the river. Valley farming is the method of growing the cucurbits along the rivers or in the floodplains with their plentiful subsurface waters. Along with irrigated farming, this is one of the most ancient types of agriculture, traditional for the territory of present-day Karakalpakstan.

Dishes to Try

Culinary traditions also contribute to uniqueness of both Khorezm and Karakalpakstan: many dishes prepared here exist in no other form elsewhere in Uzbekistan. For those who believe that plov is the alpha and omega of Uzbek, discovering these local gastronomic customs will be highly interesting.

Tukhum barak is a dish you can try almost exclusively in Khorezm. Thin dumplings of wheat flour with liquid filling of lightly beaten eggs are served cold, with cold suzma or kefir. In Karakalpakstan, this dish is known as maek borek.

Shivit oshi cannot be found outside Khorezm nowadays. Homemade green noodles with lots of dill are served with meat stewed with vegetables, and suzma. Tukhum barak and shivit oshi are staple foods in any restaurant serving national dishes in Khorezm.

Khorezm plov, usually cooked with beef and cottonseed oil, is notable for the many hours that its broth, or zirvak, is stewed. It is served without stirring, in layers: rice, carrots, and meat. This version of plov uses the minimum quantity of spices.

Ijjan is a traditional Khorezm dish seldom offered in restaurants. It is a tartare of raw lamb finely chopped by hand and thoroughly pounded, seasoned with salt, black and red pepper.

Khorezm gumma are small chebureks of thin dough deep-fried in oil.

Ushak barak are the local variety of chuchvara dumplings. They are tiny and served with broth.

Flatbreads are large and thin, made from wheat flour and baked in tandoors.

Karakalpak flatbreads, unlike their Khorezm cousins, are often made from sorghum flour, not just wheat. This low-maintenance high-yield cereal is very popular in Karakalpakstan. These flatbreads are called *zagara*, and cooks often add carrot or pumpkin to the dough. Usually they are baked in tandoors, but in rural areas, they can be baked over coals or in kozons.

Smoked fish is a Karakalpak specialty. Fish is smoked over pine or birch chips.

Bes barmak is a dish that Karakalpaks share with Kazakhs: pieces of boiled dough served with boiled meat and duzlik or cebere, onions cooked in a fatty broth. The dough may be made of wheat or joughara flour, it is rolled thinly with a pin and small dumplings are then made by hand; there is another variant called aksaulak with an extra-thin finely cut flatbread. The meat can be beef, lamb, turkey, and it can come salted or dried.

Jueri gurtik (also, jougheri gurtik or gurtuk) is another take on Bes barmak using dumplings of sorghum. The dish usually cooked with turkey.

Kauyin aksaulak is an excellent example of the many ways melon is used in Karakalpakstan: finely sliced flatbread served with melon, cooked low and slow, and suzma.

Karma is a thick chow or cereal of catfish and sorghum flour, a traditional dish of Aral fishermen.

Bayursaqs are oil-fried pieces of dough, a special dish with a ritual significance.

The popular belief is that the smoke of cooking bayursaqs will satisfy the hunger of the elders and grant them peace.

The Dastarkhan of Karakalpakstan

Traditions of the Karakalpak meal and its elements are different from Uzbek ones reflecting cultural and historical background of the region. Before the meal, the mistress of the house or one of the junior women bring the guests a jug of water and a bowl to wash their hands. Even today, when a table is laid, you will see a towel next to your plate: one dries their hands on the towel never shaking off the water. This is a living tradition once prevalent across the entire region, but only here did I see it with my own eyes. Whereas the Uzbek tradition uses the breaking of a flatbread as the signal to start the meal, in Karakalpakstan, each guests takes as much of the flatbread as they want. Actually, flatbreads and bayursaqs are the first to appear on the table. *Baslam*— "Begin"—the host says at the start of the meal. The host will never remind the guests that they need to carry on eating (while they do in Uzbekistan).

Similar to the Uzbek tradition, the meal always starts with tea. It may be brewed with milk and some black pepper. Tea, flatbreads and bayursaqs share the table with jiyda, syok, nawat, and izhan.

Jiyda are fruit of the plant known as Silverberry or Oleaster, with dark skin and a stone, rich, sweet and sugary. In Karakalpakstan, they put several dried jiyda berries per bowl of tea.

Syok is boiled and dried millet, added to tea by Karakalpaks and Kazakhs.

Nawat is crystallized sugar made from evaporated sugar syrup, or grape sugar.

So, the Karakalpak tea, black, brewed with milk, jiyda berries, syok and nawat is a rich and hearty beverage in itself.

Izhan can easily bear the name of Karakalpak energy mix or superfood. People take a spoon and indulge themselves with this mix of ground sorghum, millet, sugar and sesame with dried zagara flatbread.

The presentation and serving of dishes generally follow the Uzbek tradition: broths are served in individual bowls, while hearty dishes are placed at the center of the table in large pots and plates. The meal concludes with another serving of tea. After eating, guests pass the dish to the bowing woman of the house in a gesture of thanks and blessing.

For the Good of the Fatherland

Mirza Boshi was the title of the head of administration in the Khorezmian Khanate. The grandfather of Zeynab Abdullaeva, owner of Mirza Boshi hotel and restaurant in Khiva, had that title under the Khan Muhammad Rahim II. However, the history, culture and music of Khorezm know him as Kamil Khorezmi the musician, writer, artist, and calligrapher.
Khan Muhammad Rahim II, who had been in power until 1910, was a progressive ruler. He wrote poetry, and his court attracted persons of fine education and culture, public figures of broad outlook, for whom preservation of arts and culture of Khorezm was a matter of state importance. The Khan and the head of his administration were both students of Agahi, a poet, historian and translator of Khorezm. Together with Muhammad Rahim, Kamil Khorezmi visited Russia (St. Petersburg), and opened the first Russian indigenous school of Khorezm. Having learned the European system of musical notation, he revolutionized the traditional Uzbek music and invented a method of writing down the *makam* melodies, the epitome of Central Asian classic Sufi music. Before Zeynab's grandfather, performers had to memorize the melody after listening to it, and then, they used the system he had invented. He even wrote egantsome makams using the European notation, which was done with the blessing and the support of the Khan.

In 2019, Zeynab was awarded with the Order of Labor for the Fatherland from the President of Uzbekistan, and the photograph of the smiling President and herself, wearing an elegant suit, stands on a prominent place in the restaurant. Zeynab-opa was the first in Khiva to open her house for tourists because she had grown here, in Ichan Qala, and worked as a guide for many years. She showed the guests how bread is baked in the tandoor, and how dill is chopped finely for the shivit oshi. A small hotel opened behind the national house, and a restaurant followed a little later. When it came to giving the project a name, Zeynab had no doubts: it would be to honor her grandfather.

The recipes that Zeynab uses together with her daughters and assistants come from her mother and grandmother. They are especially careful about observing traditions here, in the city, where time seems to have stood still for a couple of centuries. In the kitchen, I watch Zeynab pour the beaten eggs from a teapot into almost transparent pockets of finely rolled dough and immediately send them into boiling water, her movements precise and efficient. She says, "Foreigners ask us to serve tukhum baraki hot, but according to the Khorezmian tradition, we serve them warm, with a good dollop of cold suzma So, we have to adjust."

One of the most delicious things that Zeynab has to offer is not even the tukhum baraki. It is a piping hot flatbread straight out of the tandoor, a bowl of hot tea and homemade apricot marmalade, where each whole fruit contains a hulled apricot pit. A breakfast worthy of a Khan!

The restaurant offers a panoramic view from a terrace on the roof; you can dine looking at the jagged city walls, and the giant Kalta Minor Minaret seems within

Zeynab Abdullaeva at Mirza Boshi restaurant in Khiva

reach. Is this an Oriental fairy tale? Yes. Just the way you have always imagined. *+998 93 569 89 89, Khiva, Pahlavan Mahmud Street, 1*

Khiva Moon Tour
One of the best restaurants in Khiva is outside the Ichan Qala walls. In the shade of the trees of the inner yard there are topchans; take a seat and watch the plov being cooked (reservation required). From the regular menu, take the Khorezm chebureks, shivit oshi and fish cooked on the open fire (you can choose the fish of your liking here, from a small pond). If you love tartare, order ljjan, the Khorezm-style tartare (order in advance). The inner courtyard of the restaurant

is a perfect place for folk performances, so ask the staff to organize everything beforehand.
+998 90 648 21 22, Khiva, Polvon Qori Street, 101

Kheivak
This restaurant is situated in the very center of Ichan Qala, in the Malika Kheivak hotel. I love the topchans in the courtyard: light curtains provide privacy and coolness. One of the best places in the city to have tea or lunch and relax during the day, or pause your excursion and wait for the heat to subside.
+998 99 427 30 03, Khiva, Islam Khoja Street, 11

Terrassa Café & Restaurant
This restaurant by the old citadel of Khivian Khans, Kunya Ark, is especially nice for its terrace and the view of the Old Town that opens from it. The coffee here is above good, so if you miss European coffee with a view, this is the place. The menu also features all the classic national Uzbek dishes.
+998 91 993 91 11, Khiva, Buyokchilar Street, 7A

Ayvon Zarafshon
Brand-new smart restaurant with a panorama terrace on the rooftop. Spicy eggplant salad and Zarafshon assorted kebabs are definitely worthy of your attention.
+99 891 278 99 91, Khiva, Islam Khoja Street, 44

To Be the One

Ayimkhan Shamuratova was the only woman of Karakalpakstan to be awarded the title of the People's Artist of the USSR. She was the grandmother of Ayzhamal Taubaldieva, who speaks thus: "She was the embodiment of a free woman. She was a queen, and always behaved this way. Having no knowledge of Russian, nor education, she achieved a lot. She is my role model."

Ayzhamal hung her grandmother's portrait on a prominent place in her hotel in Nukus, Jipek Joli. Ayzhamal's mother was the last, seventh child of Ayimkhan and Amet Shamuratov, born only one month before the premature death of her father. "Grandma became a widow at thirty-six with seven children to feed. I remember that she cooked very tasty food, and I came to learn from her,"

View from Ayvon Zarafshon

recalls Ayzhamal showing me in the hotel's kitchen how to make dumplings from joughara flour for juweri gurtik, traditional Karakalpak dish.

"Grandma left home, and they cursed her," continues Ayzhamal. Although Karakalpak women never wore burqas, the very fact of a woman performing on stage was an outrage for the traditional community where Ayimkhan had grown and been educated. Once the *aul*, where her family lived, received a newspaper with a photo of a scene where Ayimkhan's character was dying. The family slayed their only cow and sent Ayimkhan's brother with the meat to Tortkul, the first capital of Karakalpakstan, to have a funeral feast. It took him one week to get there, but when he came to the theater and saw his sister on the stage, safe and sound, he gave her blessings from the entire family. During the war, Ayimkhan Shamuratova, with two small children, gave concerts across Karakalpakstan, raising money for a military aircraft. In the first private museum of Nukus, opened by Ayzhamal's mother and father in the memory of Ayimkhan and Amet, a writer and a translator, there is a letter signed by Stalin: the Commander-in-Chief thanked her for her help to the Karakalpak theatrical community during the war. Three halls of the museum contain personal things of the spouses, a collection of Karakalpak household and decorative items and accessories. Later, the children of the Shamuratov family continued the collection. The house of Ayimkhan and Amet, as well as their history, reflect the history of Karakalpakstan in the first half of 20th century: a difficult and turbulent time that only very strong people could survive.

Ayimkhan died in 1993. In 2004, she was posthumously awarded with the order "For Outstanding Merit," the highest award of the Republic of Uzbekistan. The first hotel Jipek Joli Inn, part of which is the museum in her honor, was opened in 2003 as the first private hotel of the city. "This hotel started our business, and we opened a tourist company," Ayzhamal says. The second hotel of the same name, Jipek Joli, welcomed guests several years later. It is one of the best hotels not just in Karakalpakstan, it is one of the best in the entire country. As I talk to Ayzhamal about the details, items of interior, tableware, live flowers in the hall that impressed me so much, she smiles and recalls having ordered different things from Russia or Europe, where hardly anyone even knows where Nukus is.

The tourist market of Karakalpakstan is operated by local agencies: it is too far from Tashkent and major tourist attractions. The region has other things that people come to experience: not the blue domes or plov but rather the austere nature and the disappearing Aral Sea. The hotel owner here is not simply responsible for guest accommodation. The hotelier's efforts and capabilities directly influence the guest's duration of stay. "I do not want people to come to Aral just to tick this box," explains Ayzhamal, "because in some five or seven years there will be no more of Aral to see." She knows that the sea, the magnet that attracts the tourists to the republic, keeps shrinking, and she designs programs to show the living and growing Karakalpakstan that is true to its traditions. Gastronomy, ethnography, arts and crafts are her specialty.
+998 90 727 15 15, ayimtourtravel@gmail.com
ayimtour.com

Navruz, the Main Holiday of the Year

Translated from Farsi, Navruz means "a new day." This is the holiday of spring according to the astronomical calendar, celebrated in Uzbekistan on March 21 (as well as throughout the entire Turkic and Persian world). The tradition of celebrating Navruz is pre-Islamic and dates back to the times of Zoroastrianism. It is the holiday of renewal of nature and people, a public holiday that is enjoyed not just in a family but together with neighbors and dwellers of the mahalla in a big feast. People bring the best of their homemade food, cook plov in giant pots, invite musicians or play musical instruments themselves.

The main dish of Navruz is sumalak. All night long from March 20 to 21, they boil germinated wheat sprouts in gigantic pots. Only women cook this treat for the whole neighborhood, or mahalla, standing in turns by the pot while music is playing, young people are dancing and children are playing all around. In order to get a homogenous creamy texture, sumalak is constantly stirred. It tastes like halva or toffee. If you come to Uzbekistan in late March, you will surely try it, because often it is served with tea. In bazaars, you will see wheat sprouts.

Neo
One of the most famous restaurants of Nukus, Neo is perhaps too bright for a Westerner, but the food is cooked fast, it is always fresh and maintains high standards. The long menu has it all, from lagman to all kinds of skewers and kebabs. Unfortunately, the terrace is not large, and smoking is allowed indoors.
+998 61 224 00 03, Nukus, Kamalov Street, 21

Cinnamon Café
Located opposite of Savitsky Museum, this café offers a selection of coffees and desserts, as well as European dishes like pizza and burgers. A nice place to take a coffee or a lunch break from the many hours' tour of the museum.
+998 97 789 77 89, Nukus, Jipek Joli, 1

Sofram
A small café specializing in Turkish dishes sits between the museum and Jipek Joli Hotel. If you are tired of Central Asian cuisine, order some *pide* and lentil soup.
+998 91 388 00 05, Nukus, Sayohatchilar Street, 13A

Premier Lounge
The extensive menu of this restaurant covers it all, from Ossetian pies to pizza, pasta and steaks. Good coffee and stylish yet subdued interior add to its advantages.
+998 97 358 70 07, Nukus, Jolmurza Aymurzaev Street

FishHouse
Karakalpak and European cuisine with an emphasis on the local fish: wild carp (Sazan), grass carp (Belomor or Bely Amur), and Bighead carp, or Tolstolobik. Owners either buy fish from fisheries or from fishermen catching it in the Amy Darya. Try the karma, traditional thick fish soup of Aral.
+998 93 713 78 38, Nukus, Khojaly Avenue

Karakalpagalym
A chain of several national cuisine cafés. In Nukus, many people think that the skewers and kebabs here are the best.
+998 99 956 70 07, Nukus, M. Jumanazarov Street, 59

A table set for Navruz

DECORATIVE AND APPLIED ARTS OF KHOREZM AND KARAKALPAKSTAN:

Uzbek Exotics

Daribay Tadjimurato's studio in Chimboy

The distinctiveness of these regions, their striking difference from the rest of Uzbekistan is vividly reflected in their applied arts, largely shaped by geographical isolation and inaccessibility. The crafts and their methods of production, commonplace in Khorezm and Karakalpakstan, are utterly unique and even exotic to the rest of the country. While the applied arts of Khorezm and Karakalpakstan share historical roots, their development in the 19th and 20th centuries followed dramatically different paths. In Khiva, flourishing at the time, all forms of refined urban and palace art were thriving, catering to the tastes of the elite. Meanwhile, Karakalpakstan preserved crafts as domestic handicrafts, echoing its nomadic and communal traditions and retaining more archaic forms.

Fewer tourists (compared to other parts of the country) come to the region, which poses another challenge for the development of local crafts. Khorezm and Karakalpakstan struggle harder, than other Uzbek regions, to find authentic, original artists who continue to develop or reinterpret the old traditions. The stalls of Ichan Qala are flooded with Uzbek or Chinese knockoffs, along with items unrelated to local artistic traditions.

Researchers say that embroidery of ancient Khorezm and the Aral Region is absolutely unique; it shares more common features with specimens from the Volga and Ural Regions than those from Central Asia. Primarily, it decorated clothes, another less typical use for the rest of today's Uzbekistan. We can hardly speak of embroidery as Khwarasmian art, but the **Karakalpak embroidery** is alive and is strikingly different from anything you may see in Bukhara, Samarkand, and Tashkent. It features cruciform graphic motifs, clear symbolism of each color, and special requirements for fabrics.

Ceramics of Khorezm, regrettably, is an art that is fading away. Many potter's workshops closed in the 20th century after construction of the Khorezm ceramics factory and the overall decline of demand for handmade crockery. Local salty clay is very complicated to handle, and items made from it are heavy and fragile making them hard to transport and use, which affects both the price and the demand. The region is making more ceramic tile than tableware; the tile that adorns the inner courtyards of palaces of Khiva. The ceramic decoration resembling a butterfly knot or a tiny bird, seen only in Khorezm and Karakalpakstan, is a descendant of the Zoroastrian symbol of *faravahar*, the winged sun guiding the human soul on its path to unity with the Divine.

Modern ceramists carrying on traditions of Khorezm ceramics:
–Odilbek Matchanov
+998 91 432 04 44, Madyr Village
–Odilbek Rahimov
+998 93 744 19 10, Yangiariq District, Kattabog Village, Kattabog Street, 34

Woodcarving rose to incredible heights: the local technique is arguably the best in the country. Being a rare and exceptionally expensive material, wood in Khorezm was as valuable as ivory in Europe, and the technique is striking in sophistication and intricacy. The patterns of Khorezmian woodcarving, dominated by floral motifs, were primarily used to adorn columns and doors. The carvers worked in tandem with ceramicists, who decorated palaces and mosques with tiles. Descendants of renowned Khorezmian carving dynasties continue this craft in Khiva, fulfilling both large commissions and creating small decorative pieces that are easy to transport. In Karakalpakstan, woodcarving evolved as ornamentation for yurts with patterns covering doors, chests, tableware, and musical instruments.

Modern carvers carrying on the traditions of Khorezm school:
–Shavkat Jumanimyazov
+998 91 572 70 70, Khiva, Islam Khoja Street, 9 and 35
–Odamboy Masharipov
+998 91 996 09 00, Gandimiyon settlement, Yuz Boshi Street, 111

Another craft of Karakalpakstan is **manufacture of yurts** and their components, i.e. woven parts, traditional felted wool carpets, and mats. Yurts are in demand across Uzbekistan: they are widely popular in the tourist, hotel and restaurant business.

Shokir Abdullaev
Shokir Abdullaev represents the seventh generation of a Khorezm family of fur-dressers. “All of Uzbekistan uses skullcaps, while we wear hats,” the Usto proudly says.

Chugurma is the surprisingly versatile national headdress of Khorezmians. The hat looks massive, but, crafted in the proper technique, it is very light. It protects one from overheating in summer, and from the cold in winter. Older men jokingly call such hats “head conditioners.” In field conditions, chugurma served as a pillow, and, thanks to its thick layer of fur, it could protect the wearer from a blow. It is also a symbol of manhood, without which the national men’s costume would be incomplete.

Artisans use different kinds of fur for the hats. Usually, the visitors prefer hats with long silky fur made from sheep and goat hides; the locals, however, give preference to more modest smooth hats.

Fur dressing is a traditional men’s craft. When you pay a visit to Shokir’s shop by the main gates of Khiva, ask him to show you not only the chugurma hats but Khorezm’s signature fur jackets, or *postyn*, their fur dyed with natural pigments.
+998 91 278 99 19

Matyakub Matyakubov
The jeweler’s tradition of Khorezm is one of the most interesting in Uzbekistan for many reasons, one of them being its development in close contact with the art of Turkmenistan, Kazakhstan, and Karakalpakstan. The richly decorated costume of Khorezmian women had no random elements, each decorative method having sacred and practical meaning. If you look at the sets of jewelry accessories adorned with turquoise, corals and mother-of-pearl in glass cabinets of Khivian museums and want to try them on or even buy them, ask the dealer of antiques, Matyakub Matyakubov. His shop by the Orient

Star hotel sports a collection of near-museum-grade. He also sells ceramics and handmade puppets.
+998 91 437 90 00

Jabbarov Family Show
The circus show of the Jabbarov family in the courtyard of an old madrasah adorned with painted tiles is one of Khiva's treasures. On a tightrope fixed five meters high, the sons, daughters, grandsons, and granddaughters of the dynasty's founder, Bakhrom Jabbarov, walk on their hands, perform push-ups, and build human pyramids.
Uzbekistan has ancient, rich circus traditions. Traveling performers entertained crowds in market squares of towns and villages. *Darboz*—the Uzbek term for tightrope walkers—were symbols of a celebration for locals. High above the crowd on a slender rope, these artists executed daring acrobatics. At heights up to 25 meters, without safety gear, *darboz* performed blindfolded: walking, running, and even doing splits. The show continued with jugglers, stilt-walkers, puppet theater, and horseback riding, a craft perfected over centuries in the steppes of Central Asia.
+998 91 914 24 54, +998 91 917 98 92

Lazgi is the name of the dance born in Khorezm and spread across Uzbekistan; in 2019, UNESCO included it in the List of Intangible Cultural Heritage. Paintings depicting lazgi were discovered during excavations of the ancient settlement of Toprak-Kala, which confirms its centuries-old history. Marked by the distinctive shaking of shoulders and arms, lazgi is a vibrant, energetic dance that captivates all its spectators. Since 2025, there has been a museum of lazgi in Urgench
(+998 62 228 46 90, Khanka Street, Najmiddin Kubro Park, bldg. 7).

Unseen Masterpieces

State Museum of Arts named after I.V. Savitsky
A wind-swept desert, salt from the dying Aral Sea scattered across the gray sands under the blue sky as far as the eye can reach, with nothing else: when I first came to Khiva, a city almost on the border of Uzbekistan and Turkmenistan, I thought, that was the end of geography. As if... The true end of the world is Nukus, capital of Karakalpakstan, a city without a face, lost in the sands so far away, that Igor Savitsky, whose name marks the local museum of arts, managed to hide here the paintings that had less than zero chances of being exhibited and admired in the Soviet times. Using official money, Savitsky gathered so many works of artists rejected and persecuted by the regime, that two buildings of the museum can hardly exhibit a fraction of them. Now, do you grasp the scale of the venture?

Igor Savitsky was born in Kiev in 1915. Having strongly suffered from the new Soviet regime, part of his family moved to Moscow. Young Igor entered the Art Institute named after Surikov; during the war, the Institute was evacuated to Tashkent. Igor's second visit to Uzbekistan was within the Khorezm Archeological and Ethnographic Expedition organized by Sergey Tolstov. Igor Savitsky participated in excavations and made sketches discovering the culture of Karakalpakstan and its artifacts that nobody had collected, studied, or registered before. Igor felt a connection with this severe desert and stayed there to gather such a collection of Karakalpak antiquities that he became a cult figure for the locals. What Savitsky did for Karakalpakstan is the foundation of its national identity.

In 1966, Savitsky became the director of the newly organized museum, whose collection had to fit into a couple of rooms. For over thirty years, he was gathering an amazingly rich collection of what is known today as Uzbek avant-garde, and an incredible set of Russian artists of the first half of 20th century. The Nukus collection is like none other because it was assembled by a single person. Sometimes, people compare Savitsky to Tretyakov, considering his vision that underlies the collection. The tricky thing is that Savitsky did not choose the works, he saved them taking everything that was available, taking frameless canvases nobody needed (the frames had been burnt in cold winters), canvases with cracks and holes. When you visit the museum, the keepers will show you numerous paintings that the artists' widows and children had used to stuff the leaking roofs.

Sometimes people portray Savitsky as an eccentric lunatic who abandoned Moscow and its prospects for a dusty God-forsaken corner of the USSR. In reality, Savitsky understood perfectly what he was doing, recognizing that the remote location of the museum and difficulty of any its inspections was a great advantage in saving the works doomed to oblivion or destruction, just like their creators. Savitsky saved over forty-four thousand works of such artists as Robert Falk, Liubov Popova, Ivan Kudryashov, Kliment Redko, Alexander Volkov, and such masters of the Uzbek school as Ural Tansykbaev and Viktor Ufimtsev. The museum had the status of a state museum, the works were purchased with official money. Taking the train from Moscow, Savitsky carried away compartments full of canvases.

Every time I am in the museum, I try to comprehend, to grasp some things: how big a threat for the authorities was there in scenes from Uzbek life, like a tea party in a choyxona? What harm was there in perfectly customary abstract art? How could artists live and work without even a hope of exhibiting their work but with a grim anxiety of being thrown in prison... The Nukus museum is a memorial book of those who fell in the clash of two realities, artistic and Soviet, a book of human tragedy (died in prison camp, gone missing, executed by firing squad, served twenty years in prison), a book of a small man who had no fear of standing against the system and single-handedly saved an artistic phenomenon.

Not only he *saved* it, in many aspects, he *created* it. One of Igor Savitsky's goals was to give the artists and the emerging artistic movement of Karakalpakstan some basis, some example, some material for development. Bringing to Nukus the works found across the entire Soviet Union, he contributed to the foundation of an artistic school.

Usually, the collection of the Savitsky Museum is spoken of as a collection of Uzbek avant-garde. However, he never said he was collecting the avant-garde proper. The term is rather used to describe the diversity of art that could not have been aligned to the standards of official norm. The collection of the museum, without doubt, is broader than any artistic trend.

The reserves of the museum contain thousands of works by lesser-known artists that Savitsky purchased. Apart from the artists' relatives and keepers of the museum, no one saw them. Even those works that are considered gems of the collections are almost unknown to a general public of amateurs of art or a narrower group of experts. The remote location of the museum, its obscure reserve and lack of catalogs allow some to call the collection of the Nukus museum an unknown one. The exhibition of April 2017 in Moscow showing only 250 works reverberated in the connoisseur circles: nobody expected the far-away Karakalpakstan to have such treasures! Indeed, it was a rare opportunity to see the masterpieces of Nukus, at least a small part of them.

Igor Savitsky died in 1984. As he conceived the museum, neither he, nor the people who worked with him, had any idea of what they were creating and preserving, nor did they imagine how big the collection would become. Savitsky's dream was for people to come to the remote Nukus to see the museum. This dream became a reality.
+998 61 222 61 28, Nukus, Kaipbergenov Street, 52

Bazarbay Serekeev Memorial House
Bazarbay Serekeev is one of the most famous artists of the Republic of Karakalpakstan, whose memorial house provides a careful reconstruction of life of the popular artist. His family welcomes the guests and tells about his life and the artistic side of Nukus. His son, Bakhtiyar Serekeev (*+998 55 104 70 46*) is also an artist, so you can see the museum and the workshop at the same time. Please call in advance for an appointment.
+998 90 358 70 46, Nukus, Akkol Street, 24

Daribay Tadjimuratov
In Karakalpakstan, only the salt lies on the surface: everything else needs to be searched for, with an open heart and the readiness for surprises. This was the surprise for me and many other guests visiting the workshop of Daribay Tadjimuratov, one of the most famous artists of the republic. His workshop is in the back yard of his house in the *aul* of Chimbay, where one cannot find a patch of paved road for many miles away. Dust in the wind and cracking of shells under your feet make it hard to believe that once, there was sea around. It is even harder to comprehend that an artist with such a gift and such vigor did not leave his native soil preferring the dusty Chimbay to the glamorous Tashkent: "The place where I live gives me the energy," he says.

Daribay's workshop is like a museum: only here did I see the Karakalpak ceramics, the tradition of whose manufacture is almost gone. Here were wooden sculptures reminiscent of ancient idols and expressionist paintings with colors almost pouring out off the canvas, witty sketches of everyday life and culture of Karakalpakstan, and austere philosophical drawings. When asked about the prices, the artist refuses to sell anything and says curtly, "I want to create a museum." On the question of what his preference is, sculpture or drawing, he explains, "Most of the time, I think, then I find the themes, one, for a sculpture, that, for graphics, another one, for painting. I do not know who I am."

The works of Daribay Tadjimuratov are held in Uzbekistan's leading museums, including the Savitsky Museum collection. His art is defined by an unbroken connection to traditions and their deeply personal reinterpretation, and unfettered imagination. Following his father's path, his son Adil Tadjimuratov has embraced the same demanding artistic calling. Today, Adil stands as one of Karakalpakstan's finest jewelers, crafting traditional adornments with strict adherence to canonical forms and the symbolic meaning of every element.

The yard of Tadjimuratov's house had an old arba, household items, and a traditional tandoor. This is the ethnographic exhibition about the native land. It is an interactive exhibition, and all guests can learn to cook the plov, bake flatbreads over hot ashes, and try the Karakalpak ways of life and traditions.
+998 99 283 55 05, Chimboy settlement, Karakol Housing, J. Khamedullaev Street

Azamat Turekeev
In Karakalpakstan, the yurt served as home for both nomads and settled populations. Today, we might describe it with modern terms: quick to assemble, ergonomic, energy-efficient, and equipped with a smart ventilation system. In winter, its perimeter was adorned with felt carpets for insulation; in summer, with woven mats to allow fresh airflow. The yurts are still constructed without nails: their wooden components (crafted exclusively by hand!) are fastened with leather straps and cotton-wool fabric bands, all decorated with traditional patterns. The yurt consisted of a ceremonial and a utilitarian section, each with furnishings that were both highly functional and richly decorative. Floors were covered with carpets and rugs, including those made using the region's traditional felting techniques. Carved wooden chests and boxes added ornamentation, while the frame of the yurt held cloth bags for storing clothes, tea, salt and spoons. The entire structure typically featured a red and brown color scheme. A fully assembled yurt could be erected in five hours and dismantled in just ninety minutes.

Yurt manufacturing remains an important craft for Karakalpakstan: tourist business places high demand on them. Yurt campsites, restaurants and hotels are major customers. It takes forty days to manufacture one yurt. Azamat Turekeev represents the third generation of the family in the yurt business: even in the Soviet times, there were numerous settlements where the yurt was the major housing for people. At the same time, I saw quite a few houses in Uzbekistan, where people still have a yurt in their yard preferring to live in it from early spring to late autumn. Besides his main production facility, Azamat has a small guesthouse and a workshop for machine and hand embroidery where the yurt trimmings are made and clothes are decorated.
+998 90 593 86 86, +998 90 734 36 56, Chimbay District, Vodnik settlement, Temir zhol guzari Housing

Gulnara Embergenova
Gulnara Embergenova is a well-known designer and artist who invested a lot of time and effort into her project of restoring the national embroidery. She educated several generations of embroideresses. Her workshop manufactures stylish clothes with Karakalpak ornaments: dresses, camisoles, chapans, headgear, and household items.
+998 91 387 17 21, Nukus, Miyras Street, 19

A traditional Karakalpak felting

Altynay Naubetova
There are few women like Altynay Naubetova left. Just several decades ago, every Karakalpak girl could sew, weave, dress and spin wool to make cloth, cook tasty dishes from cereals, make ayran and butter from cow's milk, and bake flatbreads. Altynay-apa has hands of gold, and she puts a lot of love and dedication into the hardest tasks, and looking at her makes one feel the same love for the simplest mundane things. If you are in search of Karakalpak rugs that have no fluff, or tablecloths, or coverlets of patterned canvas, carpets and felt boots, come to Shumanay and visit her. It is just an hour's drive from Nukus.
+998 90 575 16 57, Shumanay District, Uzbekistan Street, 125

Aysanem
The new Nukus project focuses on producing stylized wool carpets. It offers visitors a local souvenir option with contemporary appeal.
+998 91 384 73 00, Nukus, Jipek Joli Street, 1/7, aysanem.com

Family Ceramics Studio Shanarak
A young family turned the very term "Karakalpak ceramics" from abstract to very real: Salamat Allambergenov (a young Karakalpak artisan, B.A. of Karakalpak State University, now doing his Master's at the Kamoliddin Behzod Tashkent National Institute of Painting and Design, participant of regional ceramics festivals) and his wife Gozzal Gubenova. Salamat and Gozzal are working in two directions: terracotta carved in relief, seldom seen in Uzbekistan today, and glazed ceramics decorated with traditional Karakalpak motifs. Salamat traveled around the country, met master ceramists and their workshops, and, supported by the authorities of Karakalpakstan, reconstructed his house, installed a modern electric kiln and started working with guests in May 2024.
+998 91 388 85 57, +998 91 380 85 57, Nukus, Kutli Makan Housing, Zheti uyi Street, 7

Republican society Ónerment promotes the Karakalpak decorative and applied art and supports artisans of the republic. t.me/qrhby

HOTELS OF KHIVA AND NUKUS

Lobby at Jipek Joli
Hotel in Nukus

Arkanchi
One of the city's first hotels that remains top-tier to this day. Features include a rooftop terrace, compact gym, sauna, and bicycle rentals, all claiming solid four-star standards. Located within the old city walls.
+998 55 602 32 22, Khiva, Pahlavan Mahmud Street, 10

Shaherezada Boutique Hotel
This hotel belongs to the renowned Jumaniyazov family of Khivan woodcarvers. The property features exquisite, intricately detailed decor in traditional style. Be sure to admire the magnificent hand-carved wooden entrance doors, a true masterpiece of craftsmanship.
+998 62 375 95 65, Khiva, Islam Khoja Street, 35

Farovon
True, this hotel is not in the old city center, but a property of this size and layout could never fit within the tiny Ichan Qala! With over 100 thoughtfully designed European-style rooms, a grand courtyard fountain, spacious lobby, and indoor pool, this stands as Khiva's only hotel of this caliber.
+998 62 227 78 78, Khiva, Kiyot Mahalla, Buyuk yol Street, 1A

Jipek Joli
One of Uzbekistan's finest hotels! Its thoughtful design (a refreshing change if you're weary of traditional colorful vibrancy), excellent breakfasts, and availability of any national dish for lunch or dinner upon request. The hotel also organizes Karakalpakstan tours, owned as it is by the republic's leading travel agency. For more budget-conscious travelers, the Jipek Joli Inn sits just two blocks away, under the same management.
+998 61 222 11 00, Nukus, Jipek Joli Street, 4

Pana Hotel
One of the most modern hotels of Nukus designed under international standards. Multi-room suites, or apartments, are a wise choice for travelers with children or visitors for the long term.
+998995767300, Nukus, Miymandos Street, 2

Besqala
This small guesthouse forms a part of the extensive Besqala travel network. Accommodation ranges from twin to six-bed rooms (with shared bathrooms), and includes access to their yurt camp at the Aral Sea and private fleet of off-road vehicles.
+998 91 377 77 29, Nukus, Alisher Navoiy Street, 121

Aral Sea. *The Ship in the Sand*
The Ship in the Sand is one of Rafael Matevosyan's paintings. The artist is also known as "the bard of Aral." Born in Samarkand, educated in Baku, he lived a great part of his life in the Karakalpak Muynak, and painted the sea. He witnessed the ships that traversed the sea being buried for good in the salty sands.

The sea did not disappear in a single day; it kept shrinking, yielding the water for the ambitious cotton-growing project of Central Asia. Once the fourth largest lake in the world, the Aral Sea turned into two small separate reservoirs, the shoreline moving at least one hundred kilometers from the former port city of Muynak. The wind blows the salty dust of Aral to faraway places, and they say, that one day, dwellers of Khiva saw their city covered with a deposit of white. People are trying to save the Aral Sea: they constructed a dam in Kazakhstan and are implementing a project to discharge agricultural waters in Uzbekistan. Some projects seem to

26

work, and others do not live up to their promise. The Karakalpaks try to save it from oblivion: many tourist agencies offer tours to the shoreline of the disappearing sea. However, these trips to the area of the environmental catastrophe offer little amusement. People come here to recognize that laws of nature are universal and yield no exceptions.

What was the sea like? You can see it in the Savitsky Museum: the routine life of Aral fishermen, the azure waves, squat cabins on the shore and fish packing are all alive in the pictures of Rafael Matevosyan, Viktor Ufimtsev, Ural Tansykbayev, and Mikhail Kurzin.

Tours to the Aral Sea:

–Oktyabr Dospanov, +998 90 575 32 28, karakalpakiya.com

–Ayzhamal Taubaldieva, +998 90 727 15 15, ayimtour.com

–Tazabay Uteuliev, +998 97 354 00 24, besqala.com

A yurt camp near the Aral Sea

Surxondaryo and Qashqadaryo. Land of Fire

Chapter V

Surxondaryo and Qashqadaryo Regions are actually two different areas, but for the travelers they represent the mysterious "other Uzbekistan," with Buddhist stupas instead of blue domes.

Dorus-Saodat Complex in Shahrisabz

The place where fewer tourists manage to come than to any other destination within the country. People go to see these places, separated from the rest of Uzbekistan by mountain chains, not to enjoy the architecture but to see nature, local color, and everyday life. Here, you stop being a tourist and become a part of an expedition whose goal is to deliver important information, knowledge and unfathomable riches to the mainland. For it is the land of the highest peaks of Uzbekistan, land of bakhchi storytellers and descendants of shamans, pahlavan wrestlers and chovandoz riders, the land of elements, folklore, and traditions. This is the land where UNESCO preserves not just the monuments, but the culture itself. The land that precedes memory.

No matter what the subject, Surxondaryo and Qashqadaryo will argue, like two sisters. Best tandoor-baked meat? People from Surxondaryo will vote for Dzharkugan, and the ones from Qashqadaryo will object: of course, near Karshi! Best tubeteika skullcaps: Boysun or Shahrisabz? Finally, the highest mountain of the country, Khazret Sultan, what territory does it belong to? You will definitely need some of the Oriental wisdom when people see you as a judge in this sororal dispute. The people welcoming you here are not spoiled by tourist attention: sometimes I was the only tourist, no, the only guest who made it here in a long time, and so the feast would start for me, and pages of ancient legends would come to life. If you are not afraid of bumpy roads and modest hotels, you may as well become such a guest.

You will need a guide in these places, and the value of human contact is higher than anywhere else. There will be no internet to find your way around, and not everybody will speak Russian much less English, plus, there are no decent and detailed guide and reference books. Your own curiosity, flexible timing, capability of making decisions on the spot and a guide, speaker of Uzbek language in love with his region, are your best companions.

Surxondaryo—“Red Valley” from Tajik surkh—lives up to its name: rust-hued mountains, scarlet soil, and clay like forged iron define Uzbekistan’s southern frontier.

CUISINE AND WINEMAKING:
Sweet Meat and Sweet Wine

Making keskan-osh, the traditional soup

Despite the eternal dispute between the two regions, which one cooks in a better and proper way, there are more similarities than differences in their cuisine. The type and special features of dishes here depend on the history, location, routine life, customs, and traditions of people.

Many dishes and methods of their cooking directly relate to the needs and capabilities of chabans, or mountain shepherds, which form all the specifics of the regional cuisine. This includes fast-braised lamb, **chuponcha**, **bykhtyrma** soup of just two ingredients, lamb and onions, and **kurtova** soup, made from crushed balls of kurt cheese.

The second defining feature of local cuisine is the breed of sheep traditionally raised here: the distinctive **Hissar sheep**, known for their massive fat tails, thin subcutaneous fat layer, large size, and endurance. Adapted to long migrations between pastures, these animals graze high in the mountains on alpine meadows filled with fresh, often medicinal herbs.

Next comes the local plant, **archa**. A member of the juniper family, archa grows on the mountain slopes of both Qashqadaryo and Surxondaryo. It has a lingering spicy aroma of fir needles. The use of archa to cook the **tandoor gusht** meat (lamb, most often) makes the whole country believe that the best tandoor meat is cooked in these regions. Skillfully cooked, tandoor meat stays fresh for a long time, and the tender bits of archa sprigs, dried and crushed, are added to the dry rub in which the meat is marinated before baking, giving it the tart flavor.

Both regions derive their names from the tributaries of the Amu Darya River. Access to rivers means availability of fish, such as sazan, sudak, and som, or catfish. In the mountain rivers, people catch **marinka**, a species of fish compared to mountain trout. However, there are no exquisite ways to cook the fish: usually, it is fried in a lot of oil. Simple cafés specializing in fish dishes are usually found by large water reservoirs. Fish is served with homemade hot sauce of tomatoes, onions, and garlic.

These regions of Uzbekistan receive more sun than the others and are some of the hottest. Spring comes early, and the first greens and vegetables come to markets in big cities of the country from these places.

"A lot of sun is good for the grapes," believe the local winemakers. Some of the best Uzbek wines, sweet, semi-sweet, and dry, are made in the Oltinsoy District of Surxondaryo Region, in the **Sulton Sharbati family winery**.

Dishes to Try

Tandoor gusht is meat (mainly lamb) cooked in a tandoor covered with a kozon to prevent airflow. The meat is marinated with archa, local juniper. Sometimes the whole carcass is cooked, but more often, just the shoulders and legs are baked.

Chuponcha is lamb, usually very young, fried fast in a kozon. This is one of the first dishes that shepherds cook after butchering the lamb.

Umakay jyz is tender lamb, braised and then roasted. It comes from the kishlak of Umakay in Qashqadaryo Region. It takes only an hour to get to Umakay from Samarkand, and for dwellers of the big city, *Umakay jyz* is a brand: in many restaurants of Samarkand, the jyz comes under this name.

Yakhna gusht, Yakhna chialsi, or Chiyal yakhna is the meat of young lambs stewed with lamb fat for 12 hours, then cooled off in pots wrapped in thick kurpachi blankets, served cold. The most famous place where it is cooked is the Sunday bazaar in the Chiyal kishlak in Qashqadaryo, 60 kilometers from Karshi, and it is believed this is the place where it was originally made. People eat Yakhna gusht with flatbreads, or thin manti without filling (pachok manti).

Keskan-osh, or Kesgan-osh is a light soup with homemade noodles and vegetable stock (sometimes, meat stock is used) served with katyk, greens, black pepper, and pepper paste. Local men believe that a healthy portion of Keskan-osh is the right meal to recover after a long night's feast.

Bykhtyrma is a thick fragrant soup of lamb and lots of onion. It confirms the ancient statement that simplicity is key! Originally a shepherds' dish of the simplest ingredients that are always at hand and do not require special storage, it is mainly seen in Surxondaryo.

Langar flatbreads are cooked in tandoors. They are made from rough flour and come from a mountain kishlak of Langar in Qashqadaryo. You can try similar flatbreads near Boysun. It is hard to find this rough flour, because bread is made from fine white factory-milled flour, but there are stone grinds in remote kishlaks, and wheat is still ground by hand.

Boysun butter is rich and salty. It is cured in cows' stomachs. Traditionally, chabans made this product keeping it in cool caves in the mountains. You can only buy it on the bazaar in Boysun, nowhere else.

Sherabad pomegranates are large and juicy fruit from Sherabad in Surxondaryo, considered by many as some of the best in Uzbekistan.

Sherabad pomegranates, harvested from local orchards, sold at a roadside stand

DECORATIVE AND APPLIED ARTS:

Archaic Purity

Traditional embroidery from Surxondaryo, Dmitry Inyushev's Collection

Much as in the case of the cuisine, the arts and crafts of Surxondaryo and Qashqadaryo are more similar than different, the main crafts being carpet weaving and embroidery in various techniques. Some locations still keep ceramic manufacturing and traditional manual fabric making. In many aspects, the culture of both regions follows traditions of steppe tribes, nomadic forefathers of today's dwellers of Surxondaryo and Qashqadaryo.

Located far from the center of the country, Surxondaryo Region kept its arts and crafts original. The rural population keeps timeless customs and still continues to make things for their own consumption, household use and rituals. Thus, in many locations brides still embroider their own **suzani** for the wedding. In other words, the fabrics, carpets, and embroidered skullcaps still remain utilitarian and not souvenir objects, and keep their connection with the folk. They do not adjust to the market demands that sometimes undermines the quality and dilutes traditions making the region highly important for those interested in ethnography and decorative and applied arts, and for those who collects embroidery, clothes or carpets. Here, in the regions seldom visited by many tourists, prices are much lower than in Samarkand, to say nothing about Tashkent. The well-preserved local style with numerous archaic decorative elements makes items from Surxondaryo unique.

In Surxondaryo, they never manufactured silk fabrics: clothing was made from **janda**, heavyweight cotton fabric manually woven on a wooden loom, with stripe motifs in the region's characteristic ochre, yellow and brown colors. The ochre and terracotta shades make Surxondaryo textiles immediately recognizable, including suzani stitched against a bright background.

The traditions of Surxondaryo ceramics are all but lost: urbanization, remoteness from tourist centers as well as markets have resulted in virtual disappearance of Denau and Boysun schools of ceramics. However, it has survived in Shahrisabz (Qashqadaryo Region), where the artisans of the **Muzafarov family** carry on and develop the traditions set by their ancestors centuries ago. This school bears the name of fiery for its bright ochre, yellowish and terracotta hues. Very interesting specimens of unglazed ceramics come from the artisans Bakhtiyor Sattorov (*+998 97 954 92 95*) and Mukhriddin Urakov (*+998 94 337 53 63*) from the settlement of Kasbi, some forty minutes from Karshi. Tourists visit these places rarely, and the masters will be glad to welcome guests, so, if you are around, pay a visit.

The two regions have never been strong in making tufted carpets. The products for their own in-house use and household were **double-sided palace carpets and rugs.** One of the main centers of manufacturing such flat-woven carpets was **Qashqadaryo** Region, where the tradition and the technique had been brought by the Arabs. *Arabi gilam* is the name of handmade carpets keeping the archaic pre-Islamic motifs that look very modern to this day.

The embroidresses of Shahrisabz are proud of their mastery of several techniques: along with the traditional *kanda-hael* stitch of suzani, reminiscent of dense damask stitch, they also use the *iroki* technique. The ready items (panel pictures, skullcaps, makeup pouches, and bags) look as if they were embroidered with beads. Personally, it is one of the most beautiful types of Uzbek embroidery. This is an urban sophisticated tradition formed due to the closeness to the court of the Emir in Bukhara.

Surxondaryo and Qashqadaryo: A Schedule

Day 1
Termez: Museum of Archeology, Qirkkiz and Sultan Saodat Complexes. Lunch. Departure to Jarkurgan: the minaret and Dmitry Inuyshev's collection. Dinner.

Day 2
Departure to Boysun. Hakim at-Termiziy Complex. Fayaz Tepe and Kara Tepe. Dinner in Boysun. Boysun Crafts Center. Red canyons. Return to Termez or night in Boysun.

Day 3
Derbent and its environs. Transfer to Karshi or Shahrisabz.

Day 4
A day in Karshi: sightseeing tour of the city, lunch, Arab kishlak of Jeynau. Night in Karshi or transfer to Samarkand.

Or

A day in Shahrisabz and its suburbs. Sightseeing tour of the city. Katta Langar. International Latitude Station in Kitab, Maidanak Observatory. Transfer to Samarkand.

At Caravan carpets workshop

SURXONDARYO: A BIT OF HISTORY

Buddhism, Pleated Minaret and the Military Post

Qirkkiz Complex in Termez

A voyage through Surxondaryo is a voyage into nature and artifacts of old times that have survived in some places: the Jarkurgan Minaret dating back to 1109 or the Fayaz Tepe Buddhist Complex built in 1st century. If you have experience traveling the Golden Triangle of Uzbekistan (Samarkand, Bukhara, Khiva) and then turn up in Termez or Boysun, you might look around and wonder: why are there no cities here as unified agglomerations? Why are there so few architectural monuments? Why must one need to piece this land together from separate locations?

The main cities of Uzbekistan were mainly founded near fertile oases and, for a long time, developed more or less in the same territory, rising, time and again, from the ashes of disastrous invasions. Old Termez, situated near the modern city (now capital of Surxondaryo Region), outlived Alexander the Great, flourished as a major Buddhist center in the 1st–4th centuries, and revived after the Persian rule to become a key Central Asian trade and administrative hub. Visit the **Termez Archeology Museum** and request to see not only the Buddhist artifacts but also coins excavated from this land across different eras. Examining these coins—currency from diverse countries and regions still difficult to reach today—you look at the globalized, sophisticated, and astonishing world of Eastern trade and travel. Termez could not survive Genghis Khan: its inhabitants abandoned the ruined city and resettled in its modern location. Under Timur, the new Termez became a pivotal waypoint not only for merchant caravans but also for all European and Eastern embassies *en route* to his court.

By the late 18th century, the glory of the city had faded. The Russians came here a century later: the Bukhara Emirate that included this area, was under the Russian protectorate, and Termez housed the military post to protect the frontiers, and a Russian fortress was built. Alas, it was demolished in the modern period. In the Soviet times, the city founded on the site of two kishlaks, was a military base and had restricted access due to vicinity to the Afghan border. In the years following Uzbekistan's gaining independence, the restrictions were lifted, but the location is so remote, virtually on the edge of Uzbek lands, that tourists find it hard to get there. Other cities of the region (Boysun, Jarkurgan) only received their urban status in the second half of 20th century and did not retain any unified layout or infrastructure.

Termez

Termez keeps its most interesting sites not in the center. These include the Kara-Tepe and Fayaz-Tepe Buddhist Monasteries (ask whether you need a permit to visit them before your trip, both locations are on the very border with Afghanistan); Mausoleum of the Sufi collector of khadith, Hakim at-Termezi; Sultan Saodat necropolis that reminds of Shah-i-Zinda in Samarkand; and remnants of the Qirkkiz Complex that either had been a harem or a school for girls. The center of the city is modern, loose, retaininwg almost none of the historical infrastructure. The center's main attraction is the Archaeology Museum with its extraordinary collection of Buddhist-era artifacts. The city's bazaar offers a slice of authentic local life: oil bubbles in cauldrons, plov steams, and *atala* (an ancient soup of wheat, milk, and tail fat) is poured from a battered churn

Fayaz-tepa Complex near Termez

wrapped in ten blankets into a well-worn bowl. Atala serves as traditional remedy for ailments, a restorative for postpartum women, and a hearty national breakfast for strong stomachs.

Hotels and Restaurants

Karvon Saroy Hotel
A large hotel with a restaurant and open swimming pool located in spacious green grounds. Twenty-minute drive from the center of Termez.
+998 91 909 70 70, +998 78 770 88 88, Termez Cargo Center, Airitom Mahalla, Akhunbabaev Street

Hilton Garden Inn Termez Airitom
Newest in the city, the Hilton Garden Inn Termez Airitom operates within the free economic zone on the border of Uzbekistan and Afghanistan. With contemporary design, spacious rooms (including multi-room suites), and a fitness center, this is exactly the hotel the city needed!
+998 71 205 26 26, Airitom Free Economic Zone

Within the same free economic zone, there operates a massive Afghan bazaar: a veritable city within a city, complete with merchant stalls, casual eateries, and sweet shops. It offers visitors a chance to experience Afghan culture without leaving Uzbekistan.

Comfortable Home Stay
Located in the outskirts of Termez, this guesthouse is set in a renovated private home adapted for visitors. Hospitable hosts welcome guests to a shady garden. Note: shared bathroom facilities for multiple rooms.
+998 91 586 48 33, Mukimi Street, 10

Farhod Choyxona
As I was *en route* from Tashkent to Termez, my fellow traveler told me about this teahouse. He said it was the best place in the city to try the ilik pai, braised beef bones with just a little meat, served with stewed vegetables and a flatbread. Ravshan-bobo, the chef, puts the pot with ilik pai on the fire at 7 in the morning, so that by 11 a.m., when the first guests will come to lunch, everything is ready. If you order ilik pai, they will bring you a wooden board. Knock the bone on it until the marrow comes out: this is why you order this dish. Note: the teahouse is open on Sundays, but they do not cook ilik pai, because there are not too many guests.
+998 94 464 99 99, Malik Kahor Street, 19

Yes Boss
The whole city of Termez calls Abdusalom Dizhuraev simply "Boss-aka." He is one of the most famous chefs and teahouse keepers in Surxondaryo: not only does he run his own restaurant, he finds the time to cook for out-of-city events. A great plov for a wedding? Important guests to treat? The Boss receives a phone call. His father and grandfather were both cooks. His father lived to the age of eighty-four, a true Surxondaryo person, a pahlavan wrestler and chavandoz rider. Despite its European name, Yes Boss is a true choyxona that has no menu. In the morning and after lunch the Boss puts on kozons of kovurma gusht, tender braised lamb, needing only a quarter of an hour to serve fresh Uighur lagman, and has pots of bykhtyrma and bystyrma (clear soup of lamb and chickpeas) simmering on the stove every morning.
+998 91 575 29 65, Islam Karimov Street

Jarkurgan

This small town with only 20,000 people has three wonders: the unique minaret, the delicious tandoor kabob (tandoor-cooked meat), and the "Sarmangan" folklore ethnographic group famous across the entire country. They will convince you to choose this road to Boysun, not the one that goes through the pomegranate gardens of Sheradab.

Minaret of Jarkurgan
To get to the Jarkurgan Minaret you need to go outside the city center, to the Minor kishlak taking an unpaved dusty road. Along it, gray-bearded old men in velvet chapans sit at the entrances of their homes contemplating the rare passing cars and the passing of life. Shaking on the bumps, cars and motorcycles take livestock to the market in trailers. Only 21.5 meters, or a third of the original height, is all that remained from the minaret built in 1109. One look at it hints at what a colossal mosque once stood there (closed in 14th century and later demolished) and how great that kishlak was. The minaret is of extreme beauty, and its architecture is unique for Uzbekistan: the best word to describe it would be "pleated." On a massive octagonal base, sixteen semi-pillars of fired brick are joined forming a rhythmical "herringbone" pattern, so that the entire structure seems pleated by a skillful artisan from cane or leather. Erected by the order of Sultan Sanjar, last of the Great Seljuks, this minaret is one of the region's few structures of pre-Mongolian times.

Jarkurgan Tandoor
Ask any Surxondaryo native what culinary delight their region offers, and they will definitely say it is tandoor gusht, lamb slow-cooked in this clay oven. They will also insist you need to go to Jarkurgan for the real deal. In fact, Jarkurgan's tandoor has gained fame far beyond Surxondaryo: couriers are regularly sent for it from neighboring regions, even from Tashkent. There are two secrets in Jarkurgan tandoor lamb: the Hissar lambs with their massive tail fat and lean meat grazing on healthy grass of mountain meadows, and the ground soft bits of archa, local juniper, that give the meat the subtle tart flavor of pine needles.

Rano's Tandoorxona
The café has no name: it is just a tandoor house in the Istiklal Mahalla, Jarkurgan District, where they cook tandoor gusht. When you get there, ask for Rano, and the locals will immediately show you a neat house by the road. The older generation of the family also cooked the lamb in the tandoor, traditional method of this region, so the locals see a very strong connection between the "tandoor" and the "Safarov family." The guests are taken to spacious rooms with comfortable furniture, TV sets and Wi-Fi, the diners have some privacy thanks to woven mats providing lacelike shade. Meat is served with homemade pickles, piping hot flatbreads fresh from the tandoor, strong sweet tea with lemon, and honey quince for dessert. Juicy soft lamb (it stays in the tandoor covered with a kozon to prevent air intake for more than an hour), crunchy spicy cabbage and a slice of warm flatbread is a royal meal cooked with all heart and soul. Rano, the mistress of the house, bakes the flatbreads using the lamb fat and makes the dough using the starter she got from her mother-in-law.
+998 97 747 19 05, Jarkurgan District, Mahtumkuli Street, 11 (M41 highway)

Minaret of Jarkurgan

Designer Dmitry Inyushev in his studio

Dmitry Inyushev's Collection
Dmitry was born and raised here, then left to study fashion design in Tashkent, then returned to his hometown. He began sewing for sale and altering clothes brought by neighbors from his mahalla. Even during his studies, he attended industry exhibitions in Tashkent only to realize that no one exhibited embroidery, clothing, or jewelry from Surxondaryo. Worse, when people learned where Dmitry came from, they asked, "Is that really in Uzbekistan?" Today, his workshop is stacked with boxes of treasure: suzani from all regions of Uzbekistan and all districts of Surxondaryo, Afghan, Turkmen, Tajik, and Uzbek national clothing, exquisitely embroidered *joinamoz* prayer mats, incredible seamless skullcaps, *khurjin* carpet bags (back in 2002, the team started making those specifically). His team counts twenty people: they weave carpets, embroider, sew clothes and skullcaps, and create patchwork pieces. Dmitry is also the inspiration and the driving force of the folklore and ethnographic group Sarmangan (the old name of Jarkurgan) which is an essential element of every large-scale festival in the country. Their programs are based on thorough research and reconstruction of not just the attire but the rites of ethnic groups living in Surxondaryo.

The collection Dmitry keeps in boxes and on hangers is a museum-grade one. For over fifteen years, he has been gathering it in kishlaks and remote districts. Looking through the dresses, robes, and scarves, Dmitry tells about the details giving an insight into the character and customs of the people of Surxondaryo. Women never wore burqas here, and when they went outside, they covered their faces with the sleeve of the *kurta* dress. The gowns had no pockets, and so the sleeves were sewn shut, so that keys from a chest or sweets for grandchildren could be kept there. The patterns of embroidery depicting cotton appeared in the 1950s due to a greater focus on cotton farming, motifs related to peace, in the 1960s. The special feature of Surxondaryo crafts lies in the lack of borrowings, in their originality and preservation of mwany pre-Islamic motifs.
+998 90 521 49 20, Navruz Mahalla, Crafts Center

Boysun

The cultural space of Boysun was declared a UNESCO Masterpiece of the Oral and Intangible Heritage. This project exists to highlight not the monuments, but the unique combination of factors that make a territory remarkable. Such is Boysun. As a town (it only gained urban status in 1975), it may seem unremarkable, yet it serves as the heart of a region where nature of rare beauty and diversity converges with rich folkloric and craft traditions, plus archaeological sites dating back to ancient times. Thus, a trip to Boysun is not about admiring architecture. It is an expedition to remote villages, complete with challenging roads and occasionally subpar hotels.

Boysun Bazaar
Even if Boysun had no embroidery, crafts center, Boysun ensemble, Boysun Spring Festival, and the Boysun butter could be good enough reasons to visit the place. Surprisingly, very few people know about the butter, and one cannot find it in bazaars of the remote Samarkand, not even in Termez that is just an hour and a half away. Rich, dense, salty Boysun

butter is like good cheese and can be eaten in chunks. It is made by chabans: they cure the product in cows' stomachs in cool caves in the mountains, and then bring it to sell to the bazaar.

Boysun Crafts Center
The small town of Boysun was assigned the UNESCO status of Masterpiece of the Oral and Intangible Heritage, and soon, in 2006, the Boysun Crafts Center was opened as the first museum of its type. The collection of the museum (the word *unique* would suit it best without any exaggerations) was based on findings of a scientific expedition of several years before. A team of specialists from across the country went to the very remote districts of Surxondaryo to bring fantastic items, like the *Ok Enli* carpet dating back to the turn of 19th and 20th centuries, with flat stitching over a narrow woven white strip.

There are workshops in the museum where girls weave fabrics and carpets after special training. Dilafruz Sidikova, *jandaduz* ("janda master weaver") tells that only men were engaged in weaving this cotton fabric. The grandfather of Nazira Juraeva, who is responsible for carpets in the Crafts Center, was also a janda weaver. The word *janda* originally means "dirty, ragged." Dirty and ragged robes were given by the *bai* to their servants. Today, it takes a week to make a *chapan* by hand. Dressing gowns, bags, cosmetic cases, and carpets made by women cooperating with the center, are available in the shop of the museum.
+998 97 244 39 56

Suzani Art Center
A small art center displaying a collection of embroidery, skullcaps, and old ceramics sits in the building of a former mosque. The owner is Feruza; ask her to organize lunch and a folk performance.
+998 90 907 64 76, Boysun District, Gaza Mahalla, Zarafshon Street

Folk Ethnographic Ensemble Boysun, Hamza Bozorov
One of the main events around Boysun is the Boysun Spring Festival. For several years it has gathered folk ensembles, craftsmen and musicians from entire Uzbekistan in the blossoming spring hills of Surxondaryo. It is a festival of traditions that still exist in popular memory thanks to such festivals as "Boysun." Organized in 1975, it focuses on revival of traditional of musical and poetic creativity and the art of dance. It embodies the best of the Surxondaryo folklore, from the spoken word of the bakhchi storytellers, to

At the Boysun Crafts Center

dances: women's dances are smoother, whereas men's feature many jumps and squats, and expressive movement of the arms. Each program is based on a thorough study of regional traditions, trips to remote kishlaks, and talks with the elders. I was privileged to see a performance by part of the collective: I was fascinated at the openness, emotional charge and fantastic skill of the dancers.
+998 99 679 10 05, Arik Usti Mahalla

Boysun Palace
The newest freshly decorated hotel of Boysun with spacious rooms and even a charging station for electrical vehicles.
+998 881 46 39 39

Gaza Hotel and Restaurant
For many years, Gaza has been considered one of the nicer hotels in Boysun. It is freshly redecorated, it has a gym, and the restaurant on the ground floor serves good Uzbek cuisine: the kovurma gusht, tender braised lamb, is delicious.
+998 94 464 18 27, Gaza Mahalla, Zarafshon Street, 1

Derbent

The mountain kishlak of Derbent (or Darband, the local name used to avoid confusion with the Derbent of Dagestan) lies on an important trade route along the Sherabad River. It connected the southern parts of present-day Uzbekistan, North Afghanistan and Tajikistan with the center, cities of Samarkand, Bukhara, and Tashkent (known as Shash at the time). The etymology of the name of Derbent or Darband (whether Dagestanian, Uzbek, or Iranian) is the same: a frontier post, a narrow passage in the mountains, or a ravine serving as a natural border. The ambassador of Castille, Ruy Gonzalez de Clavijo, once traveled this route to get to Timur's court in Shahrisabz in the early 15th century and described a complex of powerful fortifications, natural and man-made. The remains of the wall serving as the border between the Kushan Empire and Kangju, found near Derbent, date back to 1st–3rd centuries; in other words, it lies between two powerful empires of the period. Probably Derbent was the place where Alexander the Great married Roxana, daughter of the Bactrian warlord Oxyartes. One fact is for certain: Alexander the Great was here during the Mountain War and laid a siege to well-fortified strongholds, whose remains can still be seen today.

Boysun Ensemble performance

The land around Derbent appears scarred. Tall cliffs form grand gateways one moment, then nearly converge overhead, their reddish hues echoing

Kupkari match near Derbent

the spilled blood shed defending borders for one empire after another. These are places of raw, primal beauty and overwhelming power, where gorges (not just the famed Sogdian Iron Gates besieged by Alexander, but dozens of others) weave into labyrinths still unexplored in full. Seventy-six canyons make this area a speleologist's dream!

Kupkari

Kupkari, or goat pulling, is a popular sport of Surxondaryo and Qashqadaryo, also related to large family events. The participant riders are called *chavandoz*. They are fearless men, strong, quick-reacting, and skillful horseback riders, who train their own horses. Kupkari takes place in early spring and late autumn, in the weather that will not harm the horse or its rider with extreme cold or heat. The chavandoz tries to snatch the carcass of a goat, sometimes made heavier with a bag of sand, carry it for a certain distance or place in a special goal. Leaning down, taking the carcass from the ground, holding it tightly, at the same time controlling the horse and preventing others from pulling the goat from one's hands (hence the name, goat pulling) is quite a challenge. A seasoned chavandoz knows how to tear the carcass out of the rival's hands without losing his balance or frightening the horse. The spectators, who gather on the hills around the kupkari pitch or on tops of trucks, cheer and support. Telling the truth, I failed to see the goat as I was standing on the rusty top of a Soviet truck in the company of one referee (the second was on the pitch)

Kurash match near Derbent— just before the competition begins

and guests of honor. What I did get was the pleasure of immersion into a world of elements and primal instincts.

Kurash

Kurash is a traditional folk wrestling style popular in Uzbekistan. It allows no painful grips or kicks, only throws and undercuts. The name of the style goes back to the expression "achieve the goal by fair means." Kurash counts some 3,500 years of age and is considered one of the most ancient wrestling styles. There is the National Kurash Federation in Uzbekistan, but many boys and teenagers gather on hill slopes of Derbent, never learned from a coach or went to a gym. They learned from their fathers and grandfathers, who, in their turn, had learned from theirs. Kurash is often organized to honor important family events: the competition I saw was a part of a wedding celebration, or, more precisely, it was to honor the xatna-kilish ritual (circumcision). Four pairs of wrestlers come to the pitch at the same time, the referee monitors the process as well as spectators sitting on carpets on the ground. The winners get substantial prizes: money, sheep, or horses. The family that celebrates their son's special occasion pays for the Kurash, morning plov for the guests, and prizes.

Turdikulov Family Guesthouse Sitorai Darband

There are few places to put up for a night in Derbent. I stayed at a guesthouse wall to wall with the home where my Surxondaryo guide Shavkat was born and raised. It is a great stroke of luck to

Sultonov family

travel with him as your guide! Shavkat Turdikulov is one of the most sought-after German-speaking guides of Uzbekistan, a PhD in philology, one of the pioneers of international tourism in the country.
+998 97 919 88 90, +998 97 925 80 12, Isfandiyor Street, 8/10

Sulton Sharbati Winery
The company was founded in 2006: the Oltinsoy Factory fell into decline, and the Sultonov family bought part of it. The agricultural farm owns 135 hectares of land growing seven varieties of grapes (Cabernet Sauvignon, Saperavi, Tavkveri, Aleatico, Muscat, Rkatsiteli, and Kuldzhinskii), and buy grapes from local farmers. One of their best wines semi-sweet Muscat in an interesting amber-colored bottle. The local white variety, Kuldzhinskii produces fresh wines with a nice acidity and lemon drop flavors. The winery plans to open a tasting room.
+998 94 627 28 88, Oltinsoy District, Shakarqamish Area

Ak Saray Palace in Shahrisabz

QASHQADARYO: A BIT OF HISTORY

Timur and His Team

The remains of Ak Saray Palace in Shahrisabz

Unlike Surxondaryo, Qashqadaryo is a region that sees more tourists because it borders not on Tajikistan, Turkmenistan, or Afghanistan but on the more developed Samarkand Region attracting numerous visitors. Only the steppes around Karshi, capital of the region, end up on the Turkmen border. However, there is another problem: the birthplace of Timur, Shahrisabz, is just a couple of hours' stop in most of the tourist routes. The big buses simply do not stay here longer. Staying here for longer, unlocking the beauty of the land, feeling the balance between the dramatic nature, old customs and traditions and a quite decent infrastructure is a task not for a tourist but for an explorer and a traveler.

Timur was born on April 9, 1336, in a kishlak on the outskirts of present-day Shahrisabz. He was just thirty-four, when in the year 1370 he took control of the Timurid Empire that he created with the capital in Samarkand. Shahrisabz was the second city in the empire, but what made it even more important was that it possessed the soul of the emperor. It was here, not in Samarkand that he built the enormously large **Ak Saray Palace** famous for its complex engineering, and it was here that he spent his time after his campaigns. After the death of Timur (1405) and the death of his beloved grandson Ulugbek, an astronomer, politician, and philosopher, Shahrisabz gradually came to a decline. From the early 16th century, it was part of the Bukhara Emirate and shared all the twists and turns of history with it, first, the advent of the Russian protectorate, and later, the Soviet power. They say that in Soviet times Shahrisabz literally served as a donor for the reconstruction of monuments of Samarkand.

Old Shahrisabz fell victim to renovation without rationale. The districts around Ak Saray, unique examples of medieval urban planning for some and obsolete housing for others, were demolished to free up space to construct neat alleys devoid of former life. If you come to Shahrisabz unprepared and without a guide, you will see the frame of Timur's palace, fields of tile, rows of urns and a wall separating this space of orphaned history from the city itself. Chances are, you will shrug your shoulders and leave. One of my goals is to prevent just that.

Shahrisabz

The main sights of the city are clustered in the center, within walking distance from one another: a part of the remaining portal of Timur's palace Ak Saray and the Dorut Tilovat Complex (Timur's father's resting place, Mausoleum of the Shaikh Shamsiddin Kulol al-Keshi, Gumbazi Sayyidon, and the Kok-Gumbaz Mosque). The most beautiful place that still keeps the spirit of the Old Town, because it didn't succumb to renovation, is the inner yard of the mosque under the shade of the sycamore tree planted in 1370. This tree remembers the great Emperor.

Aziz Ahmedov
For me, the two great memories of the town are Aziz Ahmedov and the scale model of the Ak Saray he made. Aziz was born and raised in Shahrisabz. Since childhood, he has been fascinated by the two remaining pillars and the ruins of Ak Saray. He went to an art school

and, later, to the faculty of restoration of architectural monuments. It took him twenty years to prepare for the construction of the model of the palace, fully made by hand, complete with woodcarving and engraving of plaster: he made sketches of his Master's project, the façade of the palace, he worked on the town reconstruction and gathered archive materials, excavation findings, and old photographs. He guides me around the model of the entrance portal, which occupies the central position in the gallery situated between Ak-Saray and the Kok-Gumbaz Mosque. As we walk, he explains how mathematical calculations and meticulous attention to detail—combined with guidance from his teacher, Iskandar Azimov—enabled him to determine the palace's exact height. Speaking about his plans, he shows a picture on the wall of Ak Saray in full detail, with its harem, its exquisite courtyard and the great swimming pool decorated with maiolica. "We will build all of this," he says with a voice ringing with conviction.

Aziz works together with numerous artists across Qashqadaryo, supporting craftsmen from both Shahrisabz and remote villages by providing orders, organizing meetings, and fostering knowledge exchange and healthy competition. His favorite place in the region, evident from the artworks adorning his walls, is the mountain village of Gylan, nestled high in the Hissar Range within a nature reserve that is home to bears and snow leopards. His gallery boasts one of Uzbekistan's finest collections of European-style paintings, all tastefully framed. Exporting presents no issues: Aziz is authorized to arrange special permits.
+998 97 380 02 12, Amir Timur Alley, 14

Saodat Nizamova
No matter when you visit, you will spot a stall piled with embroidered bags, pillowcases, and cosmetic pouches by the walls of the Kok-Gumbaz Mosque. Behind it, a smiling woman in a headscarf, Saodat Nizamova, one of the most renowned embroiderers of the city. Her home, just nearby in a mahalla untouched by renovation, welcomes guests with vividly painted walls and floors covered in plush velvet kurpacha rugs. Four generations of the Nizamov family have lived here, and Saodat came as a bride. She learned embroidery and regional patterns from her grandmother, and now mentors others herself. She has trained over a hundred embroiderers who, in turn, passed the craft to their own students. With tourism always thriving in

Embroidery artist Saodat Nizamova at her home

Dorus-Saodat Complex in Shahrisabz

Shahrisabz, this craft has grown into a full business, supported by her entire family, including her husband. Up to forty home-based embroiderers now work under her guidance. Saodat explains how she travels with the Hunarmand artisans' association to remote villages, teaching women a trade that can sustain them.

Traditions of Shahrisabz embroidery usually date back to Timur's time, who brought artisans from the whole empire to build and develop his garden city. The weaving school of Shahrisabz was one of the most influential, and local artisans use several techniques at once. The most characteristic of Shahrisabz and the most labor consuming of them is *iroki*. Saodat unfolds a giant panel picture I have never seen before, the one depicting Ak Saray and Timur's monument. The embroidery is done in minute stitches, resembling beadwork, leaving no space of fabric uncovered. This technique does not entail the transfer of contours to the canvas; the skillful master calculates the pattern just by seeing the texture of the cloth making a pattern by using solid calculation and artistic talent.
+998 91 644 91 89

Suzani for Hermès and a Garden for Grandmothers
"I graduated from the faculty of foreign languages and speak good French, so, in 1999, after a study visit to France, I started my own school: I gathered gifted children from less-to-do families and taught them foreign languages for free. Oh, it was hard! I had to give up my salary. But, by the grace of the Almighty, we had a brilliant idea, to give a good job to the mothers so that they could buy books for their children. This is how it started." Yulduz Mamadiyorova and I are drinking tea under the medieval cupola Chorsu in the center of Shahrisabz, where she has a showroom: stalls of bags, footwear, makeup pouches, and walls are adorned with large carpets. Several women are embroidering, weaving, and sewing. "We bought 100 grams of thread, and people were mocking me: do you think that would be enough," Yulduz continues her story. She and three other women from her native kishlak started with purse embroidery. "I said, you just wait, and I will buy hundreds of kilograms!" In three months, she had 75 women working with her, 10 articles of goods, she had her own brand and label, and the pieces went to be sold in Tashkent. Now, twenty years later, Yulduz works with over 100 women in four workshops manufacturing over 50 types of products.

The suzani embroidered by hands of Shahrisabz women adorns the hall of the Hermès office in Paris. They received this commission through Gulnara Karimova, daughter of the first President of Uzbekistan. It was a gigantic canvas, 5 by 4.3 meters, and it was a rush order: the team completed the work in seven months, instead of two years. The French client pushed them without completely understanding how painstaking a job embroidery is. "I sent them a letter and attached some photographs: how women work in the kishlaks, what the situation is like in their homes... And the French customer was lost for words," Yulduz says, "Then, there was a magazine published in France, with an article and those pictures. When we received it by post, I translated it for my team of artists as we were sitting together cooking some plov. It was so inspiring!" Yulduz shows me the photos of *that* suzani, and adds that they had had no idea that their

Yulduz Mamadiyorova and her collaborators

commission was from the oldest fashion house of France until the work was completed. Now, after Hermès, there are no insurmountable tasks.

As she speaks, Yulduz often talks about God saying she cannot enter every single home and tell that life can be changed, that handiwork is worth decent money, and that women can be independent. "Money is still of no interest for me. I made a pledge to God, and through Him, to the women: to raise their standard of living so that they would be able to make their own decisions. This is a dream that we can only make true by working," she says, adding that she teaches women to see their craft as art, raising the prestige of hand labor.

Yulduz says ideas keep coming into her head: she points at her aunt standing by the weaver's loom, and explains that she started working with carpets for her sake and that of her friends, who have mastered the skill since their childhood. Yulduz laughs: "Grandmothers love spending time together," and adds she wants to open a care home where the elderly would be able to communicate and work, if they wish. She speaks about her plans to become a people's deputy and bring natural carpets back to the kindergartens, where substitutes have taken a strong position: "I believe that God helps, if you truly have a good dream."
+998 91 467 77 82, Kullolik Street, 2/1
yulduz1967@mail.ru

Zayneddin Muzafarov
The Muzafarov family is the only one to preserve the old tradition of pottery in the city: Zayneddin-aka living in Shahrisabz, and his son Rustam (*+998 97 407 50 89*), who works with Shahrisabz style ceramics in Tashkent. As late as in the 1980s, there was a mahalla of ceramists near the Ak Saray, and the only thing that remains today is the choyxona "Kullolik," from the Uzbek *kulol*, meaning "potter." "The old ones are dead, and the young ones did not carry on their work," laments Zayneddin. He calls the ceramics of Shahrisabz fiery pointing at its ochre, burgundy and scarlet tones. He represents the sixth generation of potters: his patterns and techniques come from his father, Akhat Muzafarov, an artisan known across Uzbekistan, from his grand- and great-grandfathers.

The technique used by the Muzafarov family involves a pattern applied by brush and single-stage firing at high temperature. Every item displayed in the memorial home, that has both a workshop and an elegant showroom with works of family members including 250-year-old jugs and lagans, bears the recognizable features of the Shahrisabz school and traits of personal style. Unfortunately, the family has no shop in the center. One location was offered, but the rent was too high. Zayneddin says, "Our favorite motif is fish, they symbolize wealth and friendship as well. And the Huma bird, symbol of happiness and freedom."
+998 97 774 48 53, Ak Saray Street, 7

Potter Zayneddin Muzafarov at his home

Hotels and Restaurants

Kesh Palace
One of the finest hotels of Qashqadaryo operates from a modern building in the newer district of the city. Rooms offer all standard European amenities, from electric kettles to safes. Personally, I deeply missed these comforts, especially the proper beds, during my travels through Surxondaryo.
+998 95 505 55 51, Fusunkor Street, 1

Eshon-pir Historical House Hostel
A guesthouse set in a charming old home within a mahalla just steps from the Kok-Gumbaz Mosque, accommodating up to nine guests across three triple-occupancy rooms decorated in traditional style. The host, Rashid-aka, also conducts workshops preparing plov in the courtyard and sharing insights about customs of Qashqadaryo.
+998 97 188 00 61

Anoragul Guesthouse
A small guesthouse decorated in traditional style, with exceptionally hospitable hosts and homemade breakfasts. Be sure to ask for the geotag, since finding it by address alone proves challenging.
+998 91 642 44 66, Fusunkor Street, 4A

Koba Maqom
An elegant restaurant in the old caravanserai building after the restoration of its historical appearance. The first place where esteemed guests are taken.
+998 99 318 95 99, Zingiron Street, 78 D

Chorsu Milliy Taomlar
A large restaurant offering national cuisine, popular both with locals and guests of Shahrisabz.
+998 95 681 00 03, Ipak Yuli Street, 8

Yulchi Tandoor
On the road from Shahrisabz to Guzar, about 10 kilometers before reaching your destination, you will spot a small tandoor bakery on the left. *Yulchi* means "roadside" in Uzbek. Here, they prepare traditional lamb almost identically to the method of Surxondaryo using Hissar lambs and archa, juniper branches, but the local tandoor master Tura Tursunov has his own secrets. First, the spice rub for the meat includes garlic, cumin, and coriander seeds. Second, Tura places khasip (a homemade sausage of lamb liver, meat, and fat in natural casing with the same spices) on a grill in the upper chamber of the tandoor. He explains that shepherds invented tandoors, like most other regional dishes: meat cooked this way keeps longer without spoiling. He recommends the shoulder and rib cuts as the most flavorful. Both the lamb and khasip were superb, the khasip being the best I have ever tasted. My guide Aziz, who orders meat here for family celebrations, always requests quince baked in the tandoor too: it makes a delicate side dish.
+998 90 667 60 10

Historic center of Shahrisabz

ENVIRONS OF SHAHRISABZ

A Jeynau woman dressed in Central Asian Arab traditional clothing

Hissarak Reservoir and Gilan Kishlak
The areas around the Hissarak Reservoir created in 2011 on the Aksu River are some of the breathtaking locations in the region. These are the foothills of the Hissar Range that shines its snow-capped peaks over the horizon. There, in the mountains, at the height of over 2,000 meters, lies Gilan, a picturesque kishlak, one of the highest-elevated settlements of the country, with a network of manmade canals traversing the steep slopes with gardens and fields cultivated on the stony terrain. There are old houses, where the ground floor is given to the cattle, and living rooms are in the second floor. The places around Gilan are perfect for hiking and trekking. There are no hotels, but you can stay up for a night in a family guesthouse, for example, at *Kimiy's* (*+998 99 644 79 85, t.me/guesthouse893kimiy*).

The rivers flowing into the reservoir are abundant with marinka, a local species of fish similar to mountain trout. There are numerous restaurants cooking it near the kishlak of Miraki.

One hour's drive from Shahrisabz will take you to the Kitab International Latitude Station and the Maidanak Observatory. Scientists study the Earth and the space from here: they observe the movements of tectonic plates, monitor celestial bodies and celestial garbage. The Latitude Station has been in operation since 1928, and the observatory was founded in 1970. There is a hotel available on the premises. *+998 919504916*

Katta Langar
It was believed that one of the world's oldest Quran manuscripts, the Uthmanic Quranic, transcribed during the reign of the third Rightly Guided Caliph (and Prophet's son-in-law) and now housed in Tashkent's Muyi Muborak Madrasah, has been kept since 15th century at a Sufi memorial complex in the mountain village of Katta Langar, 40 minutes from Shahrisabz. Locals still maintain that the chest which held this copy remains there to this day. A legend has it that 500 years ago, a youth from the Ishqiyya Sufi order came to these foothills of the Hissar Range. He became renowned as a sage, a mystic, and a spiritual guide who attained the highest enlightenment. Katta Langar houses his mausoleum, an austere structure of burnt brick adorned with Quranic inscriptions on the inside. Above its dome rises a spire bearing four spheres, symbolizing the stages toward enlightenment.

Jeynau
One-hour's drive from Karshi will bring you to Jeynau, a kishlak bright with Arabic colors. The vibrant clothes of local women are very different from Uzbek attire, and women wear a golden septum ring. The majority of the population here are Arabs from the Shayboniy tribe. The relocation of Arabs to the Central Asia was in several stages, staring with late 8th century continuing to early 20th century. One of the largest groups in Central Asia lives in the lower reaches of Qashqadarya River. This is a large carpet-manufacturing region inhabited not only by Arabs, but also by Turkmens, Tajiks, Uzbeks, and descendants of early Turks. Weaving was the craft of Turkmens and Arabs, and the suburbs of Karshi are considered to be the only region in Central Asia to employ both men and women in the textile crafts. In the second half of 19th century there was a veritable industry of manufacturing, mainly flat woven carpets sold in the regional bazaar that had some demand in Bukhara and Russian Turkestan. The carpet craft of Arabs kept the ancient

Arabian patterns, and the palace carpets of Karshi were famous for their elegance and strength. Only horizontal weaver's looms have been used traditionally, and are still used. The local Culture Center (*+998 91 450 16 71, Hamro Sharopov*) will be happy to introduce guests to master carpet weavers and keepers of Arabic traditions of singing, dancing, and playing musical instruments.

Karshi Bridge
The Karshi Bridge, also known as Amir Timur Bridge, spans the Qashqadarya River. This massive brick structure, built in 1583 (when Karshi served as a major city in the Shaybanid state), ranks among Central Asia's oldest and largest surviving bridges of its kind, measuring 122 meters long and nearly 9 meters wide.

Sharifjon Raupov
When I first met Sharifjon Raupov, a hereditary jeweler, over five years ago, I traveled to Guzar, once the largest city of the Bukhara Emirate, with a guide: finding his house proved nearly impossible. *En route*, Aziz, my guide of Qashqadaryo, was fuming, why did Sharif still lack a proper workshop in Shahrisabz, given that only the most determined travelers would brave these rough roads? Now Sharif finally has a place to welcome guests, though you will need to head not to Guzar or Shahrisabz, but to Karshi. Sharif represents the sixth generation of the Raupov jewelers' dynasty. He continues creating accessories using traditional techniques. His tools are a legacy from his grandfathers, who worked for the Bukhara nobility, for example, the father of the last Emir of Bukhara, Said Abd al-Ahad Khan. Sharif will show you replicas of jewelry made by his great-grandfather and kept in the State Hermitage Museum. Everything made for the Emirs was confiscated after the Revolution. "They left the molds," Sharif says, "So, I managed to restore it all." These items can help studying the history of Uzbekistan jewelry. The Khorezmian school is on the heavier and ornamental side, the specimens of Bukhara and Samarkand schools are lighter, with smoother lines, whereas Tashkent and Fergana items used a lot of gems, mainly corals and turquoise, even mother-of-pearl! One can easily imagine caravans laden with Indian treasures, from which the best of the best pieces was chosen for the ruling families. Sharif keeps a collection of clothes of Bukhara nobility of 19th–20th centuries, his family possession. With skillful movements of his hands, he forms the turban from a cut of silk up to seven meters long, and poses for a picture wearing two dressing gowns (only one was never worn!) against a collection of vintage clocks that he has been collecting all his life. While Sharif's jewelry can be purchased in Samarkand and Bukhara, visiting his workshop in Karshi remains the best option. Much of what you see here is not found even in top museums. Besides, no curator would ever let you feel the fluid drape of antique silk beneath your fingers.
+998 91 262 51 34, Karshi, Buston Mahalla

Kitab Pass
Two roads lead from Shahrisabz to Samarkand. The picturesque road goes over the Kitab Pass (also known as Takhtakaracha among locals): there, at the point where Qashqadaryo and Surxondaryo Regions meet, a small but lively bazaar sports wicker baskets full of mountain herbs, dried fruit, and kurt. In autumn, the pass wears russet tones, but its most breathtaking season is late March, when fruit trees bloom in pink

and white, and boys sell mountain tulips. Come summer, the pass offers refuge from the heat: cool off by a mountain stream or at a tandoor bakery with topchans set in welcome shade. One such spot (my favorite!) is *Sharshara: +998 95 505 02 77.*

Chiyal, Chuvillok, Arabbandy
The second road, usually taken by big buses that cannot go over the pass, leads to Samarkand along several locations highly important in Qashqadaryo. The Sunday Bazaar in the kishlak of Chiyal and a smaller Friday Bazaar in the neighboring Chuvillok, are signature places for connoisseurs of unusual dishes. Only here you can try the specialty of Qashqadaryo, the yakhna gusht cold meat. Lamb is stewed for 12 hours, together with fat and bone, and left to cool in pots wrapped in several warm blankets. The result is actually confit lamb, served here with fresh flatbreads or thin manti without filling called pachok manti. They are cooked by local women, and served with a basting of vegetable oil and a sprinkle of mixed sweet and hot pepper. Nowhere else have I seen such simple rustic manti! At this same bazaar, I finally stumbled upon rare coarse-grained flatbreads like those made in the mountains near Langar. Stone mills for flour have become a rarity these days, and with them disappeared the dark, dense flatbreads yielding to fluffy, snow-white ones.

The Sunday Bazaar of Chiyal is the largest in the region, known since the Soviet times. Coming here is worth it not only because of the local color and the cold meat, flat-woven arabi-gilam carpets are another attraction. Many women of Qashqadaryo Region know the craft of weaving them, and selling them on the market to the locals and the few tourists reaching the bazaar is one of the ways to earn the living.

Caravan Carpets
If you are in a quest for a carpet but have no time to get to the Bazaar, your destination is in the kishlak of Arabbandi, approximately mid-way on the bypass road between Samarkand and Shahrisabz, to the workshop of Sharif-bobo and Chinni-buvi Huidakulov. Almost all of their 11 children, 42 grandchildren and 12 greatgrandchildren deal in traditional carpet weaving manufacturing mass and custom items (a gift on the occasion of a wedding). Wearing a high fur hat, Sharif-bobo shows a yurt standing on elevated ground and says that he put it there, on a location easily seen from the road, as an attraction for tourist groups. The idea proved highly efficient, and Arabbandi is now visited by every other group on their way. As any other guest, I am treated to tea with hot flatbreads and cold grapes. Chinni-buvi keeps a skein of yarn in her hands, and her fingers transform a fluffy mass into a taut thread. Of course, I could not refrain from buying a carpet. Lucky thing it can be folded, packed, and checked in with your luggage.
+998 94 333 02 74, +998 93 225 41 47, Arabbandi kishlak, Chirakchinsky District

Umakai Choyxona
At the very border of two regions, two kilometers away from the highway post between Qashqadaryo and Samarkand, kishlak Umakai is famous for its authentic jyz, lamb cooked with tail fat until fall-apart tender, then quickly roasted. People from Samarkand (Umakai lies closer to Samarkand than to Shahrisabz) believe that Umakai jyz is the perfect version, and use this name in the menus of many restaurants. When we asked about the jyz, Sharif-bobo pointed to this choyxona. It is very simple, but the locals prefer it.
+998 93 244 99 44

Fergana Valley. Choyxona of Pomegranate

Chapter VI

Surrounded by mountain chains from all sides, Fergana Valley is the most densely populated, the most fertile land of Uzbekistan; it consists of three administrative areas, Fergana, Namangan, and Andijan Regions. The route from Tashkent goes through the high-mountain Kamchik Pass.

The automobile and railroad tunnels allowing fact commuting to and from the capital were opened quite recently, and the valley, proud of its free spirit, is now connected with the capital even stronger. Making a way through the stubborn mountains was a matter of ambition.

The valley is the place to feel the way of life of a large Uzbek city that sees tourists as something unusual. The chaotic maze of the old center is not hidden by a wall from the travelers' eyes. Winding gravel-coated streets of mahallas, webs of wires on posts, streets closed for crowds hurrying for the Friday's prayer. Choyxonas opening at 5 in the morning, after the morning *salah* prayer and closing just two hours later, at 7 a.m. Choyxonas are open only for men, although for sleepless women there are separate rooms, secure from foreign eyes, with floors covered with colorful kurpachas. This is the place in Uzbekistan with the most women with covered heads and most places not serving or allowing alcohol.

Fergana Valley does not have such a concentration of monuments that the traveler gets used to after visiting Samarkand, Bukhara, and Khiva. Madrasahs, mausoleums and mosques are sometimes scattered over remote kishlaks or hidden in the chaotic old districts. It makes them all the more valuable, for, not frequented by tourists, they have not been touched by restoration. They embody the spirit of the valley, they are all by themselves, with their chipped and cracked walls, just the way they are. This is why the monuments of Kokand stand out so bright and new on their background. A few steps away from the old center reveal the second layer of the city: the Turkestan Art Nouveau, mansions of cotton magnates, eyewitnesses of the era when Kokand was one of the most important cities in the Russian Empire.

The Art Nouveau and the Sufism, the poetry and painting, cool choyxonas and noisy bazaars, old arts and crafts and avant-garde trends, rivers of pomegranate with shores planted with grapes, the valley lives a life of its own, sometimes looking back, because the capital is staring at it. The valley keeps a well-sharpened knife from Kokand or Chust: what if guests are coming? That calls for butchering a sheep and cutting carrots for some plov... Extreme hospitality that immediately pulls you in a whirlwind of feast and personal contacts is another phenomenon complimenting to the overall picture of the valley.

View over Kamchik Pass

A BIT OF HISTORY

Celestial Horses, Revolts, Leech Tax, an Attempt at Autonomy

Khudayar
Khan Palace

As a geographical area, Fergana Valley is currently separated between three countries. The greater part belongs to Uzbekistan (I am using the term Fergana Valley to denote the Uzbek territory), and there are smaller parts that belong to Kyrgyzstan and Tajikistan. The powerful Kokand Khanate with the capital in Kokand in 18th–19th centuries included parts of Tajikistan, Kyrgyzstan, and China. Along with Bukhara and Khiva Khanates, it was one of the three Uzbek states of Central Asia. In the pre-Islamic times, there existed a state known to us by Chinese sources as Dawan or **Dayan**, with the capital in Ershi, the remains of which are on the territory of the Andijan Region. A key part of the global trade process, Dayan became known as the place where famous racing horses were bred, valued in China for their endurance and beauty and hence bore the name of "celestial horses." (Though another name was known too—"blood-sweating horses" for their thin skin and blood vessels, that could rupture due to extreme strain or attacks of parasites.) In the middle of 7th century, the territory of the country was conquered by Turks, and in the late 8th century by Arabs.
In 1709, Shahrukh Bek became the first rules of the young Kokand Khanate that started its bloody process of separation from Bukhara. By the early 19th century, Kokand's rule embraced not only Namangan, Andijan and Margilan but also Tashkent. We can speak about the period of prosperity of the region between the early 19th century and first decades of 20th century; at the same time, from 1868 the Khanate was under the protectorate of Russia (similar to Khiva and Bukhara Khanates). Inside the Kokand Khanate, popular unrest was brewing due to the plundering policy of the Khan (e.g., he introduced a tax on leeches, and the time between 1873 and 1875 is marked by numerous revolts. Khudayar Khan fled in 1875, and a mix of total war for power and desperate chase broke out: both the Russians and the local elites wanted to seal the fate of the escaped Khan. In the year 1876, the effort of General Mikhail Skobelev resulted in Kokand losing its independence and ascending to the Russian Empire as part of the Fergana Region. In the same year, a city was founded near Margilan that became the administrative center of the region. Its name was New Margilan, today known as Fergana. The Soviets came into power in the region in 1918, after the widespread Civil War and an attempt of forming the Turkestan Autonomy. However, this did not stop unrest and revolts. Whatever the regime, the local population was always in opposition to it. Thus, it happened historically that the popular moods in the valley are closely monitored by the administration and the people from other parts of the country, marking even slight deviations from the norm.

Kokand, Rishtan, Margilan: A Schedule

Day 1
Full day in Kokand. Old city: Khudayar Khan Palace, Jami Mosque. Modari Khan and Damoi Shahon Mausoleums. Lunch. Art Nouveau of Kokand: historical building of the Kokand Branch of the Russo-Asian bank, Vadyaev House, Simkhaev House. Dinner.

Day 2
Departure to Rishtan (one-hour drive). Visit to one or several ceramics studios. Khoja-Ilgar Mausoleum. Lunch. Departure to Margilan (forty-minute drive). Visit to Yodgorlik Factory. Sayyid Ahmad Khoja Madrasah. Return to Kokand.

CUISINE AND WINEMAKING OF FERGANA VALLEY:

The Gold Standard

Cooking traditional plov in Kokand

For many enthusiasts of Uzbek cuisine, the culinary traditions of the Fergana Valley represent the gold standard, the benchmark against which all else is measured. Uzbek cuisine is essentially understood as Fergana Valley cuisine. That iconic plov made with the distinctive dark devzira rice, the accompanying tomato-and-onion salad, the fiery peppers in every dish, the hefty samsa, the sugary grapes are all signatures of the Fergana Valley.

Plov is cooked here with local and "imported" types of rice; at the same time, the more expensive fermented types are used in a festive plov cooked for special occasions, a plov that not only is costly, but also requires special skill. In choyxonas, the conventional white rice is used, most often, the lazer from Khorezm. Chickpeas, quince, dolma, and quaxs' eggs may be added. What I found most interesting was that there are no stereotypes as to when plov may be cooked. While an evening plov may be absurd in Samarkand, it is perfectly normal for cities and towns in the valley.

Red hot peppers are an indispensable condiment to many dishes in the Fergana Valley. Of course, it is common in other regions of the country, but the amount it is eaten in the valley is something special. Whatever you order, a salad, a samsa, or some plov, it will come with a hearty helping of sliced hot pepper. The local word for it is "bitter" pepper.

More than elsewhere in Uzbekistan, people in the valley favor the organ meat. A breakfast in a Kokand choyxona may include kalla gusht, cold pressed meat of a lamb's head, sometimes pressed together with tripe. In Andijan, a piece of lung boiled in milk goes over a slice of bread. In Margilan, near the O'Ram Choyxona, you will see long stalls of homemade sausage and meat products made from tripe and parts of the animal that are not usually eaten.

The soil of Fergana Valley is considered most fertile not only in Uzbekistan but across all of Central Asia. Here, they cultivate pomegranates, grapes, apples, quinces, peaches, apricots, cherries, and sweet cherries, much of which is exported to Russia. It is said that the village of Altyaryk alone sells $50 million worth of grapes in Russia during the harvest season.

In Fergana Region, Fergana France is processing some fruit, a winery producing both grape wines and **fruit wines** (a rarity for Uzbekistan), along with classic and fruit brandies.

Dishes to Try

Fergana plov. Despite the numerous varieties of plov in the Fergana Valley, the authentic is the plov cooked with lamb and dark fermented devzira rice with carrots, garlic and onion; the only spice used is cumin. The carrots are rather fried than steamed, so the Freghana plov is sometimes called kovurma palov (fried plov). Before serving, the ready plov is stirred.

Pirozhok (literally, little pie). The pirozhok of Fergana has nothing to do with pies. It is another variation of lamb and potatoes, a dish that is said to be the result of a cook's mistake (the kozon with potatoes and meat was left unattended on the coals). The secret of this dish is the long time required to braise the potatoes in the lamb fat. In the rest of the country, the same dish is known as kozon kabob and as kotirma in Namangan.

At the same time, the **kozon kabob** in Fergana Valley is not a stew but a soup of lamb, potatoes, chickpeas and tomato.

Kalla gusht is the pressed meat of the lamb's head served cold. It is an important part of the breakfast served very early in choyxonas near large mosques, after the morning salah, or prayer.

Kokand halva is a sweet treat similar to toffee, made from powdered milk, butter, and sugar, with nuts and dried fruits.

Kokand flatbreads are called patir or patir cookie. Their edges are fluffy, and the center is hard and slightly dry.

Shurpa in a jar is a rich soup of lamb and onion cooked low and slow in a glass jar covered with a lid over an electrical stove. A very popular dish in Namangan choyxonas.

Shirmoy non are thick flatbreads from Namangan leavened not with yeast but with aniseed and chickpea infusion. They are glossy with a fine, herby, slightly sour flavor.

Braised neck of lamb is a traditional dish for choyxonas in Asaka, Fergana, and Andijan: the meat is braised low and slow in a kozon and served with crispy golden roasted potatoes.

Andijan flatbreads are thick and fluffy, sprinkled with nuts, which is not common in Uzbekistan, with a glossy surface. One flatbread may be up to two kilograms!

Gushtli non are bagel-shaped flatbreads with filling of coarsely chopped lamb and onion that I only saw in Andijan.

Samsa. In the Fergana Valley, samsa is hefty. Made with soft, non-layered dough, the best samsa in the region is considered to be from the Romanqa District in Kokand, and in Altyaryk, located between Rishtan and Margilan.

At Yodgorlik Silk Factory

DECORATIVE AND APPLIED ARTS:

Ceramic Soul and Silken Heart

Potter Bakhtiyor Nazirov

The tradition of art pottery of Fergana Valley continues in Rishtan, Andijan, and Gurumsaray. The most influential is the Rishtan School famous for over two centuries. In this city lying between Kokand and Fergana, the clay is very pure, almost with no contaminants, very plastic and fusible. With the advent of the Soviets, the artisans of Rishtan (almost 80 families) were united in a cooperative later transformed into a ceramics factory. Discussing Rishtan ceramics today, one needs to draw a line between factory-made mass products and artistic pottery. The latter not only upholds long-established traditions of craftsmanship and design but also reflects the aesthetic visions and creative explorations of its makers including hereditary potters and first-generation masters alike.

With the readily recognizable white and blue ornaments of Rishtan, the bright yellow and green colors of pieces by the Andijan artisan Mirzobahrom Abduwahobov look as if Rishtan is much, much more than 130 kilometers from Andijan. The history of uninterrupted tradition of pottery runs in the family for seven generations only according to documents, while in reality it may as well be fifteen. Another school of ceramics, that of Gurumsaray, near Namangan, was brought back to life by the effort of one artisan. There are more ceramist artists in the Fergana Valley than elsewhere in Uzbekistan, so for those interested in ceramics this region is the destination of choice.

The second pillar that makes Fergana Valley renowned is its **silk and silk textile production**. In Margilan, it is seen as a full-fledged industry, or at least as industrial as a centuries-old craft reliant on meticulous handiwork can be.
Even large Russian museums have only a few samples of Fergana **embroidery**; at the same time, the tradition, although second to the bright and vibrant style of Bukhara and Nurata, is alive. I was able to meet the master artisan and see the strict, austere floral motifs stitched with silk on silk, in Namangan.

The valley still produces vast quantities of **embroidered skullcaps**, worn more widely here than anywhere else in the country. The black *duppi* skullcaps with white hand-stitched embroidery, crafted in Chust, are worn across Central Asia.

Chust, near Namangan, is even more famous for its **knives** than for its skullcaps. The town is the home to one of the country's oldest metalworking centers. Kokand, too, boasts renowned blades; while Chust draws those seeking practical household and work knives, Kokand attracts collectors of artistic masterpieces.

Ceiling at Jami Mosque in Kokand

Kokand

Of all the cities in the Fergana Valley, Kokand enjoys most of tourists' attention: it is more colorful than its neighbors, and it is closer to the capital. People come to see the brightly ornate palace of Khudayar Khan, to meet the artisans; sometimes, people choose it as the starting point for travel to Margilan and Rishtan. If you are traveling to the Fergana Valley from Tashkent for a couple of days, Kokand will be an excellent choice for a first trip to the region.

The country's largest **Handicrafters' Festival** is held in Kokand once every two years, gathering artisans from across the country and all the world. It is a unique opportunity to see everything (and everyone) at one, and participation in it is prestigious. More than once in my travels, the artisans I met proudly showed the diplomas and medals they had won in Kokand.

Kokand is an ancient city, documented since at least the 10th century, though nearby archaeological excavations suggest human presence here some 2,000 years ago. One should not expect the compact charm of Bukhara or the monumental scale of Samarkand here: Kokand is a modest, loosely structured town, typical of much of Uzbekistan.

The golden age of Kokand was in the 18th century, when it became the capital of the Khanate. Its crowning relic from that era is the **Khudayar Khan Palace** (also called Urda, the citadel), constructed between 1845 and 1875. A person accustomed to the tiles of Samarkand will marvel at the faceted minarets and unconventional multicolored patterns of ceramics. Some of the major treasures of the palace are its painted ceilings above the halls, more lavish than one could expect, rich is gold tones and filigree detailing. The two asymmetrical parts of the façade were built by two competing masters; one was local, and the other, as the legend has, it, was from Namangan. With Eastern cunning, the Khan told each artisan that his work pleased him more than his rival's.

Today the palace houses the museum of local history, a large, exquisitely decorated museum that serves a great aid in studying the architectural, stylistic and decorative techniques characteristic for the Fergana Valley, much like the **Modari Khan** and **Damoi Shahon Mausoleums**. Of course, they do not have the scale of the Shah-i-Zinda of Samarkand, but these complexes date back to the early 19th century, not XIV. When inside, look at the contrasting snow-white walls of the mosques symbolizing the futility of the earthly existence and the vibrant decorations of the ceilings, promising the joys above and out of this world. At the entrance to Damoi Shahon, in an intertwining of Islamic and pagan beliefs, shamans work with their visitors.

The **Jami Mosque** is the cathedral mosque of the city, frequented on Fridays, dating back to the early 19th century. Its modern structure is very interesting: its spacious courtyard is enclosed with iwans built in different periods. The oldest, built in 1816–1818, is to the right of the entrance, a terrace supported with ninety-eight carved pillars, with a brightly ornate ceiling, each part of which features a unique drawing. To the left are workshops of artisans, and in the center is a small museum featuring items of Kokand decorative and applied arts. Exactly in the middle of the courtyard stands the minaret: such an unusual location is characteristic of Fergana Valley.

What sets Kokand apart from both other Fergana Valley cities and the rest of Uzbekistan is its concentration of buildings in the **Turkestani Art Nouveau** style. After the Kokand Khanate was annexed to Russia, the regional administration moved to the newly built Fergana, yet Kokand retained greater strength and significance as the valley's financial (and, of course, religious) center. Cotton was the major source of money. Cotton and banking were in the hands of the Germans and the Jews: it was a rather colorful multinational landscape resulting in a multitude of stylistic preferences sprinkled with local color. Big, fast money had luxury palaces and mansions appear in Kokand. The house of the cotton magnates, **Vadyaev Brothers**, made from the typical yellow brick, now houses the mayor's office. The building of the **Russo-Asian Bank** on the opposite side of the road, with its voluminous dome, decorative pillars and round windows, still functions as a bank. The post office now occupies the **Potelyakhov House**. The **House of Simkhaev**, who also made their money on cotton, looks as if the proprietor could not decide on what they wanted: classic pillars, façade in the manner of Dutch cities, or a dome for everyone to envy. This part of the city is very nice for walking (elegant avenues shaded by tall trees), and very original due to architecture so unconventional for Uzbekistan; my advice is not to lose the opportunity and enjoy the fantastic exterior of Kokand of early 20th century.

Sights to See: Kokand Art Nouveau

Kokand Branch of the Russo-Asian Bank
Vadyaev House
Simkhaev House
Mandalaka (Mindelaki) House
Branch of the State Bank
Kraft Brothers' House
Siegel House
Commercial School Building
Knabe House

Khasan Umarov

The Uzbek word for a knife is *pichak.* Master knife manufacturers worked across the country: each region needed them to skin the animals or chop the carrots for plov. There were simple household and kitchen knives, and there were expensive knives fit for a Khan, with exquisitely patterned steel, encrusted blades and handles, decorated sheaths; such knives are museum exhibits. There were weapons, too, for instance, sabers. Fergana Valley is leading in the number of workshops still maintaining the ancient craft. The knives you will see in the bazaars of Tashkent and Samarkand, and in the stalls of Bukhara all come from the valley, from Chust of Shahrikhan. However, those are mass produced; but what Khasan Umarov makes is pure art.

His knives have not just encrusted handles, but blades as well; sometimes they are adorned with patterns similar to the national embroidery or Cuphic script. The master uses wood, ivory and goat's bone for handles, as well as jade, brass, and silver. He seldom takes orders: "It is difficult to create when you work not out of the yearning of the soul but out of a customer's will," he says.
+998 91 141 68 89, Khamza Street 5, Jami Mosque

Interiors of the Russo-Asian Bank in Kokand

Kokand halva—a rich, toffee-like traditional sweet

Mirzayunus Umarov and his son Jamshed
They are followers of the great artisan Kadyrzhan Khaidarov, an undisputed authority, founder of the Kokand school of artistic woodcarving, laureate of numerous awards, master of the intricate carving technique *pargori*. When in the Khudayar Khan Palace, pay special attention to the exhibited works of Usto Khaidarov.
+998 91 696 50 26, +998 91 156 4 02, Khoja Dodkho Street, 45

Botyr Baratboev
The works of this ceramics artist demonstrate a striking difference from the ceramics customary in the Fergana Valley. The art of Botyr Baratboev is bold and nonconventional: the well-recognized delicate thin brushwork meets Greek meanders, and oriental beauties are gazing through half-closed lids from the lagans; his still lifes are executed in the abstract manner.
+998 91 201 81 40, Saykhon Street, 2

Avicenna Garden
Plantations of Mehrigiyo are sometimes called one of Avicenna's gardens. A ten-minute drive from the center of Kokand will take you to a stroll in a field of lavender, you will see the olives, coffee, and guava trees, have some herbal tea in a yurt, and replenish your life forces in an aroma therapy room. Of course, you can buy something to take home: how about a cushion made from hand-woven silk and stuffed with dry lavender?
+998 99 888 31 03, Uchkoprik District, Urozimergan Street, 94

Kokand Bazaar: Halva, Flatbreads, and Kurt
The signature sweet treat of Kokand known across the country is the **sweet milk halva**, quite different from the sunflower seed halva that we know. This dessert with a clear milky taste is quite soft but firm and keeping its shape for months (provided that the people keeping it have strong will power). Halva may come packaged from factories, but the greatest selection of it is in the bazaar, where you go from stall to stall, trying each variety (you are in the East, so it is expected) to choose the most delicious one.

Another unique find of Kokand bazaars are **patir flatbreads**, their dry and crispy center stamped with the baker's name and phone number. Who was the first baker to turn a flatbread into their visiting card is a matter of history, but such "branded bread" is now a signature thing of the Fergana Valley.

Kurt (kurut) is a dry fermented milk product sold not only across Uzbekistan but in the entire Central Asia. It is known for its long shelf life, spicy and tart flavor, and its special property: it relieves symptoms of motion sickness. The most scrumptious and massive balls of kurt I saw in my trips over the country were in Kokand: they were the size of a good fig. To prepare kurt, people curdle the milk. The resulting *katyk*, resembling very thick sour cream, is hanged in muslin bags to drain all the liquid. The balls are rolled by hand and dried, indoors or out, to achieve the desired hardness.

Where to Eat: National Cuisine

O'rda Café
A modern two-story café directly opposite the Khudayar Khan Palace features spacious communal dining halls, private booths, and even a terrace with views of the palace. The menu blends local and European cuisine.
+998 73 541 50 50, +998 91 685 50 50, Turkistan Street, 4A

Kokand Choyxona
One of the oldest and most beloved teahouses of the city, Kokand is situated along the highway leading from Kokand toward Tashkent. This multi-format venue welcomes walk-ins for meals, accepts advance plov orders, and offers seating at regular tables, on shaded topchans beneath trees, or in private booths. Be sure to try their tandoor-baked fish, sazan (wild carp) or Bely Amur (grass carp), a rare preparation method.
+998 95 400 65 29

Sharshara Choyxona
The classic city choyxona near the Norbyt-biya Madrasah now used as a mosque. It is only open for a couple of hours in the morning, after the morning prayer offering a solid breakfast of kabobs, kalla gusht, boiled chickpeas, kaymak, and tea. Like many choyxonas in the valley, it is a men's only establishment.
+998 91 655 15 15, +998 97 555 15 15

Karvon Choyxona
One of the oldest and most popular teahouses of the city with a blossoming garden, a fountain, dining halls designed in the national style, and shaded topchans. Signature dish: Kokand plov.
+998 91 200 70 73, Rakhima Aminova Street, 3A, karvonchoyxona.taplink.ws

Oilaviy Kafe
A popular inexpensive café offering traditional Uzbek food within a walking distance from the Khudayar Khan Palace, with a playground for children.
+998 91 201 49 09

Samsa at Romanka
These cafés feature neither official names nor name plates, and the locals find them by the codewords "Samsa at Romanka." Near the Knabe Mansion in the Istiklal Street, there are several tandoors and topchans under the sprawling trees next to some fountains. The samsa is hefty, made from soft non-flaky dough with lots of meat and less onions. The right way to eat it is to turn it upside down and cut off the bottom: you will have a bowl of meat. Sprinkle a couple of teaspoons full of fiery hot tomato sauce—and enjoy.

Urumchi
A simple yet modern café serving Uyghur cuisine: five types of lagman, manti, chuchvara, ganfan (traditional Uyghur rice-and-meat dish), dapanji (a spicy mix of chicken, vegetables, and spices), and other traditional dishes.
+998 88 627 00 20, +998 90 550 59 59, Baka Chorsu Street, 1A, Kattagan t.me/urumchitaomlarikokand

Samsa from the tandoor at Romanka

Hotels of Kokand

Silk Road Kokand Hotel
Hotels in Kokand outshine the rest of the Fergana Valley. This is a benefit of the Handicrafters' Festival that draws many guests including international visitors. The Silk Road Kokand Hotel stands as the finest in the city (maybe, even in the valley). Its minimalist yet cozy rooms feature excellent lighting, spacious shower cabins, and impeccable cleanliness. The finely tended garden with pavilions adds significant appeal.
+998 99 363 33 66, Turkistan Street, 57 A

Asmald Palace Hotel
A new hotel within a short walking distance from the Khudayar Khan Palace and Jami Mosque features a conference hall, just in case you might be visiting Kokand for business.
+998 73 541 70 00, Yangi Hayot Street, 62A

A Dance of Discourse
Askiya is the name of humorous conversational battles, an original form of spoken folk craft found only in the Fergana Valley. It is a men's craft: pawky improvised jokes, skill of quickly finding the rebuke to the opponent's utterance and making the audience laugh. It is a dialogue, a game that two can play, or a verbal genre, a dance of discourse reflecting observations of life. Askiya is worth seeing and listening (in the Uzbek language) during the Navruz and other great festivals.

Fergana

Fergana is the "most Russian" of all cities of Uzbekistan. Founded by General Mikhail Skobelev in 1876 for the efficient administration of the lands of the defeated Kokand Khanate, it was an oasis of European culture in Central Asia. Fergana was actually a satellite city of Margilan, its original name being New Margilan. Its location was chosen strategically to ensure comfortable connections to the largest cities of the region.

The city was built according to the meticulous plan of the military engineer Ivan Zhilin. The plan provided for a fortress, a grid of streets and avenues, neat green residential quarters with gardens and bath houses. Contemporary architects famous in the region made their contributions to the design of the city, e.g. Georgy Svarichevsky designed the building of the grainage factory and men's gymnasium. The military engineer Sinclair designed the building of the Military Assembly (think of the level of engineers' training!). The **mansion of the Military Governor** still amazes with a combination of classic architecture and Oriental mullion windows. Fergana served as the regional administrative capital despite lagging behind other cities in both population and commercial activity. The city boasted a cycling track, Orthodox and Protestant churches, a Catholic chapel, coffeehouses, confectioneries, and milliner's shops. In short, it was a colonial hub far from the imperial center, with its own comfortable way of life.

In 1886, **Alexander Nikolaevich Volkov** was born in the family of a doctor of a regiment quartered in Fergana. Later he became one of the main personalities in the art of Uzbekistan. Passionately devoted to his exotic motherland, a Russian by origin, Volkov studied in St. Petersburg. He had the Silver Age running through his veins, with its attention to mysticism, to the East, to the synergy of arts (Volkov was not only a painter, but a poet of no small merit reading his verses aloud in the streets and from tops of minarets). His European gaze on landscapes and people of Uzbekistan, infused with curiosity and affection, and an ability to find poetry in cotton and corn harvesting, construction sites, teahouse gatherings, caravans, and potters at work defined his artistic signature. Alexander Volkov taught young artists, directed several museums, and made invaluable contributions to the art culture of Uzbekistan. His works are exhibited in the Savitsky Museum (Nukus), the State Art Museum of Uzbekistan (Tashkent), State Tretyakov Gallery and the Museum of Oriental Art in Moscow. Volkov's legacy remains a cornerstone of the artistic identity of the country.

In the Soviet era, Fergana Region was one of the country's most important cotton growing and processing locations. The majority of population spoke Russian; even today, the locals say that knowledge of Russian is a matter of personal dignity. The city had well-developed cultural scene: the Russian Drama Theater was one of the symbols of Fergana; and Gavriil Abdulov, who lived the greater part of his life in Fergana, was one of its directors and, actually, its main figure. Here, in Fergana, his son Alexander Abdulov was born and raised. There was the Higher Teacher-Training Institute in the city, and it used to be one of the most reading cities of Central Asia and the first in the numbers of sold books. To this day, there are more book stores and press kiosks in Fergana and across the Valley than anywhere else in Uzbekistan.

Where to Eat: National Cuisine

Tulpor Oshxona
In Uzbek, *tulpor* means a racehorse. Horses and *kupkari*, traditional Central Asian sporting competition, are the main interests of the owner, Ilkhom Madiyarov. This is a simple, no-frills roadside spot with open-air topchans and indoor tables. Primarily frequented by men, it draws crowds for its kabobs, Fergana-style plov, rich bone-in shurpa, and fried liver in a fragrant sauce of tomato and herbs, the latter prepared to perfection.

Charkhpalak Choykhona
A spacious, highly popular teahouse near Fergana airport. The murmur of water and rustle of willow crowns fill the air. They serve both plov and samsa, but the real standout is their tandoori meat, prepared in the style of Surxondaryo or Qashqadaryo, with archa, or juniper branches.
+998 91 105 64 05

Oybek Osh Markazi
A very popular oshxona with arguably the best (the locals say so) wedding Tashkent-style plov (wedding plov means lots of ingredients!)
+998 93 184 80 08, Oybek Street, 1

Hammabop Choyxona
One of the best known teahouse in the city featuring an extensive national menu and Oriental vibes: carved lighting fixtures, a fountain, and some quails in cages, plus, impeccable plov.
+998 99 996 45 54, Bakhor Street, 20A

Choyxona 777+
Another location where dwellers of Fergana go for some plov themselves and where they take their guests.
+998 95 402 87 07, Alisher Navoiy Street, 55

Brown Sugar Coffee House
A modern café with vintage charm and jazz music playing in the evenings. The menu extends beyond coffee and desserts to full meals, including dishes cooked over an open flame.
+998 55 804 56 37, Khudjant Street, 4

Wine Garden

Fergana Winery (Fergana France LLC) is one of the most up-to-date and best-equipped enterprises that I have seen in Uzbekistan. It owns 300 hectares of plantations. Its products include grape wines and fruit wines, that are quite rare in Uzbekistan and that are worthy of your attention. Wines of quince, cherry, apple and pomegranate are available in four levels of sweetness; and both sweet and dry fruit wines are well balanced and enjoyable, this being an unexpected surprise for dry fruit wines. Their brandy, Napoleon, could hardly contest originality, but the Lady Brandy line of fruity, sweeter and less alcoholic distillates, can become a notable discovery.

The winery has it all to welcome tourists, for example, a cellar paved with stone with neat rows of barrels of Maykop oak. The spacious Wine Garden Restaurant, a few steps away from the entrance to the winery, is an excellent spot for tasting food and wine specialties of Fergana Valley. Finally, the winery owns a hotel under the same name: seven guest rooms in the midst of vineyards reaching far beyond the horizon just a quarter of an hour's drive from the center, with a finely tended garden, open swimming pool, and a sports ground.
Wine Garden Restaurant: +998 90 407 00 27, Okibat Street, 1
Wine Garden Hotel: +998 98 150 21 12, Shekshura settlement, Yangi Asr Street, 1

Hotels of Fergana

Emin Hotel
A new European-style business hotel in the city center. Stylish yet understated, with no gilded excess.
+998 73 244 22 88, B. Marginali Street, 22

Tantana Hotel Fergana
One of Fergana's newest additions. Freshly renovated, with restrained European-style decor and spacious rooms, the hotel is conveniently located: a twenty-minute walk to Central Park and just 10 minutes by taxi to the airport.
+998 99 349 78 78, Al-Ferghani Street, 122A

Asia Hotel Fergana
A hotel from an Uzbek chain with an excellent reputation, now after a fresh renovation of one of the city's oldest accommodations. Features a sauna and an open swimming pool.
+998 73 244 13 26, Alisher Navoiy Street, 26

Voyage Hotel
A family hotel in the center of the city with a beautiful courtyard overgrown with vines. The owners and the staff can be your guides and advisors in the region.
+998 73 226 45 70, Timur Street, 33A

Margilan

One of the most ancient cities of the Fergana Valley, Margilan is known as the place where mulberry silkworm was cultivated and silk was produced. In today's Uzbekistan, Margilan has the reputation of the silk capital of the country, although manufacturing of the fabric was developed in other regions as well. According to a legend, a Chinese princess, married off to a man she never loved, smuggled several silkworm cocoons hidden in her hair *en route* to her husband's place in Bukhara. This brilliantly orchestrated act ended China's global monopoly on silk production: a fiercely guarded secret held for 3,000 years, suddenly was revealed.

Another legend that you are sure to hear in Margilan tells about Alexander the Great, who feasted on some chicken and bread here, *murg-i-non* in the Tajik language. It is established, however, that Alexander never set foot in the city, and the etymology of its name points at something similar to a "green meadow."

Margilan had never been a particularly large city of the Fergana Valley, but its position near the intersection of trade routes made it a bustling trade hub. Manufacturing of silk fabrics in Margilan is dated back to 3rd century. One of the main locations where the guests are taken is the **Sayyed Akhmad-Khoja Madrasah** built in 19th century, now functioning as a crafts center. Artisans process fabrics, decorate them with stamp printing, and carve the wood. This place houses the workshops and the showroom of *Rasuljon Mirzaakhmedov* (*+998 99 608 43 30*), the most famous *abrband* of Uzbekistan. His workshop manufactured fabrics for several collections of the house of Oscar de la Renta. The first of them dated back to 2005, it had *adras* (cotton mix fabric with a noble matte sheen) and *bakhmal*, a material brought back from oblivion (silken velvet manufactured using the abra technology).
The operations of the workshop of Usto Mirzaakhmedov look like those of any other designer studio: the customers browse catalogs of traditional designs, choose the pattern in the desired color scheme using the computer. Following that, the weavers receive a sketch and start the process of manufacturing, marking the pattern on the threads on the loom isolating the parts that are not to be dyed. Then, the dyeing process starts with natural or artificial pigments; after which the weaving starts using antique looms with up to 8 pedals depending on the complexity of the pattern.

You can observe the entire process of silk manufacturing by hand, like in the old times, at the **Yodgorlik Factory** (*+998 90 302 08 73, +998 90 561 01 05, I. Zakhiriddin Stteet, 138*), largest in the country. The flagship of traditional fabric manufacturing and almost the economic mainstay of Margilan, the factory was founded with the effort of Turgunboy Mirzaakhmedov, Rasuljon's father. His story is dramatic, as that of revival of many other crafts in Uzbekistan: in the Soviet times, private manufacturing was not encouraged, and processing and sale of fabrics made by hand according to ancient samples cost many artisans their freedom in the late 1980s. Turgunboy Mirzaakhmedov was no exception... When he was free and got back home, he did not abandon his ideas: he recreated the extremely complicated *eight-pedal adras* loom, wove the silken fabric, and opened the first independent cooperative.

For those interested in Margilan cuisine, **O'ram Choyxona** is the right destination: at the entrance, vendors sell homemade chickpeas, meat, soups, and organ meat dishes; in other stalls, you will find glossy flatbreads, and kebabs are frying nearby. Choose what you like, order some tea, and take a place on a topchan inside a dining hall with large windows.
The richest selection of fabrics, made in Margilan and beyond, is available on the **colorful Kumtepa Bazaar**, 5 kilometers

Traditional weaving

away from the center of the city; it is open on Thursdays and Sundays.

Nurmukhammad Valiyev
A weaver in the fourth generation, he combines the local heritage and the trends of the new age in patterned and single-colored canvases, and experiments with materials (not only silk and cotton, but wool, for example).
+998 93 980 66 39, Al-Farobi Street, 8

Ikathouse
A guesthouse owned by the Mirzaakhmedov family offering top-level hospitality and possibilities to learn first-hand information about the silk industry of Margilan.
+998 90 303 38 00, Ipak Yoli Street, 133

Altyaryk Samsa
Treat yourself for some special samsa and make a stop in Altyaryk, Mustakillik Street, *en route* from Margilan to Rishtan. It looks like a bigger twin of Jizzakh samsa, with non-flaky dough, coarsely chopped beef, a generous helping of tail fat, and low on onions. The locals say that Jizzakh samsa enjoys an unfair advantage and is known better, but they are sure: Altyaryk is famous not only for its grapes, but tandoor samsa as well.

Rishtan

Each region of Uzbekistan was manufacturing ceramics: every family in any part of the country needed crockery and large *khuma* jugs to store provisions, and lamps, also made of clay. It was in Fergana Valley, however, that the traditional style managed to survive so well. In the late 19th and early 20th centuries, the center of ceramics production was Rishtan, a small kishlak, now a town, one hour away from either Fergana or Kokand. It carries on its destiny, maintains its positions and relies on continuity of old traditions and creative reconceptualization of its legacy. Much longer than in any other regional center of ceramics, Rishtan continued manufacturing not just everyday crockery, but expensive items that could stand in a prominent place to show the status of the home and its owner.
As you look at the impeccably decorated Khudayar Khan Palace in Kokand, glittering under the sun in a rainbow of colors, you see the work of the legendary ceramic masters of Rishtan, Usto Jalil and Usto Kari. They and their apprentices led the tilework, and their legacy includes establishing the still-dominant production techniques, revived using the recipes brought by artisans from Kashgar.

The potters of Rishtan, like all other artisans of Uzbekistan, had a world of trouble with the Soviet regime that tried to bring unification everywhere and make everyone work in collectives. A ceramics factory was established (no longer working today), leaving an abundant legacy of mass-produced off-the-press crockery produced to this day, sold in every bazaar and market and often called *Rishtan ceramics*. It is catching the eye, but it is not the ceramics that brought about the name and glory of Rishtan.

What sets the *artistic* ceramics of Rishtan aside is the technology of its making. First, the local red clay is highly plastic, and, in the potter's words, it *hears* its master potter; the pieces made from it withstand firing at high temperatures becoming especially durable. Second, local masters use a special kind of glaze made by burning the grass growing in the wilderness that leaves a special alkali or *ishkor*. Once copper oxide is added to this colorless mixture, the lagan or a bowl immediately spring to life bursting with turquoise, and iron oxide produces an intricate play of ochre and golden hues. The old technique was revived in the 1970–1980s, when the country experienced a booming interest towards traditional crafts. Modern ceramics of Rishtan exists, in a lot of ways, thanks to the effort of the great Sharafiddin Yusupov, who was able to make a success with the traditional ishkor-based glaze.

Khoja Ilgor Complex at the edge of the town is a place filled with transient beauty. A cemetery, a mausoleum and a mosque special for the ornamentation of the central part of the ceiling, where patterns of dark-green, blue and azure make an intricate play with the colors of Rishtan ceramics. The story goes that when on their pilgrimage, local women brought here broken or defective crockery made by Rishtan potters, considering it to be sacred.
There are about twenty potters and ceramics artisans in Rishtan, whose pieces deserve the name of works of art. The **International Ceramic Center** (*Fergana Street, 222*) was founded to bring them together in one place giving the travelers the opportunity to have a full view of entire Rishtan. Many of artisans still prefer to have guests in their workshop homes. Please arrange your visit in advance.

List of master potters continuing traditions of Rishtan ceramics:
Muzaffar Saidov
Ismailjon Komilov
Mukhamadali Tadzhaliev
Mahmud Azizov
Odiljon Nigmatov
Alisher Nazirov
Rustam Usmanov
Bakhtiyor Nazirov
Odiljon Azizov
Akrom Isakov
Ganizhon Elibayev
Numon Dehkanov
Diyorbek Nazirov
Navruz Dehkanov

Workshops of these artisans are located in the International Ceramic Center of Rishtan. Their vision is best described as author's transformation of traditional regional styles.

Islimi style patterns (minuscule ornament based on spiral and bindweed motif covering the entire surface of a plate) and *girih* (geometrical patterns) are novelties for Rishtan ceramics, and it is generally the style of choice of younger artisans. Crockery depicting tourist sights, people, fruit (pomegranates or figs), large patterns resembling ones found on textiles, ceramics with brown background and loose white patterns, as well as plates, saucers and teapots fully covered with minute ornaments are factory made; they have nothing in common with the authentic Rishtan ceramics.

House, museum and workshop of Bakhtiyor Nazirov
Bakhtiyor Nazirov is the younger brother of Alisher Nazirov. Together with his son Diyorbek, he continues the dynasty. While the works of his older brother are exquisite and conceptual, Bakhtiyor's pieces demonstrate a perfect balance of aesthetics and utility. His crockery brightens up the household life every day, therefore, it makes all life brighter. Traditional *ishkor* glaze, well-recognizable turquoise

and blue colors shine in his smaller articles: small bowls, plates, and glasses. Bakhtiyor-aka loves guests and cooks impeccable plov.
+998 93 640 58 69, Fergana Street, 197

House, museum and workshop of Rustam Usmanov
Rustam Usmanov graduated from the Tashkent Institute of Arts and Theater and worked at the Rishtan Ceramic Factory for several years in various positions, including that of Chief Artist. He studied the old ceramics of the Fergana Valley, and gathered a worthy collection of old Rishtan pieces in his workshop. He was among the first to open his house to the guests.
+998 91 681 23 91, Roshidoni Street, 230

House, museum and workshop of Sharafiddin Yusupov
A Fellow of the Uzbekistan Academy of Fine Arts, Sharafiddin Yusupov was one of the best-known ceramists of the country. His achievement is the rebirth of the blue ceramics of Rishtan.
+998 90 131 10 81, Roshidoni Street, 55

Asliddin Choyxona
This choyxona is known in Rishtan as the "Choyxona on water"; indeed, the topchan platforms hang over the turbulent stream that ensures coolness even on hottest days. This is an authentic roadside choyxona standing by the highway leading to Kokand. They cook some very good Rishtan plov here: with tail fat, small pieces of lamb, with light *chungara devzira* rice.
+998 90 409 97 97

Terrassa Restaurant
A modern spacious restaurant on the ring-road that you can't miss. Rishtan plov cooked to order, and oxtail shurpa is definitely worth trying.
+998 88 538 88 88, +998 91 200 66 66, Fergana Street, 54A

Ceramics is not the only signature craft of Rishtan: bordering on Kyrgyzstan, the town is home for 150 Kyrgyz families, and almost each of them is skilled in working with sheep's wool: looming, weaving, and felting. The family of *Bakhrom and Gulkhobor Gafurov* welcomes guests to demonstrate all the stages of a small family business: fleecing, making the thread by hand, weaving carpets, making gelted cloth and other pieces.
+998 91 106 10 83, Rishtan District, Oq-Yer Village, Okpamir Street, 12

The Alchemist
"Back in the Soviet days, Rishtan had a Ceramic Factory," recalls Alisher Nazirov, "but people working with ceramics were considered second-rate, odd men. You were a potter, you found it hard even to get married." Alisher, now one of the most famous ceramics artists of Rishtan, never had prestige as a reason to chose his profession. "Well, at the age of twelve I did not think about getting married," Alisher says laughing, while we walk around the courtyard of his workshop, filled with golden sunlight. He was on a school excursion to the local ceramics factory and made his decision; his father, a teacher, did not object. Thus, Alisher went to learn his art, not to a vocational school, but to a master ceramist, the Usto. Many times in his story, and the story is as colorful and easy-going as the ornaments of his pieces, Alishr Nazirov recalls secrets of technology never described in books. In a spoken tradition from master to the disciple, the secrets of glazing, shaping, and painting are handed over. His story mentions wild herbs for shiny surfaces,

stones for fireproofing, red clay of Rishtan that becomes alive under skillful fingers, and oxides of metals reacting differently with the glazing to produce different colors... True alchemy!

Among potters, there are *kuzagars*, specializing in shaping the items, and *nakkoshi*, doing the painting. Alisher Nazirov says he is an artist, in the first place, but he trains his students in such a way that they could be able to work by hand only: in his words, a true master needs to feel the shape by their fingertips. I have a good example to prove it: I see a fifteen-year-old boy working blindfolded, and perfectly shaped jug comes out of his hands. The way his fingers move reflect hours and hours of training. The patterns are also painted by touch after being scratched on clay. This is how Alisher Nazirov's workshop creates dimensional multi-layered Rishtan ceramics.

Every piece created in this workshop is decorative and functional at the same time, each piece is multi-dimensional and alive. Some are covered with a glaze that has almost no shine, like the museum anti-reflective coating, providing a clear view of the tiniest details. Some are covered with glossy glaze that stands out when oily plov is placed on a lagan. The master even took care of the people who would wash that lagan, provideding a sophisticated pattern on the side usually not seen by people's eyes; at the same time, the glaze and the clay are extremely robust. My heart skips a beat every time I see how casually the master treats his valuable pieces. This is another difference of artistic ceramics of Rishtan from mass-produced factory items: the latter is almost single-use, quickly covered with scratches and chippings.

Alisher Nazirov spent a few years in Japan. "The Master we worked with could not believe that my glaze comes from ash," the Usto recalls the story of how the Rishtan *ishkor* met the *suzuyaki* ceramics from the Noto Peninsula. He remembers his admiration at the way the Japanese preserve the technology itself, the kilns, the potter's wheels, and shows a 150-years-old wheel of stone and apricot tree that miraculously survived the turbulent 20th century. Alisher Nazirov met the famous Master Asakura Isokichi, chevalier of the Order of Cultural Merit. "Our masters deserve such orders, too, and there are many of them across the republic," the Usto says. Who—if not they—contribute to the Cultural Merit?
+998 94 659 59 08, a.n.nazirov@gmail.com

Andijan

Historical threads connect Andijan with India and reach the Crown of the British Empire. It was in Andijan, in the year 1483, in the family of the Fergana Emir, a son was born: his name was **Zahir-ud-Din Muhammad Babur**, who became the Padishah of the Empire of Baburids, also known as the Mughal Empire. One of the symbols of India, the majestic Taj Mahal, was built by a descendant of Babur—and of Timur, because Babur was his great-great grandson.

Babur was a Timurid by his father's ancestry and a Genghisid by that of his mother. The city of Samarkand, that he attempted to conquer three times, was his blood calling him, not just the vanity or greed. He failed to defeat Shaybani Khan who controlled those areas in the late 15th century. He chose a different route, made his way through

Rishtan potter Alisher Nazirov in his workshop

Ceiling at Jami Mosque in Andijan

Afghanistan, reached the North of India and founded his own empire that had survived until 1858, when English troops stormed Delhi. The Koh-I-Noor diamond, now the Jewel of the British Crown, came into the hands of Babur in his conquest of India and for several centuries adorned the throne of his dynasty. Babur rests in a garden complex that was made in Kabul, his residence and safe haven in times of wars. In Andijan, there exists a symbolic tomb of Babur in a mausoleum in the **Babur Park** on a slope of a hill.

For Andijan, Babur is as much a *genius loci* as Timur for Samarkand. The merit lies not in the monuments he built or conceived, but in his journal known as **Babur-name**. His memoirs reveal his native city as the largest fortress of the region famous for its sweet pears and melons, fatty hares and men of great beauty. He wrote of the terrible fever that seized Andijan, of the cities around, of his own victories and failures, about campaigns and peaceful life. His journal is an extremely valuable document, a witness of the era providing us with information about the history, daily life, culture, flora and fauna. The museum in the Babur Park concentrates on the literary heritage and life of Babur.

Andijan is known for the **Devonaboy Mosque** with its two high minarets. Not quite usual for Uzbekistan, it was built in the late 19th century and reconstructed in the present times. It stands next to the large **Jomi Complex** featuring the painted ceiling of the summer mosque and the minaret standing 32 meters tall right in the center of the courtyard, following the tradition of the valley. A few years ago, the rooms in the central part of the complex were occupied by artisans' workshops, but today the jewelers, tailors, embroiderers and metalworkers returned to the **Sayyid Ahmad Khoja Hotel** (*+998 93 781 96 77, A. Fitrata Street, 256*). A rich merchant built it as a venue to welcome his business partners; it included a mosque, a hammam, guest rooms, and conference rooms: everything it takes to do successful deals. After the devastating earthquake of 1902, the newly built complex featured restorations that showcased the vividness of colors and exquisiteness of ornaments adorning the details of interior and exterior decorations.

Potter Mirzobakhrom Abduvakhobov in his studio

The Dynasty

The giant lagans made in the family of the Andijan artist ceramist Mirzobakhrom Abduvakhobov were used to serve the plov in the best choyxonas in the city. *Spinning* the great plates, as the master says, and painting them to make the plov taste even better, was a secret guarded in the family. Fifteen generations of potters is not a joke, it is a veritable dynasty! The lagan is considered almost the most difficult piece to manufacture: hard to make and hard to fire in the kiln, it requires close attention, to say nothing about the intricate painting: traditionally, lagans feature symbolic ornaments providing protection from the evil eye and securing good luck, strong health, and an ample family...

"I was ahead of my time in 1973," he says, as he recalls his work in Tashkent in the experimental ceramics shop, inventing souvenirs that traveled across the USSR and abroad, near and far, in the luggage of people who came here as holidaymakers or as business travelers. He participated in the 1974 Central Asian Seminar for artists dedicated to preservation of the valley's traditional blue ceramics. At the same time, the master remembers all styles that the local artisans used, including his father and grandfathers: the robust utilitarian unglazed ceramics, pieces slightly touched by white, and the traditional yellow and green color scheme.
A visit to his workshop produces and impression similar to an experience one gets in a museum, as one looks at the unique shapes of items standing in the niches in the ancient brickwork of his grandfather's living room. One can see the goblets placed in prominent places

to show the wealth of the house to the guests, suspended vessels to sell kaymak, deep bowls for plov standing on a tall stand to allow the oil gather in the center, kozon lids called *damtavok* that prevented the steam from escaping and making the rice exceptionally soft, and *taksuma*, rotating layered bowls to serve jams and nuts. Many of these shapes are only existent because Mirzobakhrom remembers them and keeps making them maintaining the dynasty. He explains, "My father and grandfather made even the utility items as pieces of art." In the courtyard, I see his granddaughter next to the chicken pen: she feeds the birds, sprinkling the seeds from a brightly painted bowl, ideally fitting the child's palm: in Andijan, such bowls were traditionally made on a small stand for the sake of ergonomics.

Usto believes that his son Ulugbek will continue his craft; at the same time, he says that each of his sons and grandsons knows their way with the potter's wheel. On the table, there are samples of ceramic tile, modern, but with recognizable Oriental motifs, highly demanded by designers of hotels and restaurants. His son does not manufacture traditional Andijan ceramics: he works in Tashkent looking for a balance between the craft and the commerce. Mirzobakhrom himself still uses hand-operated millstones to grind the pigments. These mills have been with the family for centuries. He continues spinning, or shaping, the gigantic lagans, up to 75 cm in diameter, by hands, never with a mold. He still fires them in a wood-fired kiln, because Andijan has problems with gas and electricity. This is why he does not manufacture his pieces to order: his production capacity is not enough. "This is why everyone gives up," says the master potter. "I am the only one who remains."
+998 93 257 12 95, Magzhuri Street, 307

Shakhrixon
If you have even half a day to spare, take a trip from Andijan to Shakhrixon, a town famed for its knives. Its brand new craft center houses 32 workshops, market stalls, and a small museum displaying a collection of traditional skullcaps and blades.
+998 94 397 10 10

One of the prominent *pichockchi* of Uzbekistan, master knifemaker Rakhmatkhoja Alikhujaev (*+998 94 102 79 42*) is known in the town as Eshon-aka. He lives in the mahalla named after his grandfather, legendary Ubaidullokhuji, in the street named after his father, also a legendary master, Alikhuji. The majority of his knives are nothing less than works of art, each in a handmade sheath decorated in the lacquer miniature or woodcarving technique; at the same time, he makes handy tools for everyday work, such as carving knives, slicers, and shears, some of them cutting through metal.

Where to Eat: National Cuisine

The Eski Bazaar of Andijan is one of the best in the country! It is huge and vibrant, and it consists of two parts. The first section meets you with long stalls of rice, kilometers of delicious flatbreads, piles of juicy apples, crates of grapes and so many more gifts of the generous Fergana Valley. Its second section is a market of crafted goods, with stalls and workshops located in the ground floors of houses on either side of narrow streets of the Old Town. Where one part of

Sweet Fergana Valley figs at Andijan Bazaar

At Andijan Bazaar, selling home appliances

the bazaar flows into another, there are stalls with Andijan street food: boiled chickpeas sold in paper bags, organ meats and sausages of all kinds and sorts.

The Andijan Bazaar is *true*. Seldom visited by tourists, it stands before a traveler in all its raw natural beauty, telling so much about the local people, customs and habits as to defy any guidebook. Pans for hammam, pails to boil the laundry, samovars for choyxonas, outdoor washbasins, kozons, rolling pins of all shapes, stamps for flatbreads, long-handled ladles to take samsa out of the tandoor... What else? Warm leather *mahsa* boots, worn indoors and outdoors, with galoshes; Andijan black-and-white skullcaps; knives and cleavers; *kapkyr*, special flat slotted spoons for plov, featuring long handles; wooden cribs and baby walkers... Many of the items sold on the bazaar are manufactured right here, in the workshops, smithies and carpenters' shops.

Eco Fish Restaurant
While they serve meat here, the real draw for Andijan locals is the fire-grilled fish: trout, carp, and zander. Guests can dine in one of six yurts set up on the grounds.
+998 97 339 30 00, Oltyn Kon Street, 14

Bo'ston City Choyxona
A classic Andijan teahouse, one of the most beloved in the town. Its tiled courtyard, finely tended garden, and soaring fountain (offering some respite from the heat) create a serene atmosphere. Spacious private rooms and open-air pavilions accommodate groups of all sizes, even large gatherings. And the plov is simply excellent!
+998 95 201 00 04, Uzmon Yusupov Street

O'rikzor Choyxona
A beloved teahouse for many, located behind the Golden Valley (Oltin Vodiy) Hotel, boasts authentic plov and a huge pool in the grounds. Ask a local, and chances are that one of their best childhood memories have something to do with this choyxona.
+998 90 253 37 73, Microdistrict 3

Tandir Kabob Bog'ishamol
An incredibly popular Andijan café specializing in tandoor-cooked meats. Its sprawling green grounds feature private dining cabins and halls of varying sizes, plus a children's play area. Be sure to ask for a guided tour to see the multi-tiered racks used to lower meat into the tandoors!
+998 91 612 00 05, Bog'ishamol Ring Junction

Cho'ntak Choyxona
This well-known choyxona is in Asak on the way from Fergana to Andijan; it stands on higher grounds offering a spectacular view of the area. One of the main dishes is **braised neck of lamb**, a signature dish of Andijan. With less connective tissue than beef neck, it is cooked low and slow for 3 or 4 hours until very tender. The rich stock is served in a separate bowl.
+998 94 106 30 83

O'rdak Choyxona
A famous teahouse specializing in poultry. A very simple venue for the locals with incredibly delicious food.
+998 93 243 00 11

Academy of Rice
In every bazaar of every city and town in the Fergana Valley, you will see some varieties of rice you have not seen before.

If you ask an oshpaz or a foodlover about the difference of the Kokand plov from the Andijan plov, one of the answers will surely be "rice." The popularity of rice depends on what kind of rice is cultivated in the area. It is always better to learn the specifics of rice while visiting a bazaar, strolling along the stalls with dunes and barkhans of rice, reading the price tags and talking to salespersons.

Devzira is the best known rice from the Fergana Valley recognizable for its longitudinal groove on each grain. It is delicately hulled. While cooking, it absorbs much water and increases in size considerably, but it takes in little oil. Another special feature of this sort is its curing in dry hulls for a year (and more!), the grains getting a darker color and malty flavor. All types of devzira are known for increasing in size by up to seven times when cooked.
The white devzira is called chungara: light-colored rice of a pearly, creamy or yellowish color with less solid structure due to a larger content of starch as compared to classic devzira, yet with the same liquid-absorbing properties. Chungara is usually cured for several months.

Devzira bapardoz, devzira qora qiltiriq, devzira nim dasta: these varieties feature grains the color of dark amber due to lengthy fermentation; they are more expensive and seldom seen in regular choyxonas. Usually, they feature in for custom orders of plov; many think that such rice requires great experience and skill. Some of these varieties are not only fermented but slightly smoked as well; one can usually find them only on bazaar of the Fergana Valley.

Lazer rice remains the most popular variety for everyday plov in Uzbekistan. Historically cultivated in Khorezm, this light, long-grain rice contains minimal starch and expands two to three times during cooking.

Alanga rice also comes from Khorezm; this low-maintenance inexpensive grain features rounded shape and minimal starch content.

Avangard rice from Khorezm is beige in color, with medium content of starch.

Hotels of Andijan

Chinor Hotel
A new hotel in the city center, decorated in a restrained European style. Features generous breakfasts and an outdoor pool.
+998 74 226 11 33, Chinobod Street, 1

Premier Hotel
Another novelty on the hotel map of Andijan: gilt excess and exquisite flourish gives way to laconic designer solutions; the hotel features a sauna and a closed swimming pool.
+998 55 202 00 10, Milliy Tiklanish Street, 24

Mosque on the Water
A detour *en route* from Andijan to Namangan in the direction of the border with Kyrgyzstan will bring you to the kishlak of Izbaksan. It has one of the most beautiful architectural monuments of the Fergana Valley: the **Ota-Kuzi Khoja Mosque**. Originally built as a madrasah, now serves as a mosque. The courtyard for the worshippers is covered with a contemporary roof for comfort's sake. However, on the outside, the building that dates back to 1914, with its several elegant minarets and ideally preserved carved wooden

doors, sustained no change. The genius of the builders lay in the fact that the turbulent stream passes directly through the courtyard, forming a *hauz* that gives delicious coolness. Alas, today it is covered with planking for collective worship. It is believed that the same master architect worked on the Ota-Kuzi Khoji Mosque and the Mulla Kyrgyz Madrasah in Namangan.

Namangan

Namangan in the second largest city of Uzbekistan following Tashkent; at the same time, it has so little tourist attention, that occasional visitors of a bazaar form lines of people wishing to share a piece of advice what exactly to visit and to see. No keeper of a mausoleum or a mosque will let you go until you sign the guest book.

Namangan was first mentioned as a fortified city in the late 15th century. It grew in the shadow of the much bigger Akhsikent destroyed in 1620 in a powerful earthquake. The survivors of the catastrophe moved to Namangan. The population of the city began growing rapidly in the beginning of the 20th century, when a railroad connection between Namangan and Kokand was opened. A large archeological park now welcomes guests on *the site of the ruins of Akhsikent* (*Turakurgan District, Shahand settlement, +998 99 993 77 02*). The ground still keeps remains of unique cultural artifacts; and visitors can find ceramic shards and other items from the past. The new director of the historical complex, Rustam Mamadiev, puts every ounce of energy in the development of the project: the archeologists deliver excursions in several languages telling about the first sewage systems made of ceramics, and other engineering advancements that had been ahead of European technology.

Old city Namangan is authentic, unkempt and unpolished, sometimes even lacking asphalt pavement. District mosques, small choyxonas for the locals, women wearing head scarves, long-bearded men, a bazaar of absolutely gigantic proportions, selling everything at once: prayer mats, skullcaps, bunches of isryk (or wild rue, that all-Uzbekistan cure for everything), heavy flatbreads... This established patriarchal community does not seem to have changed over the past century.

Mulla Kyrgyz Madrasah, at the foot of which the bazaar is bustling with life, is one of symbols of Namangan. It bears the name of a rich factory-owner, patron of arts, and architect, whose money—and design—ensured the construction of the building. Erected in 1910–1912, the madrasah with its three domes is classic in shape, featuring the well-recognizable yellow brick (so-called *Nikolaevsky* for its stamp of the coat of arms). At the same time, the ceramic tile, the brickwork of Cufic script, and the design of portals testify to the deep synergy of the traditional Central Asian architecture and the Art Nouveau trends brought by the Russians. Inside the madrasah, the crafts center is open. Marina Dzhabbarova (*+998 93 400 00 43*) started bringing together the best artisans of the city and the region in early 2025. Her plans include master classes of making plov and shirmoy non flatbreads unique to Namangan.

Ota Valixon To'ra Mosque, one of the biggest in Central Asia with its 14-meter dome, now houses an art gallery showcasing the works of local artists. The dome alone is worth your attention, but do not miss the exquisitely carved doors with a fantastic combination of three traditional ornaments: *islimi* bindweed, *girih* geometrical patterns, and calligraphy.

Mausoleum of Khoja Amin in the depths of the old city dates back to the 18th century, although it bears resemblance to pre-Mongolian structures. Looking at its carved finishing, you will be reminded of one of the oldest mosques in Uzbekistan, the Magoki-Attari in Bukhara. Its façade is executed in the technique of carving of unglazed matte terracotta, reflecting the architectural principles of 11th–12th centuries to be pushed out by 15th century with colorful glazed tiling. This is an amazing treasure of ornaments featuring inscriptions, geometrical and floral motifs, and traditional grid and star *girih* patterns. We know the name of the artisan architect, Usto Muhammad Ibrahim, son of Abdurahim, because his work is signed; what we do not know is why this carved mausoleum appeared in Namangan at the time of absolute prevalence of glazed ceramics. The multicolored glazed tile is only used to decorate the entrance portal. On the inside, the walls are covered with a continuous carved decoration against a vibrant background, the centerpiece of which is a Quranic inscription, large and dimensional. Without doubt, this is one of the most beautiful monuments of the Fergana Valley.

Latif Sadriddinov
Latif Sadriddinov is a Namangan master embroiderer. Not too much is known about the art of embroidery in the valley, although here, similar to other parts of Uzbekistan, girls made suzani for their wedding both as a demonstration of the bride's talent and as a charm for the new life. Even the ethnographic expeditions of the 19th–20th centuries, whose findings form the textile collection in the State Museum of Oriental Art in Moscow, brought little embroidery to the imperial capital. The laconic, modest, reserved style of Namangan embroidery with its fine ornaments leaving the most of the surface free stands in the shadow of the vibrant colorful pieces from Bukhara and Nurata. Therefore, Latif and his workshop, employing over 30 people, work little in the traditional Namangan technique, doing custom orders from Bukhara and Samarkand.
+998 90 552 90 36, latif25@mail.ru

Hakim Tajibaev
Creating suzani, clothes and accessories of natural silk with organic dyes for more than twenty years, Hakim Tajibaev continues the family tradition. His workshop trains over 200 students. Hakim's goal is to preserve the authenticity and revive the handiwork techniques of old times. His works are shown in museums of Tashkent and international exhibitions. His son, Abdulbosit Isakzhanov, carries on the family business.
+995 91 340 80 76

Silk Granat
A stunning showroom in the Valley of Legends Theme Park, backed by the tireless entrepreneur Marina Dzhabbarova. Here you will find

Mausoleum of Khoja Amin in Namangan

Gurumsaray ceramics, Chust skullcaps, suzanis from across the country, and bags of silk *bakhmul* fabric. Marina will gladly share contacts of artisans of Namangan. *+998 93 400 00 43, Valley of Legends Theme Park, silkgranat.uz*

Gurumsaray Ceramics
Despite the azure colors, customary for the valley, the ceramics of Gurumsaray are very distinct from Rishtan pieces. Its décor is more archaic, monumental and solemn, and a trained eye will at once notice the influence of the steppes, Kyrguz felted carpets and their background-free ornaments. In case of ceramics, the background and the ornament are equal, and the space between the elements of color itself plays the role of a pattern. Gurumsaray ceramic items are heavier than their Rishtan counterparts. The artisan who raised this unique tradition from the ashes is Vakhobzhon Buvaev. One can say Gurumsaray was lucky: its remote location from large centers of ceramics and tourism helped the local tradition retain its purity and its archaic features. The attention of Usto Buvaev to the authenticity and his great heart prevent the tradition from sinking back into oblivion. So, if you seek the real treasure, you need to head to Gurumsaray: an hour and a half from Namangan... almost in Tajikistan. *+998 93 373 28 49, +998 95 033 08 69, Niyazi Street, 23*

The Miracle of Chust
Artisans of Namangan Region are sure: Damascus steel does not come from Damascus. The Damascus steel is not the most durable steel. The secret of strength and durability was known in Akhsikent, where the blacksmiths knew how to raise the temperature in the furnaces to the required 1600–1700 degrees. The archeological findings confirmed that the ancient Akhsikent was a large center of metallurgy supplying high quality steel to the entire Middle East. Every year, it produced some 5,000 sabers that were taken worldwide by the caravans of the great Silk Road. The largest market was in Damascus, which glorified the brand name of *Damascus steel* in Asia and in Europe. The technology used in Akhsikent was not known anywhere else, and it would take hundreds of years before the Russian metallurgist Anosov would be able to recreate the hard *bulat*: Damascus steel.

In the Western terminology, Damascus steel and *bulat* are not differentiated between, but Uzbek professionals know that the two materials are not the same, even though the patterns on the blades may be characteristic of either. *Damascus steel* is a composite material whose optical effects are the result of heretogeneity of material and technology of manufacturing. *Bulat* is a composite material produced without multiple welding. The pattern of *Damascus steel* is orderly, and that of *bulat* is chaotic; in either case, it is not an embellishment but a proof of extra durability. Nevertheless, as a brand, *Damascus steel* enjoys more popularity than *bulat*.

Knives of Chust are as important a brand of the Fergana Valley as the Rishtan Ceramics. Of course, Chust is not the only knife-making center: many masters work in Shakhrixon, some remain in Andijan and Kokand. The shapes of the blades and handles vary from town to town, and an expert's eye will distinguish an Andijan blade from a Kokand one. It was in Chust, however, that a large factory was situated in the Soviet period,

Potter Vakhobzhon Buvaev in his studio

hence the tradition: a knife, is it? Must be a knife from Chust.

On the Chust bazaar, there are long stalls of knives. The items presented there have no glamor or glitter, no fancy ornaments of expensive knives scattered across the country's souvenir shops to attract visitors. Expensive *bulat* is not sold here, either. The most reliable knives for household needs that are always in high demand are made from old rasp-files and stainless steel, and they sharpen them so well that you can set your mind at rest about them for three or four years.

If you have come this far, do not spend too much time by the stalls with knives; ask someone to take you to the depths of the market, to the smithies. There, in the deafening staccato of hammers and whirring of grinding machines, master knife-makers are to be found. My personal recommendations for renowned Chust masters go to Shukhratzhon Gaffarov (*+998 97 256 77 25*) and Rakhim Ubaidullaev (*+998 90 555 08 58*).

Duppi is the Uzbek word for the skullcap. Traditionally, young women used to wear the skullcaps embroidered with colorful ornaments, but now these items are made to be sold to tourists. However, almost all men continue wearing them, especially here, in the Fergana Valley. The most popular design is white embroidery against the black background: four pepper pods (kalampir) to protect the wearer from the evil eye. The band is embroidered with arcs of varying height, and different regions of Uzbekistan favor different designs. In Chust, up to 80% of women work in skullcap embroidery since they are sold so well across Uzbekistan and many countries of Central Asia. What's more, the *duppi* are foldable! What a practical way of carrying such a tall and elegant headgear!

Where to Eat: National Cuisine

Namangan Region boasts two local signature foods: **shurpa in a jar and shirmoy non flatbreads.** Shurpa is traditionally served in numerous oshxonas across the region and demonstrates the wit of local cooks. One needs a liter glass jar, a metal lid, some lamb, onions, maybe, some garlic to taste, definitely, some salt and water. The most important ingredient is the time: the soup is cooked low and slow on an electric stove for three or four hours, until the meat is tender and the broth is rich. It is delicious as it is, but the shurpa is always better the next day, when all flavors have fully developed.

Shirmoy non flatbreads require serious skill: they are leavened not with yeast but with chickpea and aniseed infusion. The aniseed is boiled for an hour, and the brew is poured over chickpeas and left to ferment for several hours in a warm place (a large bowl of husk and bran over a scarcely warm oven). The chickpeas start foaming, and the foam is mixed with flour to create the starter. The starter also ferments for 5 to 6 hours. Afterwards, flour is added, the flatbreads are formed and baked in a tandoor. You can recognize the shirmoy non by their delicate herby aroma rising from the dough. You can try and but these flatbreads in the Chorsu Bazaar in Namangan or in the *Guzal Kulcha Nonlari* bakery (*+998 90 597 00 06, Guzal Residences*), a true flatbread paradise offering not only the shirmoy non, but a couple of dozens of other varieties.

In the blacksmith's workshop at Chust Bazaar

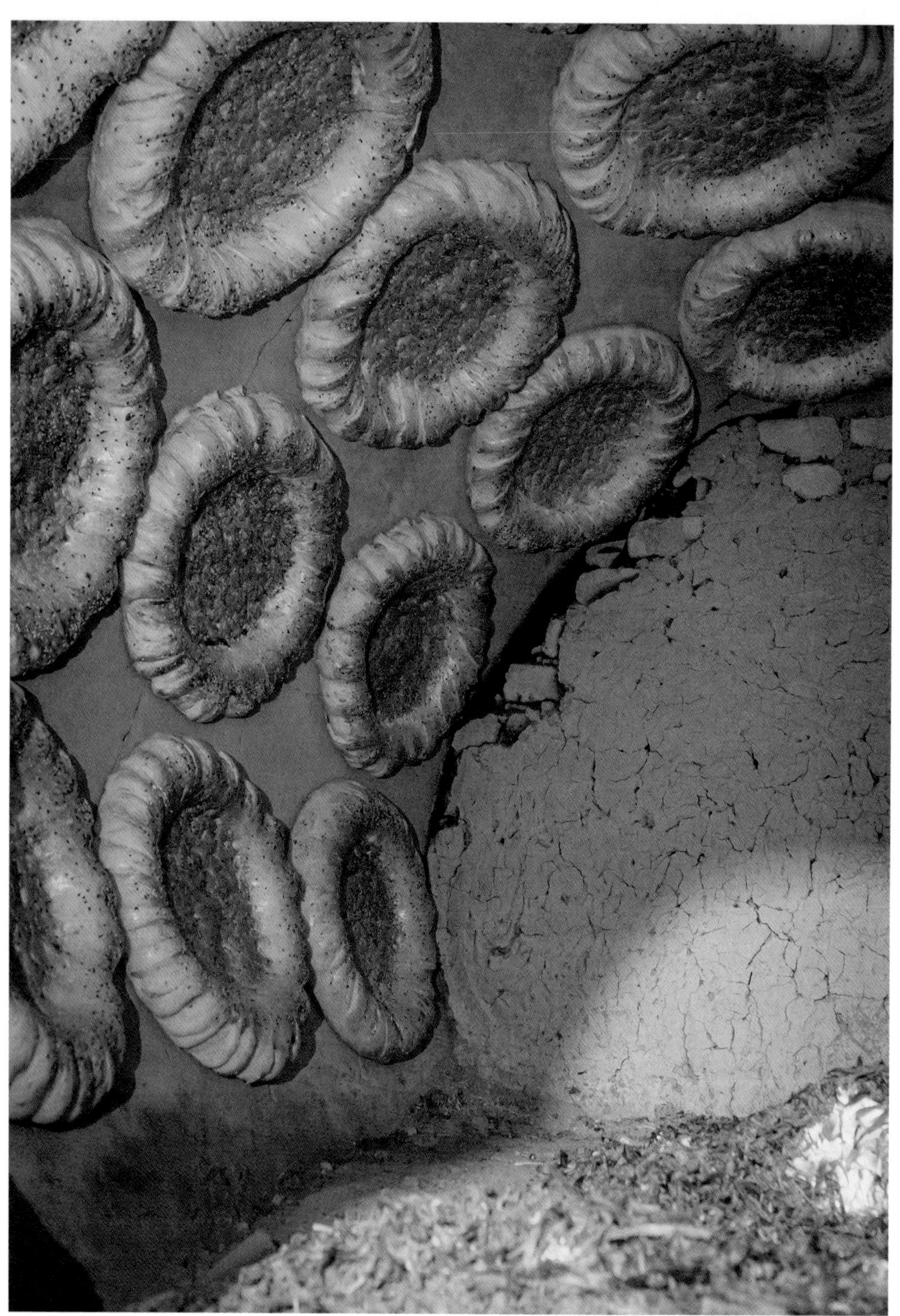
Flatbread baking in a tandoor oven

Kurashxona Bazaar
This is the culinary epicenter of Namangan: a bustling market nestled between the walls of a grand mosque and a roaring canal. Vendors' stalls feature with khasyp, assorted flatbreads, katyk, and nohut shurak. The bazaar opens early: after morning prayers, men gather here for breakfast. What is breakfast in Namangan? Fragrant tea, rich cream, homemade sausages, and piping-hot flatbreads.

Afsona Crepe House
A modern restaurant whose menu features so much more than crepes: yes, they have thirty varieties of crepes with different fillings, but guests come to try the borsch and rassolnik (exotic dishes for Namangan!), for excellent kebabs, khinkali, chebureks and vareniki dumplings. The crepe house, or Blinnaya is in the Valley of Legends Theme Park.
+998 99 222 00 43, Girvonbulok Street, Valley of Legends Theme Park

Al-Mashrik
A spacious, affordable restaurant in the newer district of Namangan featuring a large garden with sprawling persimmon trees and a murmuring fountain. The menu spans everything from a glass of kefir and breakfast pancakes to Turkish pide, expertly prepared kozon-style meats, and kebabs.
Diyonat Street, 26

Sardoba
A traditional oshxona by the Babur Park with delicious devzira rice plov.
+998 90 261 02 00, Nodir Koriev Street, 3

Sayohat
A classic Namangan teahouse with expansive green grounds, soothing murmur of cool water, and private booths for groups of all sizes. The dish to try? Without doubt, the dark rice plov.
+998 99 130 66 66, Navoiy Street, 63

Guliston
A very popular choyxona on the side of the canal. Order shurpa in the jar and kotirma, lamb and potatoes cooked in a kozon.
+998 98 771 30 30, Zhaloliddin Manguberi Street, 1

Sulim Café
One of Namangan's most famous cafés, Sulim masters multiple culinary domains: shashlik, plov made-to-order, and fire-grilled river fish. The venue offers private booths, outdoor seating, and a large event hall.
+998 91 295 22 22

Sarbon Oshxona
A simple oshxona on the side of a bypass road outside the center of Namangan. The shurpa in the jar was almost perfect: rich and fragrant, with fall-apart tender meat.
+998 99 936 20 00, +998 91 342 76 65

Mahmudzhon-Ota
The classic, exemplary, true choyxonas are situated in the Chust Park, in the shade of tall trees. The plov I tried here, at Mahmudzhon-Ota, was one of the best in my entire travel of the country: made with lazer rice, lamb, hot pepper, dolma, quail's eggs and even lemon. Purling water, chittering quails, bright purple kurpachas, and tea-drinking babai added to the bliss of the picture.
+998 88 825 25 86

Tog' Shabbodasi
As you go back to Tashkent from Fergana Valley, make a lunch break at this café on the Kamchik Pass

(Namangan Region), order jyz or kebabs and enjoy the mountain views.
+998 93 410 59 95, +93 643 11 11, Pop District, Chadak Village

Hotels of Namangan

Akhsikent Hotel
A new hotel in the modern part of Namangan, 15 minutes by taxi from the city center.
+998 78 777 07 77, Yangi, Namangan District, Shimoliy Aylanma Yuli Street, 46

Atour Hotel
One of the latest additions to Namangan hotels, featuring spacious rooms, European décor, and hearty breakfast, located close to the airport.
+998 69 211 10 10, Davlatabad District, Airport Street, 1

Nanay Family House
A complex of several modern guesthouses with a beautiful garden, open swimming pool and billiards, located in the Nanay kishlak, a popular recreation area.
+998 91 271 00 00, Yangikurgan District, Urban settlement Nanay

Chodak Kemping
Chodak is the Switzerland of Uzbekistan. The foothills of the Pop District feature clean air, coolness and picturesque landscapes. The elevation of 2,000–2,100 meters above sea level ensures temperatures some 12–15 degrees lower than in the valley. One of the best recreation areas, with a shady garden and a swimming pool, is managed by Naimkhon Abdurakhmanov.
+998 93 400 45 05, t.me/kempingchodak

About the Author

Dariya Sirotina is a traveler, author, photographer, and expert on food and wine. This book distills her seven years of rigorous research into Uzbekistan's cultural, culinary, and winemaking traditions.

For her contributions to the development of tourism, she has been awarded two honorary distinctions by the Republic of Uzbekistan. Since 2018, she has designed and led specialized private and corporate tours across the country.

Instagram: *@darsik*
Email: *d.sirotina@gmail.com*